GW00853432

GW00853432

1st NEWRY (EARL KILMOREY) SCOUT GROUP

FOUNDED
1910

The Life and Times of 1st Newry Scout Group

Published in 2012 by
1st Newry (Earl Kilmorey) Scout Group
Newry
County Down
Northern Ireland

www.1stnewryscouts.org
info@1stnewryscouts.org

All rights reserved. No part of this publication may be reproduced, stored in a retrieval system, or transmitted, in any form, or by any means, electronic, mechanical, photocopying, recording or otherwise, without the prior permisson of the publisher and copyright holder.

ISBN 978-0-9539601-9-4

Acknowledgements

Grateful thanks are due to Clive Scoular who edited the book and to Thomas Johnston for its design.

We would also like to express our special thanks to:
The National Lottery Heritage Fund
Newry and Mourne District Council
Noreen Cunningham, Newry and Mourne Museum
Ken Abraham, Newry and Mourne Museum
Betty Whiteside, Newry
Ken Gillespie and staff, Northern Ireland Scout Council
The staff at Scout Association, HQ, London
The Hodgett family, *Newry Reporter*
S.E.L.B. Library staff, Newry and Armagh
Andrew Totten, 10th Belfast
David Mahood, Craigavad
Rev. Brian Colvin, Downshire Road Presbyterian Church

Thanks are also due to many former members who forwarded images and who provided information and the names of Scouts in a number of photographs in the book. And finally we wish to express our gratitude to the many other people, too numerous to mention, for their help and information in the compilation of the book.

© All photographs copyright.

Printed by GPS, Alexander Road, Belfast, BT6 9HP

For all the Scouts of former generations who made 1st Newry great;

for the present day Scouts who continue that fine tradition;

and for the Scouts of the future who will carry the 1st Newry baton forward into the 21st century.

Memorial window in Downshire Road Presbyterian Church

Contents

Message from the Chief Scout

2 August 2012

Dear Scouts,

On your 100th Anniversary, I am so proud to send you huge congratulations for your wonderful Scouting celebrations.

Scouting is an incredibly powerful Movement, and it is such a privilege together to be a part of the life enhancing adventure to inspire and encourage young people.

Together, we help provide totally unique opportunities to learn both life and outdoor skills and to make a real difference in our own communities.

I wish you many more years of fun and success.

Well done!

Bear Grylls
Chief Scout

The Scout Association
Gilwell Park Chingford London E4 7QW **T:** +44 (0)20 8433 7100 **F:** +44 (0)20 8433 7103 **E:** scout.association@scouts.org.uk **W:** www.scouts.org.uk
Patron: HM The Queen **President:** HRH The Duke of Kent **Founder:** Robert Baden-Powell OM **Chief Scout:** Lt Cdr (Hon) Bear Grylls RN
Registered Charity numbers 306101 (England and Wales) and SC038437 (Scotland) Incorporated by Royal Charter
Printed on 100% recycled paper

Introduction

This book is a celebration, recording just over a century of Scouting in Newry. Any group which survives and flourishes for 100 years – and there are very few – is fully entitled to celebrate its longevity, for it has something special. 1st Newry is justified in feeling pride in the sustained quality of the work done by the Group over those years and in the benefit conferred upon successive generations of Scouts in Newry. Like the flame in this Olympic year, the tradition and spirit of the Group have been handed on by each generation to its successor and kept alive by the continued effort and dedication of its leaders and supporters.

The novelty and excitement felt by those who were part of the early Troop come across clearly in the records dating back to its foundation in 1910. As in so many places around the country, boys flocked to join the new Movement, which grew and developed so quickly that in 1911 there was a 'grand review of Boy Scouts by His Majesty the King at Windsor Great Park'. By that time the fledgling 1st Newry troop was flourishing. It now enjoyed the patronage of Lord Kilmorey, with his name as part of its title. An early photograph taken in August 1911 shows a total of 24 Scouts, smartly turned out in full uniform (very recognisable to those of us who were Scouts in the 1940s and 1950s) and equipped with Scout staves, under the command of their Scoutmaster. The record continues over the next 100 years, with a large gallery of photographs cataloguing the Group's many and varied activities, including a continuous succession of summer camps, the centrepiece of Scouting life.

Countless Scouts over these years have derived immense benefit from the work of the Group. The multiplicity of their activities and the happiness of their demeanour are manifest in the pages of the book and the photographs. They are testament to the positive effect on the lives of so many young people who have passed through the ranks of the Group over its first century. Those young people have themselves passed on the values of Scouting by their own lives and in the work which many have contributed to the Movement (one might single out for mention that paragon William Johnson, one of our great Chief Commissioners, who joined 1st Newry as a Scout in 1915).

The continuity of a century requires the leadership of a large and devoted cadre of people over the years, with the back up of a supportive body of parents and friends. 1st Newry has been fortunate in both respects. It has had a succession of dedicated leaders, none of whom has contributed more than the evergreen Mervyn Ferris, who has put sustained and determined effort into producing this book. The Group has deep roots in the Newry community, which has given it support and encouragement since its foundation.

1st Newry deserves its celebration, and this book will be a tangible reminder to future generations of members of their history and heritage. Northern Ireland Scouting rejoices with them and sends warmest good wishes for the Group's next century.

Robert Carswell

Robert Carswell
The Rt. Hon. The Lord Carswell
President, NI Scout Council

Message from the Chairman

We are extremely proud to have produced this very fine work on the history of one of the oldest Scout Groups in Northern Ireland which is published under the auspices of 1st Newry (Earl Kilmorey) Scout Group. This is one of very few such publications from Scout Groups in Northern Ireland and certainly the first ever by 1st Newry. The publication of this book was only made possible by the very generous funding provided from The National Lottery, Heritage Lottery Fund, Young Roots scheme together with some additional funding from Newry and Mourne District Council and from the Group's own resources. To these organisations the Group is greatly indebted.

The concept of this book arose some years back even before the Group decided upon the plans for its centenary, when the Scoutleader, Mervyn Ferris, who had already undertaken the production of booklets for the Group's 75th and 90th anniversary celebrations, decided to take the bold step to produce a book about the history of the Group since its inception in the early 1900s.

Over the past two years much work has been involved in the collection of information, articles, memorabilia, personal reminiscences and photographs to allow the book to be produced to the high standard which you see before you.

Mervyn has been assisted over the years by a willing band of helpers in the collection of this vast amount of information. Special thanks must go to Colin McElroy (Assistant Cub Scoutleader) for his research into the past history of the Group through many days and weeks of diligent labour into the archives of Newry Library and the *Newry Reporter* and *Newry Telegraph* newspapers. Billy McAlpine MBE, who has photographed the many and various activities of the Group over the past fifty plus years, has provided numerous photographs contained in the book.

We would also wish to express our grateful thanks to our team of Explorer Scouts — George Bingham, James Kernaghan, Harley Stinson, Sheehan Poucher, Toby Girvan, Christopher Bagnall and Andrew Hodgett — who have helped with this and other projects by collecting and organising the information for the book and our exhibition centre.

Many others have contributed information, photographs, images, memorabilia and personal reminiscences as well as advice on the content and format of this publication. Among these are; the editor of our book, Clive Scoular (former County Commissioner for County Down) and Thomas Johnston for the design and layout; our Committee members, Alan McGaffin (Chairman), Linda Bingham (Secretary) and Jim Baines (Treasurer) and of course our leaders, Carol McWhirter (Beaver Scoutleader), Alison Kernaghan (Assistant Beaver Scoutleader), Lee McWhirter (Assistant Cub Scoutleader), Gavin McCullough (Assistant Cub Scoutleader), Robert Henry (Assistant Cub Scoutleader), Garry McWhirter (Assistant Scoutleader) and Colin Whiteside (Assistant Scoutleader).

Alan McGaffin

Chairman, 1st Newry
August 2012

Editor's Note

From this fascinating and interesting chronicle of 1st Newry's first one hundred years Scouting, readers will quickly appreciate that the story is not in narrative form but rather comes as a series of notes written down year by year, often for the annual minutes of the Group's activities. In the early years the detail is impressive and at times over wordy, especially with the lengthy lists of participants at their jamborees, or annual concerts, and the names of every boy who won a prize or took part in a multitude of races at sports day. Other years, however, give only very brief mention of the Scouting highlights of that particular year. Some years do not even warrant a single entry. In my estimation it does not matter whether much or little is written; it just proves that priorities change as time goes on and the main point is that the story of this outstanding Scout Group moved on apace.

The magnificent efforts made by so many leaders over the years and the impressive achievements of hundreds of boys tells its own eloquent story. It is thanks to their hard work and their obvious enjoyment in what they were doing that makes this record so engaging. Yet the real story is probably best illustrated by the vast array of photographs – from the old black and white and rather formal ones to the remarkable colour ones, most of them taken over the past fifty years by the indomitable Billy McAlpine. The stalwart efforts of Mervyn Ferris, sometime Scout, Scoutmaster, District Commissioner and Scoutleader also must be fully recognised. He has, apart from all those years of leading the boys of 1st Newry, worked tirelessly to put together this book which clearly describes the fun and commitment undertaken by 1st Newry Scouts throughout the past 100 years.

For all of you who read this book it will be for you a step back in time to appreciate how young boys of Newry spent their spare time; for those of you who have had descendants and relatives pictured and mentioned, it will be nothing short of a trip of pure nostalgia.

It has been a pleasure, as it has been for my partner, Thomas Johnston, to have turned these words and photographs into this book. But the real thanks must go to the leaders and boys of 1st Newry for giving us all the opportunity to spend such pleasurable time reading through the stories of their camps and concerts and to enjoy the photographs which surely complete the story of those who were, and of course still are, members of this great worldwide brotherhood – the Scout Association. And now they begin their second century, carrying on from the achievements of their worthy predecessors in this superlative Scout Group.

Clive Scoular – a one-time County Commissioner in this great county of Down.

Killyleagh
August 2012

In the beginning

There is evidence that Scouting under the Boy Scouts Association, with its Imperial Headquarters in London, commonly known as B.P. Scouts, started in Newry as early as 1908 with information being contained in *The Scout* magazine, page 452 and dated 22 August 1908.

The Scout magazine, published by C. Arthur Pearson Ltd., records; 'The Scouts are going strong in Dublin and Belfast, and this week we hear of a new Troop being started in Newry, 'more power to them', under the able captaincy of Mr John Kavanagh. We wish every success to this new Troop and hope to hear more of its doings as it goes on'.

Northern Ireland did not exist as a separate entity at this time as partition of the island of Ireland did not take place until 1922 so this new Troop would have been formed under the banner of The Boy Scout Association at Imperial Headquarters, London. In later years the name of the Association was changed to The Scout Association. This was to reflect the need to drop 'boy' from the title as the Movement had within its ranks young men of sixteen years and upwards and the title Boy Scout did not truly reflect the nature of the developing Movement.

Unfortunately it has been extremely difficult to establish either the name of the Troop or its meeting place but one could ask whether this was the forerunner for the commencement of the Scout Troops known as Chequer Hill Boy Scouts and 1st Newry Troop.

We do know, however, that 1st Newry Troop was in existence during the latter part of 1910, and possibly even 1909, with the Troop, as we know it today, subsequently coming under the auspices of Downshire Road Presbyterian Church in the early part of 1911.

The Scout from 22nd August 1908.
The formation of a Boy Scout
Troop in Newry is mentioned at
the bottom right of the page.

1910s

1st Newry, 7 July 1915

1911

On Saturday, 29 April, the following article concerning the formation of Boy Scouts in Newry in 1910 or earlier appeared in the *Newry Reporter*:

The Movement formulating a corps of Boy Scouts, inaugurated by Lt. Colonel R.S.S. Baden - Powell K.C.A., has spread to Newry, and already two corps have been formed, one called the Chequer Hill Boy Scouts and the other connected with Downshire Road Presbyterian Church. The former body is sometime in existence, while the latter is the outcome of a meeting held in the Downshire Road Church Lecture Hall. The meeting, presided upon by the Rev. J. Paton, elected a committee to look after the corps, in which 40 boys were enrolled (invested). Their meetings are to be held in Downshire Road Lecture Hall.

Prior to the formation of 1st Newry, the Chequer Hill corps had been very active under the leadership of T. Armstrong (Captain) and T. Cartmill and S. Moorehead (Lieutenants).

From information gathered from the local paper, the *Newry Reporter*, the Chequer Hill Boy Scouts took part in a number of weekly marches to Millvale, Craigmore and Moorvale as well as to other outdoor events during May and June 1911, but there is no mention in the press at this time of the activities of 1st Newry.

Old photographs of the Chequer Hill Scouts show them in what appears to be Boys' Brigade uniform and this would not have been unusual as many Scout patrols were in fact formed within existing Boys' Brigade companies. Baden-Powell had written his early version, around 1906, of the book 'Scouting for Boys' to provide more information and ideas for the Boys' Brigade but after it became available from 1908 Scout patrols were initially formed within the Boys' Brigade Companies. Subsequently these patrols of Scouts would separate from the B.B. companies and form Scout Troops under the banner of the Boy Scout Association.

This is most likely what took place in Newry because not long after the inauguration of the Downshire Road corps (Troop), later to be known as 1st Newry Boy Scouts, the Chequer Hill Corps slowly declined in numbers, their members being attracted to 1st Newry Troop. The increase in membership of 1st Newry was no doubt aided by the fact that the Troop was under the care of Downshire Road Presbyterian Church and the minister at that time, the Rev. Paton, who took a great interest in the Troop.

Later in 1911 the *Newry Reporter* contained information regarding 'Boy Scouts' in its article on Thursday, 6 July, when it reported on the grand review of Boy Scouts by His Majesty the King at Windsor Great Park. It was reported that over 32,000 took part and came from all parts of England, Scotland, Ireland and Wales as well as contingents from Overseas Dominions.

The same article contained the information that Boy Scouts had even extended to Newry where there was an excellent corps, (now referred to as a Scout Troop).

On Saturday, 5 August 1911, 38 Boy Scouts from Staffordshire arrived on the *S.S. Iveagh* and held their camp in Warrenpoint Town Hall under the care of Scoutmaster Young. A Sunday afternoon

W. H. SCOTT,
FIRST SCOUTMASTER & CO-FOUNDER
1ST NEWRY (EARL KILMOREY) TROOP BOY SCOUTS
1910

The first known photograph of 1st Newry Boy Scout Troop, August 1911

service was held in the Warrenpoint Town Hall and there was a good attendance which included a contingent from 1st Newry. Scoutmaster Young of 2nd Stafford Troop Boy Scouts gave the address. The collection was in aid of the hospital cot kept by the Scout Bible class. Arrangements were made for a concert and display in the Lecture Hall, Downshire Road Presbyterian Church, on Thursday evening beginning at 7.45 p.m. with the proceeds of the entertainment being devoted to the camp fund of 2nd Stafford Troop and to 1st Newry (Earl Kilmorey) Troop. The honorary treasurer of 1st Newry Troop was Mr W. H. Scott of the Newry Model School, to whom subscriptions for the development of the organisation would be gratefully received and acknowledged.

A photograph, perhaps the first ever taken of the Scout Troop, was printed in the *Newry Reporter* dated Tuesday, 8 August, shows a section of 1st Newry (Earl Kilmorey) Troop Boy Scouts in which 24 members were represented along with Scoutmaster Dick Scott. Unfortunately, despite many efforts to obtain a good copy of this photograph, the only place where it could be found was among the archived *Newry Reporter* issues and on microfiche held by the Southern Education and Library Board in its libraries in Newry and Armagh. Obviously after some 100 years, the quality and clarity of the photo have suffered over the years but it is the best that could be obtained.

On Thursday, 10 August, 1st Newry Boy Scouts under the leadership of Mr Dick Scott marched through Newry to meet the Stafford contingent of Boy Scouts, encamped in Warrenpoint Town Hall. The two Troops joined up on the edge of the town and together they marched accompanied by a big crowd through the town. One can only imagine the scene as these Scouts in the then familiar B.P. style hat marched through the town up the main street (Hill Street) through Kildare Street and Trevor Hill to arrive at Downshire Road Church. What a sight that would have been. En route handbills were distributed advertising the fact that the English Troop was giving a display in Downshire Road Presbyterian Church Lecture Hall at eight o'clock. Several policemen accompanied the Scouts on their march but, far from objecting to their presence, the South Ward contributed quite a crowd of juveniles, who accompanied the Scouts through the town and cheered the visitors on leaving.

The concert and display, at which there was a good attendance, commenced with Mr R. Kerr presiding as chairman for the evening. After expressing the pleasure it gave him to take charge over the evening's events, he went on to say a few words about the Scout Movement in Newry and wider afield. He added that the local Troop was known as 1st Newry (Earl Kilmorey) Scout Troop - his Lordship having kindly given his consent to his name being used in the Troop's title.

There were now sixty members connected with the Troop and attached to it was a patrol of eight boys from Warrenpoint. Fifty of the boys had passed the Tenderfoot Badge and had been supplied with uniforms. Great progress had been made thanks to the training of Mr Paton, Mr Scott and Mr Dick Scott, secretary. Mr Scott, Headmaster of the Model School, took a great interest in the Troop and, but for his exertions, they would scarcely be so far advanced. In his opinion the Scout Movement was 'one of the greatest taken up for many a day'. Mr Kerr further reminded all that he understood 'there were now about 80,000 enrolled in Great Britain and Ireland and, as they all knew, Baden-Powell was the Chief Scout and initiator of the Movement. Baden-Powell had said he refused to die until there was a million Boy Scouts in Great Britain and Ireland'. Mr Kerr said that he hoped BP would be spared to command them for many years to come. In conclusion, Mr Kerr having stated that as the Movement was not carried on without money, he appealed to those present who perhaps had a surplus of money to make a donation to Mr Scott, treasurer, at Newry Model School.

He then handed the rest of the evening's programme into the hands of Scoutmaster Young (2nd Stafford). The programme continued with a rally of the Scouts who were very smart and precise in obeying the different calls and patrol formations. Songs were sung, followed by conjuring acts, a fencing display, physical drill and signalling, and all were loudly applauded. Scout Brown convulsed the audience by singing 'Liza had hold of my hand' and Miss F. Yates recited 'Mother' very feelingly. Both acts received enthusiastic encores. Scout W. Scott, 1st Newry, sang 'Blue Bells' followed by a quartet of members of the Kangaroo Patrol (2nd Stafford) who sang 'We don't want a girl'.

The second half of the programme was equally enjoyable. It consisted of a song, 'I've rings on my fingers' by Scout Perry (2nd Stafford); a recitation, 'The Rose' by Miss F. Yates; a boxing display by 2nd Stafford; bridge building display by 2nd Stafford and a humorous song, 'How I saved my life' by Scout Brown. The proceeds from the event were in aid of 2nd Stafford camp funds and also to assist 1st Newry (Earl Kilmorey) Scout Group. Scouts from 1st Newry took charge of the hall and acted as doorkeepers and stewards. The evening was brought to a conclusion with a general vote of thanks to all the Scouts and leaders proposed by the chairman. The Scouts responded with three cheers for the chairman.

During the week the secretary of 1st Newry received a letter from the Great Northern Hotel, Warrenpoint requesting help at a large fete to be held at the hotel on Wednesday, 16 August. The following appeared in the pages of the *Newry Reporter* on 12 August, 'Scouts wanted at Warrenpoint'. Mr Dick Scott, secretary to 1st Newry (Earl Kilmorey) Troop of Boy Scouts, had received the following letter:

Great Northern Hotel, Warrenpoint, 10 August 1911
'Dear Sir, - Can you send your Scouts to Warrenpoint on Wednesday to give us a hand to keep the ground? We have a large fete on that day and, as you will see, there are two prizes for Boy Scouts. Kindly do your best for me and oblige.
Yours faithfully,
G.B. Morgan.
P.S. - I will get passes for them from Newry to Warrenpoint and return'.

Great Northern Hotel, Warrenpoint, circa 1911

It was recorded in the report to Downshire Road Presbyterian Church annual meeting that the Scouts turned out to this event, not only carrying out their duties very well, but also winning first prize for the smartest turned out squad of six Scouts.

In September 1911, 1st Newry and Scouts from Dundalk travelled to Warrenpoint where they acted as stewards at a pageant being held in the town.

On Sunday, 1 October 1911, a special sermon was given to Boy Scouts during the evening service at Downshire Road Presbyterian Church. The service was conducted by Rev. D. D. Boyle of McQuiston Memorial Presbyterian Church, Belfast. The evening service was in the nature of a special service in connection with 1st Newry (Earl Kilmorey) Boy Scout Troop, an organisation which embraces within its ranks lads belonging to the different Protestant churches in Newry, and which is gradually extending its membership. Special seats were reserved for the boys, who wore uniform, and the remaining portions of the church were packed with other worshippers. The Scouts sang the collection hymn. At the end of the service a collection was taken up in aid of 1st Newry Troop and a sum of £4/10/0 (£4.50) was realised.

It was also around this time that the Troop managed to establish a bugle band but it is not known how this came about or where the bugles and drums came from. However later on in the year these instruments were put to good use when the Troop paid a visit to Rostrevor.

The Troop outside Downshire Road Presbyterian Church. Note the bugles held by some of the members.

1912

In March Mr R. J. H. Scott gave the Scout report for the year to the annual meeting of Downshire Road Presbyterian Church in which he indicated that there were 56 Scouts on the roll and everything was working well. He indicated that the Earl Kilmorey had kindly consented to become patron of the Troop. Mr W. H. Scott was the Scoutmaster, Mr J. Smith acted as Commissioner and Mr Dick Scott was Assistant Scoutmaster and, under these very capable hands, the Troop had prospered. Since its formation the Troop has taken part in the life of the town. The first major public appearance was at the Coronation fete for King George V, during which Scouts were stationed along the course on which the races were run to keep the course clear and they did their duty very well. Subsequently our Scouts performed a similar duty at the summer fete and carnival held in Warrenpoint and won first prize for the smartest turned out squad of six Boy Scouts. Later on the Troop assisted at a fire-extinguishing exhibition and on the same day rendered first aid to a man who fell from his bicycle. Two of the Scouts gave valuable assistance in stopping a serious fire and one Scout stopped a runaway horse. During the year the Troop attended a church parade to St. Mary's Church of Ireland where they received a hearty welcome from Rev. S. Smart. Scouts also assisted with a jumble sale and sale of work in Downshire Road Church. The services of a military instructor were obtained to help the Troop become efficient in drill. The Troop was now fairly efficient in first aid, signalling, boxing, fencing, stave drill, dumbbells, singing, fire lighting and plain cooking. Mr Scott went on to say that he thought the Troop had received an all round training in general efficiency and that they are now able to make themselves useful in any emergency. Scoutmaster Mr W. H. Scott expressed grateful thanks to Earl Kilmorey for all his help and to the public for the support and recognition that had been extended to them.

The next mention of 1st Newry appeared in the newspapers on 9 April 1912 when it was recorded that the Earl Kilmorey Troop Boy Scouts had a most enjoyable day at Rostrevor, despite the inclemency of the weather. The Troop paraded in full strength under Scoutmaster Scott and with bugles and drums proceeded to Dublin Bridge station where they entrained for the rendezvous. It is also recorded that numerous onlookers were pleased with the creditable turnout of the boys and their manly bearing told of the good effect of their training. The Troop had, since its formation, made wonderful strides and, under the patronage of a nobleman like Earl Kilmorey, had made itself felt. The outing was so enjoyable that it would surely prove the forerunner for many others.

In 1912 the Troop camped near Portrush at Dhu Varren when nineteen Scouts under the leadership of Scoutmaster Scott had a very successful camp. During the camp the boys entertained one of the local Scout Troops to tea and buns with the help of Mrs Scott who came along to see the boys in camp.

Later on during the year a large audience filled the lecture hall of Downshire Road Presbyterian Church on the occasion of a concert and display. This was enjoyed by all those attending and the Troop was looking forward to future events.

1st NEWRY (EARL of KILMOREY'S) TROOP B.P. BOY SCOUTS
DHU VARREN CAMP, PORTRUSH, 1912.

Jack Scott, T. Bond, L. Maitland, T. Grills, W. McKinley, W. Johnston, W. Weir, W. Graham, D. O. Mahood
Mr W. H. Scott (S.M.)   W.J. Wylie.
Hamil Scott, J. Baker, R. Graham, C. Hall,   E. Bond, W.S. Scott, C. McAnuff.
Cecil Smith,   T. McCullough, O. Rodgers.
Presented by D. O. Mahood, Esq., April 1959.

1st Newry (Earl Kilmorey) Troop travelled to Kilkeel on Boxing Day 1912 to play the Juniors in a football match which took place at 1.30 p.m. The Juniors were quickly on the move when Galbraith scored. Half time saw Kilkeel two goals up, Galbraith having scored again. After the change of ends play became very fast with the youngsters going for all they were worth and Newry scored. However Kilkeel were not to be denied another and Sydney Heron added no. 3 to the list. There was no further scoring and the game ended with Kilkeel winning by 3 goals to 1. The match was brimful of excitement from beginning to end. The visitors, 1st Newry, were entertained in the Temperance Hotel where Mrs Talbot looked after all. It was recorded that the winning Kilkeel team members were: H. Hanna, J. McVeigh, W. Owens, W. Devonport, P. Ferguson, B. Cowser, S. Heron, G. Grills, W. Galbraith, C. Talbot, and J. Ferguson. The Rev. A. Eadie, B.A. acted as referee.

During this period it was noted that the Troop had a very successful and active football team.

1st. NEWRY (EARL KILMOREY'S) TROOP B.-P. BOY SCOUTS
FOOTBALL TEAM
1912-13.

| HENRY LYONS, | JIM SCOTT, | W. WEIR, | TOM BOND, | W. JOHNSTON, | JACK SCOTT |
| DICK SCOTT, | HAMILL SCOTT, | TOM GRILLS, (CAPTAIN) | | ALBERT MEGAW, | W. McKINLEY |

Presented by T. Grills, Esq., J.P., April 1959

Original Scout flag presented to the Troop by Countess Kilmorey in 1910.

1913 - 1914

From 1913 to 1914 other camps were also held at Bushmills, and Sandhills, again under the leadership of Mr W. H. Scott.

In those early days of Scouting, the Scout uniform consisted of the characteristic khaki B.P. hat, khaki shirt, green scarf, and blue or khaki shorts. The weekly subscription from each Scout was 1d. (the equivalent now of a half of one new pence).

1st Newry Troop at Sandhills, 1914

With the onset of the First World War in 1914 the activities of the Troop were severely interrupted, due to many of the older members and leaders joining the Armed Forces and going off to serve their country in what was supposed to be 'the war to end all wars'.

Those who served their country were as follows:

Chaplains: Rev. J. G. Paton, Rev. P. McKee.
Scoutmaster: R. Scott.
Assistant Scoutmasters: W. H. Scott, J. C. Lambe.
Bugle Major: S. McCrum.
Patrol Leaders: J. Campbell, D. Cloughley, G. Grills, W. Livingstone, O. Mahood, B. McAnuff, R. McNeill, J.Scott, J. K. Scott, H. T. Scott, W. J. Sterritt.
Seconds and Scouts: J. Baker, W. Beggs, S. Beggs, J. Carter, H. Clarke, R. Crozier, V. Griffin, S. Gibson, W. Harshaw, E. Holden, W. Johnston, J. McKinley, S. E. Magowan, W. McCleary, H. Masson, W. McElroy, H. McElroy, J. McGrath, W. McKnight, J. Mitchell, S. Moffatt, R. Murray, D. Pinkerton, F. Rigby, O. Rogers, C. Smith, W. J. Wylie.

During the war years the Troop managed to remain active under the leadership of a Mr Maitland and assisted the Army authorities in Newry by acting as messengers, but unfortunately it was also around this time that the bugle band appears to have disbanded as no further information concerning its appearance at parades was available from any source.

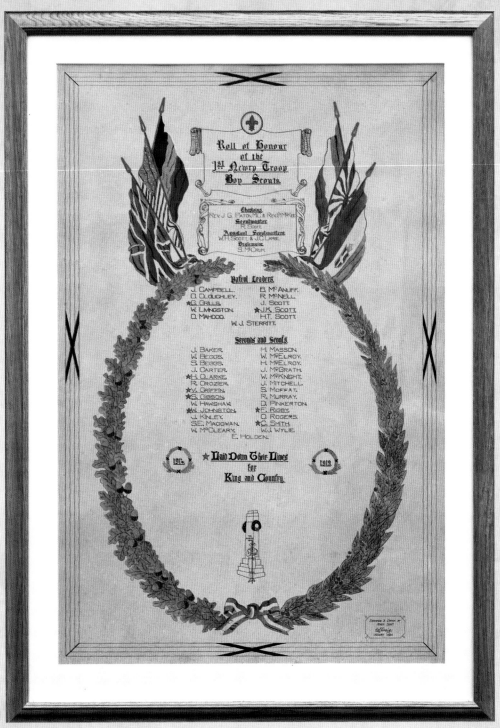

1914-1918 War Memorial

1915

On Wednesday, 14 April, a Scout night was held in Downshire Road Presbyterian Church Lecture Hall and a big gathering assembled to witness a grand display and concert by the boys of 1st Newry (Earl Kilmorey) B.P. Boy Scouts. The evening began at 7.30 with the inspection of the Troop by Major Pearse of the Royal Army Medical Corps who was delighted with what he saw. Following the inspection the concert began with the chair being occupied by Captain Magill, also of the R.A.M.C., who was moved to that position on the proposal of Mr William Johnson, solicitor, seconded by Dr. Henry Smartt. The hall was in charge of the Scout stewards with the programmes being sold by Wolf Cubs, Tom Scott, Fred Bell, Alan Rowland, Sydney Sterritt, Arthur Agnew, George Ferris, Donald Wilson, Tom Graham, Jack Crozier, Victor Crozier and Jack McKinstry. During the evening the boys were under the command of Scoutmaster Richard Scott and from all reports acquitted themselves admirably during the evening. Miss Kingham provided the musical accompaniments most proficiently for the various musical events over the evening.

The first item on the programme was the singing of the Scout Chorus by the entire Troop which by all accounts was done musically and well and reflected great credit on the musical abilities of the boys. This was followed by an exhibition of Troop drill and then Patrol Second Sterritt gave a rendition of 'The Soldiers of the King' which he gave in great style and left the stage amid uproarious applause. There followed a fencing display given by the Senior Patrol Leader W. Sterritt and Scouts Joe McKinley, W. Wylie, S. Livingstone, H. Mason and W. J. Wylie. Scout William Johnson (in later years to become Northern Ireland Chief Commissioner), son of Mr William Johnson, solicitor, then showed that he had inherited his father's musical talents in singing 'Roamin' in the Gloamin'' in character. Semaphore signalling was then carried out by Patrol Leader Scott and Patrol Second Smith both of whom showed their accuracy and speed in sending and receiving a message given to them by a member of the audience. A number of other events were then performed, such as a boxing bout between Patrol Leader Magowan and Second Smith, the song 'Who killed Kaiser Bill'

1st NEWRY (EARL of KILMOREY'S) TROOP B.-P. BOY SCOUTS at WARRENPOINT, 7th. JULY 1915

H. HEATHER, R. STERRITT, S.E. MAGOWAN, W.H. SCOTT, W. MAGOWAN, E. BOND, D. CLOUGHLEY, R.J.H. SCOTT, B. CROZIER,
J.A. CRAIG, R. GRAHAM, W.L. CRAIG, Serg. M. O'LEARY, V.C., R. CROZIER, J. FISHER,
T. GRAHAM, T. SCOTT,
A. McCULLOUGH, G. AGNEW, G. SMITH, W. BAKER, E. ROWLAND, D. GRAHAM, S. STERRITT, C. CROTHERS,
R.A. FISHER.

by Scout McKinley followed by an amusing interlude by Scouts McKinley and Livingstone. Thereafter the Raven Patrol of Patrol Leader W. Scott, Second R. Sterritt, Scouts W. Baker, D. Graham, William Johnson and Bobbie Crozier gave a surprisingly accurate display of musical club swinging. The next contribution to the programme was the tit-bit of the evening. It was a chorus of 'Slattery's Mounted Fut' in character by the Scouts. This was performed by J. McKinley as the Captain, W. Sterritt on the piccolo, W. Wylie on the side drum, B. McNeill on the bass drum, W. Magowan as Bones, B. Graham on the triangle, A. Irwin on the trumpet, W. J. Wylie on the French fiddle and S. Livingstone as the standard bearer. It was most amusing and topical with the Kaiser getting it hot both in dress and song. The first half of the programme was brought to a conclusion with a junior boxing bout between Wolf Cubs Scott and Graham. They went at it in earnest from the start with it being noted that Johnson and Willard (Jack Johnson and Jess Willard were well known international boxers at this time) could hardly have put more effort into the world championship than did these two manly little chaps.

The second part of the programme was equally enjoyable being opened with a well-executed piano duet 'The Primrose' by Second Sterritt and Scout William Heather and a very successful display of Morse Code given by Patrol Leader Scott and Second Sterritt. Near the end of the evening Scout Magowan delighted all by reciting 'Maguire's Goat' which was followed by Scout William Johnson who received another ovation for his rendition of 'Tipperary'. The evening was brought to a close with some Scout games and a presentation by Captain Magill on behalf of the Scouts of a gold medal to Miss Kingham as a token of their appreciation of her services at the piano during the evening's events and throughout the rehearsals. At the close a hearty vote of thanks was passed by the chairman on the motion of the Rev. Phineas McKee, B.A. and seconded by Dr. Smartt.

1916

It was during this year that the Boy Scout Association admitted young boys from the age of eight years into the Movement as the demand for Scouting from the younger generation had become so popular and many Troops had already taken younger boys into their ranks. Indeed 1st Newry was no exception as old photographs of the time show that Wolf Cubs had actually joined the ranks of the Troop as early as 1915.

Although the Troop had continued to meet on a fairly regular basis during the war years, there was difficulty in getting leaders to help with the various activities. Mr Maitland and others managed to ensure that Scouting still continued to function regardless with activities being held in the 'Cut Field'. This field was used by Newry Intermediate School for games and is now the location where Windsor Hill Primary School is situated. Several formal parades were held during this time. During these difficult years the Troop still managed to hold a number of short camps at Mourne Park. It is also known, from records made available from Scout Headquarters in London, that the Troop was under the care of a Mr Robert Judge of the Intermediate School in Newry for a period of time. Registration papers from October 1919 show that the Troop had 28 members and was 'under the control' of the Intermediate School.

Newry Reporter, 23 May 1916

On Saturday, 20 May 1916, the Troop took part in the district inspection and rally held at Mourne Park, the seat of the Countess Kilmorey, under the auspices of the South Down Boy Scout Association. 1st Newry, under Assistant Scoutmaster William Scott, took part with Troops from Annsborough, Newcastle and Bessbrook. Mr R. Patterson, the Commissioner for county Down, inspected those present. The various Troops gave displays in ambulance work, tent pitching, fire lighting, cooking and general Scouting activities. Following these events, the Troops were entertained to refreshments by Lady Kilmorey. Afterwards a grand rally took place in the presence of Lady Kilmorey and the large house party at Mourne Park House. Commissioner Patterson, in the course of his address to the boys, said that in his report to the chief, General Baden-Powell, he would tell him how pleased he was with the turnout and with the performance of the various Troops. He urged the boys to remember that they were representatives of a great Movement and that they should do all in their power to uphold the principles of that Movement. He thanked Lady Kilmorey for her kindness in granting the use of the grounds and providing refreshments for all present. Mr J. J. Maitland, secretary of Newry Boy Scout Association, had charge of the arrangements and the manner in which he carried out his duties left nothing to be desired.

1920s

The Troop at Crieve, 20 May 1920

1920

Following the conclusion of the war the Troop started to camp on a regular basis at Mourne Park, Kilkeel, the home of Earl Kilmorey and, as a result, the Earl granted the Troop a number of camping sites adjacent to the Whitewater river. Mourne Park is still being used by 1st Newry Group right up to the present day. After a short period, the Troop moved to the hall belonging to the Protestant Workingmen's Club. However since the 'Troubles' in the Newry area, this building had not been used as such and is now owned by Downey's. The time spent in the Protestant Workingmen's Club did not last for long as the Scouts and Cubs then moved to their next hall in Sandys Street. This building, owned by Downshire Road Presbyterian Church, was a small outhouse used to keep a pony and trap downstairs while upstairs was the hayloft. With some effort, the upstairs area was converted for use as a Scout hall with wooden steps leading down to the entry below. 1st Newry were to continue to run very successful programmes from this building and go from strength to strength for the next fifty five or fifty six years before making a move to larger premises.

The Boy Scouts and Wolf Cubs moved into this old stable and hayloft to the rear of Downshire Road Manse in Downshire Place. Renovations were carried out to make habitable for Scouting use.

However in April 1920 the Troop once again came under the auspices of Downshire Road Presbyterian Church with the Rev. Phineas McKee as chaplain. There were now thirty boys in the Troop and, judging by their keenness and enthusiasm, the future of the Troop was assured.

On Wednesday, 6 April 1920, the Troop held an attractive outdoor event comprising of races, jumping and tug of war. The Troop turn out was exceptional and all the Scouts were as keen as mustard in so far as every one of them expected to lift a prize. However some were to be disappointed. Scout C. Ferris was the winner of the 100 yards flat race for boys under 15, in which some twenty-five took part, with Scout G. Graham taking second place. The 220 yards flat race proved to be a very good contest. 18 Scouts took part in this very strong competition which ended with Patrol Leader E. Megaw and Rover Scout W. Parkinson finishing many yards in front of the opposition. The three-legged race, which proved to be exceedingly humorous, showed that the winners, Scouts A. McColl and W. Moncrief, had had plenty of practice. Patrol Leader E. Megaw was the winner of the long jump for boys over 15 and he was also the winner of the high jump for boys in the same category. He certainly was no mean athlete as he won the foregoing event with ease – 17 feet being the length of his long jump. Second W. McWhirter was the winner of the high jump for boys under 15 while Scout G. Graham was the winner of the long jump for boys under 15. Both McWhirter and Graham deserve special mention as there were about thirty boys who took part in each contest. The blindfold race, which was a humorous item, had the whole Troop taking part. Troop Leader David Graham was the easy winner practically completing the course twice before he could be stopped. Scout G. Graham was second. The only difficulty with the race was that the field was scarcely large enough to hold the competitors. The tug of war was won by Second W. McWhirter's team. The 'Go-as-you-please race', whatever form this took, was unavoidably abandoned owing to lack of time, although it was rearranged for the following Tuesday evening at 7.30 p.m. The prizes for all the above events comprised of a silver medal, fountain pens, leather wallets, pocket books, butter knives and silver cases. One can only imagine what Scouts would do with some of those items, particularly the butter knives, but I suppose these were presented to Mum when the Scout arrived home. The field for the occasion was lent by Mr James Thompson of Crieve to whom the Troop expressed their very best thanks. Captain Audrey Smartt of the Girl Guides, who was the judge for all of the events, was very ably assisted by Patrol Leader Bertha Sanderson, also of the Girl Guides. Scoutmasters W. J. Sterritt and W. J. Wylie were responsible for the arrangements which were carried through without a hitch. At the conclusion the prizes were presented by the Rev. Phineas McKee and Captain Smartt.

Uniforms were issued to the Troop on Friday evening, 23 April 1920, and all Scouts were required to wear these at all future parades and Scouting events.

On Wednesday, 28 April 1920, the Troop spent the entire afternoon and evening at outdoor work, while on the following Friday, 30 April, the weekly parade was very well attended and, after the usual indoor instruction, two hours of Scouting were held outdoors around Ashgrove. Three Scouts who overlooked 'seeing without being seen' were promptly rounded up by the Lion Patrol and spent the remainder of the evening tied to their staves. This activity is one where a number of Scouts are sent out into the surrounding countryside, within limits set, and have to disguise themselves and hide from the other patrols searching for them. It was reported that the Woodpigeon Patrol Leader was game to tackle the other three patrols the following Friday evening.

Saturday, 29 April, although wet, was a busy day for the Troop. From 3.30 p.m. until 8.00 p.m. the countryside around Craigmore and Mullaghglass was covered in different Scouting formations. A rest was called at around 6.00 p.m. when the Scouts lost no time in getting fires lit and tea ready. It was reported that one Scout was so frisky that he consumed no fewer than four dixies of tea which clearly adversely affected his running form soon afterwards. The Troop had now four patrols in good working order and steady progress on the Scouting programme was being made. Scouts without hats were informed that those previously placed on order had now arrived. The Troop is still without an official Scoutmaster and Assistant Scoutmaster so anyone keen on taking up these posts would be made most welcome to come along. There was still room for more boys to come and join the Troop, so anyone wishing to do so was encouraged to come along on Friday evenings at 8.00 p.m. to the Troop meetings.

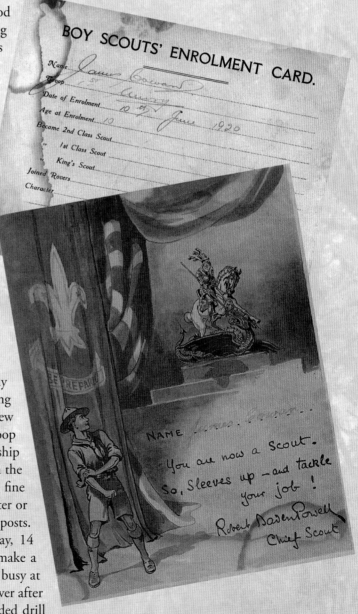

On Wednesday, 5 May 1920, the Troop spent four hours around Crieve and Damolly at map reading and marching by the map. I suppose this is what we would now call orienteering or perhaps the Scouts actually marched along the roads and across fields using the map to guide them on their way.

The following Friday evening, 7 May, the weekly parade was held as usual after which bridge building and some outdoor activities took place. Two new members were enrolled and members of the Troop congratulated Scout Reilly on winning a scholarship to Newry Intermediate School. After a test held on the Friday night, it was noted that, among so many fine young men who had applied to become Scoutmaster or Assistant Scoutmasters, none were eligible for the posts. A similar test was to be held the following Friday, 14 May, when it was hoped it would be possible to make a selection. The Saturday afternoon found the Troop busy at Craigmore. Some time was given to bridging the river after which a halt was called for tea, followed by extended drill and Scouting until 8.00 p.m.

Scout James Cowan's enrolment card from 10 June 1920

Thursday, 20 May 1920, and the Troop was still progressing in leaps and bounds. Last week and this week had seen the boys as keen as the proverbial mustard. An excellent signalling class had been formed and the Troop had engaged the services of an ex-army signalling instructor. This was a rare opportunity for the Scouts to make themselves proficient in the art of signalling. A church parade is an event of great importance and one had been arranged to take place at 6.30 p.m. on Sunday, the eve of Empire Day, in Downshire Road Presbyterian Church. Some of the Scouts were pleased to hear that Scout Jack Clarke, (sloppy's mate) had succeeded in clearing up the mystery of the sick goat – 'Sexton Blake the second'.

Warrenpoint Scouts were looking for a football match so that they could beat 1st Newry, but Newry was confident that Patrol Leader Sam Crozier and company could deal with them.

It was reported that some of the Scouts were anxious to restart the bugle band but funds were low. An appeal was made to the 'Old Boys' of the B.B. by 1st Newry Scouts asking them either to return their bugles or to offer them for sale to the present members.

Further information on the Troop was contained in an article in the *Newry Reporter* dated 31 July 1920 when it was noted that 'although the weekly notes have been conspicuous by their absence for some time, the fact was not due to any falling off in the numbers in the Troop, which was pleasing to note, and that they were still progressing with leaps and bounds'. The Troop held some excellent outings, the most successful being on the General Holiday, when a proper field day was held around Sheepbridge. On this occasion the Scouts did all their own cooking, which was quite passable and must have been good, as all the partakers had survived the event. The Scouts were sorry to lose their Scoutmaster, Mr J. Irwin, who sailed for Canada last week. As he had been a very popular figure in the Troop he would be sadly missed. The Scoutmaster, Mr W. J. Sterritt, was officially appointed together with Mr F. C. Lambe and Mr W. J. Wylie as Assistant Scoutmasters. Mr Harry Masson, whom the boys were all very pleased to see looking fit and well after his operation, had been appointed as gymnastics instructor. Harry was an all round athlete and would prove an ideal instructor.

Wednesday, 3 November 1920

1st Newry (Earl Kilmorey) Troop B.P. Scouts held an enjoyable entertainment evening in the Lecture Hall, Downshire Road Church in aid of Troop funds. During the Great War the Troop's activities were severely hampered with many of its members answering the clarion call to duty - some alas never to return. The muster spoke well for the popularity of the Movement in Newry, a Movement which inculcates healthy manliness, self reliance and uprightness in the boys. The entertainment was more than of ordinary interest to the Scouts, in that the occasion was marked by the presentation of the old Troop Colours which had been laid up during the war. The Rev. Phineas McKee, B.A., chaplain to the Troop, presided and there was a very large attendance all of whom enjoyed the full and varied programme for the evening.

The Scouts under Scoutmaster Sterritt appropriately opened the programme with a realistic camp scene depicting flag break, breakfast, and inspection – a programme presented with commendable smartness and precision and which evoked enthusiastic applause. This was followed by barbells, dumbbells, Indian clubs and boxing exercises. The Scouts also contributed to the second part of the evening's entertainment with a realistic campfire scene - the leading parts being taken by Scouts McCullough, Agnew and Heather, while a song was contributed by Scout Graham. Thereafter followed a sketch entitled 'What is a Scout?', the main participants being Scouts McWhirter, Atwell and Ellacott while all the Scouts contributed to the official Scout song 'Scouting'. At this point in the proceedings, the Rev. Phineas McKee made the presentation of the Colours, the Troop standing to attention on the well-arranged and artistically decorated platform. Addressing the Troop, the Rev. McKee, in feeling terms, alluded to the boys of the 'Old Brigade', seven of whom had laid down their lives in the late war, and exhorted the boys to carry the flag unsullied through the days and years to come. He went on to say that the Movement was one that tended to the physical and moral welfare of the boys if they faithfully lived up to the traditions of the Scout Law - a book that ought to be in the home of every boy. The Rev. McKee then formally presented the Colours to the Scouts who received them at the salute amid applause.

The concert part of the evening, or Jamboree as it was called, included songs by Captain A. Smartt, Miss L. Sterritt, Mr Campbell Gray, Mr E. Bond, and Mr Jack Heather and monologues by Mr W. R. King. All the vocalists were recalled and particularly good were the character songs of Mr Jack Heather who, in grotesque costume, was keen to win for himself more than local fame as a comedian and singer. Mr King, whose reputation as an elocutionist was so well and favourably known, added in no small degree to the pleasure of the evening by his humorous contributions. Especially good was 'The tarring of the cow' into which he introduced a touch of local colour that made the audience rock with laughter. An instrumental quartet by members of St. Mary's Band was also well received and the entertainment was brought to a close by a rollicking sketch entitled 'Slattery's' by the Scouts, followed by the National Anthem. During the evening the accompanist was Miss Sterritt.

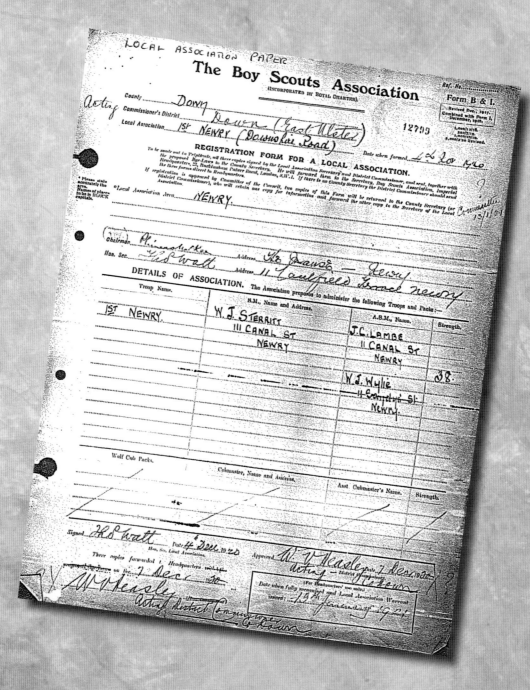

Newry Local Association Registration, 4 November 1920

1921

O n Friday evening, 11 March, a memorial service took place in the Lecture Hall of Downshire Road Presbyterian Church with the purpose of unveiling a memorial to the memory of members of 1st Newry (Earl Kilmorey) Scout Troop of B.P. Boy Scouts who served their country during the war. An article in the *Newry Reporter* dated Tuesday, 15 March 1921, indicated that the service attracted a good attendance, and was led by the Rev. Phineas McKee, B.A., chaplain to the Group, assisted by the Rev. R. E. Sherwood from Newry Methodist Church. The proceedings were characterised with a solemnity that befitted the occasion.

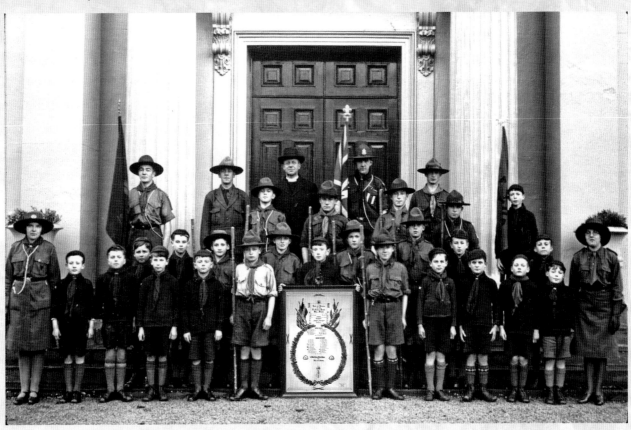

1st Newry Scouts at the front of Downshire Road Presbyterian Church, with Rev. P. McKee, at the dedication of the 1st Newry World War One Memorial

What appears to have been an annual event, the 'Go-as-you-please race', was held on Tuesday, 12 April 1921, with more entrants than anticipated. The route was from the Scout hall via Ashgrove, Upper Damolly, Savilbeg to the finger post at the Hilltown - Rathfriland road. In all the distance was roughly three miles which was covered by Troop Leader Graham in twelve and a half minutes. A good second was Patrol Leader Megaw who was only half a minute behind the winner, closely followed by Rover Scout Hunter, Scout McColl and Scout Ferris. It is recorded that the prizes for this event were not very costly, as the Scouts took part more for the honour of winning than for the prizes. However the prize winners were: 1st place - Troop Leader David Graham, silver medal; 2nd - Patrol Leader Edwin Megaw, fountain pen; 3rd - Rover Scout J. Hunter, fountain pen; 4th - Scout Allan McColl, pocket book; 5th - Scout Charles Ferris, pocket book. There was also a prize for the last person home. This was in fact the most skilful part of the race as, after some very artful and brainy moves, Scout Gordon Graham succeeded in coming in last and so winning the 'Cup'. After the event, all retired to the hall where the prizes were distributed by the Scoutmaster. Following the distribution of the prizes the Scoutmaster announced that the next meeting would take place on Tuesday evening at 8.00 p.m. and he expected all to be present in full uniform. The Troop had now formed two new patrols and those boys on the waiting list could now join and make sure of coming to summer camp. Before closing the meeting it was announced that the County Down Challenge Flag competition would take place on 25 June at Bangor. All agreed that the Troop should enter a patrol for this event with the members being chosen next week. It was expected that more than twenty patrols would take part but, even so, all hoped that 1st Newry would bring the flag back home with them after the event.

It was recorded, by 'Clove hitch' in the *Newry Reporter* on Tuesdays, 26 April and 3 May 1921, that a football match would take place on Wednesday evening, 27 April, at Damolly, the Scouts versus 'the Specials'. He went on to say that 'this will certainly prove a very interesting match as the Scout team is of a heavier nature than would naturally be supposed'. He also reported that a church parade would probably take place next Sunday evening. The same person ('Clove hitch') mentioned in his article of 3 May a request for a full attendance of all ranks at the next meeting, as there was some important business to discuss. Another football match was being arranged with Bessbrook Juniors the next Friday. He said 'this match should prove very interesting especially as the 'Brook lads see no obstacle in their way as winners'.

During the month of August this year the Troop organised a charabanc tour to Newcastle which was enjoyed by all who took part.

In early December 1921 it was recorded that the latest addition to the Troop was a fretwork class which was proving very interesting for the Scouts with some excellent models, such as picture frames and photo frames, being turned out. When sufficient numbers had been made it was hoped to display these for sale so as to help Troop funds which at this point in time were not too good. Preparations were also under way for the Scout annual concert which it was hoped to hold early in 1922. Something entirely new to the people of Newry was being aimed for. It was also noted that the following promotions had been confirmed by Imperial Headquarters in London: - Troop Leader David Graham to be Assistant Scoutmaster. Seconds A. McCullough and B. Atwell promoted to Patrol Leaders, while Scout Dick Bell is promoted to Second. The future programme for the Troop is: Monday - Lion Patrol P.L. Atwell, Second A. Agnew; Tuesday - Woodpigeon Patrol P.L. S. Sterritt, Second T. Graham; Wednesday - fretwork class; Thursday - Tiger Patrol P.L. E. Reilly, Second Ellacott; Friday - Wolf Patrol P.L. A. McCullough, Second Dick Bell.

Later in the month, on Tuesday 27, the Scouts held a very enjoyable social event which was entirely confined to Scouts. Tea was served at 6.30 p.m. accompanied by a plentiful supply of Christmas fare such as currant buns and pastry. The tea was made by Patrol Leaders E. Reilly, S. Sterritt, A. McCullough and B. Atwell. It was amazing that the Scouts survived the evening as Scouts were renowned for neither making nor serving tea successfully but obviously all went well on this occasion, as there were no reports of any illness following the event.

After tea the programme included:

1 - One - legged fight - one can only take a guess at what manner of game this was, but it proved to be one of the most interesting competitions of the night. Every Scout took part and the winning Scouts were; 1st. - Scout W. Niblock and 2nd. - Scout R. Agnew and both deserve credit for coming first and second out of thirty competitors.

2 - Beauty competition - won by Scout Armstrong as 'Tired Tim' with Scout J. Niblock, as 'Weary Willie' taking second place. Far from being a beauty competition, the contestants had to make comic faces and some of the attempts caused howls of laughter whilst others drew sympathy and tears.

3 - Whistling competition - the test piece for this event was the first verse of the National Anthem and, as the performance of all the Scouts was very good, the judge, Mr D. Sterritt, had a difficult task in adjudicating but declared Scout A. Armstrong the winner with Scout T. Graham taking second place.

4 - Drill down - this competition strenuously tested the Scouts' knowledge of the drill previously learned over weeks past and instructions were given on the 'O'Grady' principle. Scoutmaster D. Graham had all his work cut out but finally, after an hour of hard drilling, an exhausted Scout Dick Bell, who must have excelled, was declared the winner.

5 - Singing competition - after the previous events this must have proved to have been a relatively easy competition and Scout G. Graham took first place with Scout C. Armstrong coming second.

The above competitions were the principal events of the evening but other games and songs were enjoyed during the evening. After some four hours, yes four hours, (somehow or other I cannot imagine the Scouts of today having the stamina shown at this event) and the singing of 'Auld Lang Syne' followed by the National Anthem, the evening came to a successful conclusion with all the Scouts giving three cheers for the Scoutmaster and the Rev. Phineas McKee.

1922

On Wednesday, 15 February, the Group held an evening of entertainment, officially styled as a Jamboree, in Downshire Road Church Hall with the entertainment being provided by the members of the Group. It was noted that their efforts reflected no small degree of credit on the versatility and skill of the boys who were present in their natty and workmanlike Scout uniforms under Scoutmaster W. J. Sterritt. There was a large audience in attendance with the Rev. Phineas McKee, B.A. chaplain of the Troop presiding over the evening's events. In his opening remarks, the Rev. McKee complimented the Troop on their smart appearance and referred in terms of praise to the good qualities of the Troop and of the Boy Scouts in general. He expressed regret that some members, including Assistant Scoutmaster Graham, were unable to be present on the evening and hoped that they would all have a speedy recovery from the prevailing epidemic of colds and influenza. As the Troop had a very successful past year and as they had not called upon the public during the year, the proceeds from the evening's entertainment would go towards Troop funds. The Rev. McKee then introduced the programme and, at an interval during the programme, the Rev. H. B. Swanzy, amid applause, presented Troop Leader Sydney Sterritt with a silver watch as the prize for the Scout who sold the most tickets. The Rev. Swanzy also went on to compliment the Troop and gave the boys a few kindly and thoughtful words of advice on duty. The programme was excellently diversified and included several meritorious items. Miss E. McCullough provided the musical accompaniment while the Troop provided displays and individual members had the audience 'in stitches' with some really clever and humorous sketches.

Friday, 24 February 1922, once again saw the Lecture Hall at Downshire Road Presbyterian Church filled to capacity when a repeat performance - by special request - was provided of their very successful concert given the previous week. The chairman on this occasion, Captain Stewart, M.C. of the R.I.S.C. in his opening remarks said that it gave him the utmost pleasure to preside at the evening's event, as he was himself an 'old Scout' and took a keen interest in the Movement and secondly because the night fell just two days after the 65th birthday of the Chief Scout, Sir Robert Baden-Powell. He wished B.P. on behalf of the Troop and himself another sixty five years, if that were possible. Captain Stewart then introduced the programme which closely followed the previous week's event but lost none of its excitement or enthusiasm from those taking part. Once again Miss McCullough provided the musical accompaniment while many, if not all of the Scouts, played a role during the evening. At the conclusion of the programme Captain Stewart complimented Scoutmaster W. J. Sterritt on the Troop's very smart appearance and voted the performance as the best boys' concert ever witnessed.

In July 1922 the Troop held the annual camp at Mourne Park, Kilkeel at the invitation of their patron, Earl Kilmorey. The week long event was well attended with quite a number of new recruits experiencing the joys of camping under canvas for the very first time. Events during the week camp included swimming in the Whitewater river, signalling, fire lighting, cooking, games and bridge building. All arrived home safe and well after a very enjoyable camp and looked forward to another such event.

1923

In February it was reported that the Troop membership was now in excess of sixty boys and had never been in a better position. As the numbers attending on each Troop night was proving difficult for individual instruction, it was decided to divide the Troop into two sections. Section 'A', under Assistant Scoutmasters D. Graham and S. Sterritt, would meet every Monday and Thursday evening at 8. 00 p.m. while Section 'B', under Assistant Scoutmasters G. Agnew and S. Crozier, would meet every Tuesday evening at 7.30 p.m. Rover Scouts would meet every Friday evening at 7.30 p.m. under Rover Scoutmaster S. Crozier.

1st Newry Boy Scouts at their annual camp in Mourne Park Kilkeel in 1923. This is the earliest photograph of the Group's camping activity at Mourne Park.

During the month of March 1923, leaders and former members of 1st Newry Troop helped with the training and reformation of 1st Bessbrook Scout Troop which had been existence some years past but had closed down due to the war. With the growth of Scouting in South Down, the number of groups in the district had increased to ten and Scoutmaster W. J. Sterritt, 1st Newry, was promoted to the role of District Commissioner.

On Easter Monday, 2 April 1923, the Troop turned out in full strength and marched to Mr Nat. Henry's, Walden Lodge, where a most enjoyable time was spent. Mr and Mrs Henry and family did everything possible to ensure that each and every Scout enjoyed himself. In the afternoon the Troop formed up and marched further afield to Mr Joseph Ferris's farm at Cloughinny, where he kindly placed a large field at the Troop's disposal. Here a series of sports were held, which were thoroughly enjoyed by all the boys. The following were the prize winners: - 100 yards flat race (Scouts under 13) – 1st Second R Agnew; 2nd Scout A. Ferris; 200 yards flat race (Scouts over 13) - 1st P.L. A. Agnew; 2nd Scout A. McColl; High jump (Scouts under 13) – Second R. Agnew and (Scouts over 13) – P.L. A. Agnew. The above were the principal events, but others were so arranged that practically every boy won a prize. After the sports the Troop was kindly entertained to tea by Mrs Ferris which, needless to say, was thoroughly enjoyed around the campfires by all the boys. As dusk drew nigh, the Troop again formed up and all returned to town happy, having spent a glorious ten hours in the beautiful countryside.

Following the successful Easter outing, members of 1st Newry Group took part in a Scout display and entertainment in Warrenpoint Town Hall on Friday, 6 April 1923, when part of the programme comprised an inspection by Brigadier-General A. St. Q. Ricardo, the Ulster Commissioner. Boy Scouts and Wolf Cubs from Warrenpoint and Rostrevor took part as well as 1st Newry. During the

STANLEY GRAHAM   B. Mc KINSTRY   P. GRAY   B. BRIGGS   J. SMITH
JOE BRIGGS   M. REILLY   B. WEIR   W. V. HOGG

1st Newry Wolf Cubs at Mourne Park, 1923

evening there was an interesting display of a Scouting nature as well as spar fighting, Morris dancing and campfire scenes. The evening concluded with an interesting sketch entitled 'A pair of lunatics' presented by Mr and Mrs Lester Jackson. It is noted that there was a late train to Newry and a bus to Rostrevor at the conclusion of the performance. Admission was 2/- (10p) for reserved seats and 1/- (5p) for unreserved.

On Saturday afternoon, 2 June 1923, in a field at the back of the Mineral Water Works, Newry, kindly lent by Mr D. Ferris, a competition in connection with the County Down Challenge Flag took place in fine weather. The Bessbrook, Newry, and Warrenpoint Troops entered for the competition. Banbridge and Rostrevor Troops were represented, but did not compete. There was a large crowd of spectators who witnessed with much interest the display by the boys. Mr W. V. Heasley, Commissioner for Down, Commissioner McCrum from Armagh and Sgt. Major Connor were in attendance. The result was announced as follows: 1st place went to the home Troop, 1st Newry; 2nd place to 1st Warrenpoint and 1st Bessbrook came 3rd. The visiting Troops were afterwards entertained to tea and the pleasant evening was wound up with the singing of the National Anthem.

The leaders of 1st Newry Troop of Boy Scouts had now finalised arrangements for a fortnight in camp at Mourne Park, Kilkeel (kindly lent by Earl Kilmorey, patron of the Troop), commencing on 13 July. The work of the Association among boys had won general recognition and the annual camp was one of the most important schemes for their enjoyment and benefit. The ordinary expenses of the Troop were met by the contributions of the Scouts themselves and by the proceeds of a concert, but the camp expenses for around sixty Scouts and twelve Wolf Cubs were naturally considerable and were beyond the means of most of them. As the boys of the Troop at that time were drawn from all the Protestant Churches in Newry an appeal was made to members of those congregations for assistance. The appeal was, as far as we are aware, met with a generous response as the camp went ahead and no one was left behind due to financial difficulties. Mr W. J. Sterritt was the Scoutmaster and District Commissioner at that time.

On Monday, 30 July 1923, the members of 1st Newry Group met in the Scout hall, Sandys Street, to bid farewell to an esteemed member, Cubmaster Edgar Reilly, who was severing his connection with the Troop, consequent upon his departure for Waterford to take up an appointment in the

Provincial Bank in that city. In order to mark the esteem in which he was held, the boys presented Cubmaster Reilly with a solid leather attaché case, the presentation being made by Rover Scoutmaster Samuel Crozier. Cubmaster Reilly suitably returned thanks.

On Thursday, 2 August 1923, the *Newry Reporter* contained the following report concerning the annual camp of 1st Newry:

'The members of the 1st Newry Troop Boy Scouts recently concluded a most successful twelve day camp at Mourne Park – the residence of the Earl Kilmorey. The site for such a venture was ideal, inasmuch as every possible requirement for the boys was met within the actual campgrounds – bathing, cricket, football, fishing and games of every description, as well as mountain climbing. Every boy climbed Knockcree at least twice whilst in camp. The view from the top of Knockcree was magnificent and on a clear day Manx Land (the Isle of Man) was clearly discernible to the naked eye.

In round figures seventy boys attended the camp, including twelve Wolf Cubs who were under the care of Cubmaster Edgar Reilly. The whole camp was under the command of Mr W.J. Sterritt, District Commissioner, assisted by Scoutmaster John McMullan of the First Bessbrook Troop and Scoutmaster D. Graham, 1st Newry. The cooking arrangements were carried out by the boys themselves. The Troop was divided into patrols and responsible Patrol Leaders and Rover Scouts placed in charge of each. Patrol Leaders estimated their day's rations and at a given time drew these rations from the Quartermaster's stores. This system made each patrol an entirely separate unit as regards cooking and other activities. The competitive spirit was always to the fore as to which section prepared the best dinner and woe betide any cook who was a slacker – he was required to cook again the next day with the leader's instructions. On the whole really good cooking was the rule during the course of the camp.

A typical day's programme whilst in camp was as follows:

7.30 – Rouse; Patrol Leaders draw rations for day, cooks prepare breakfast, other Scouts clean up tents and tidy kits.

8.30 to 9.30 – Breakfast and wash utensils used at breakfast.

10.00 – Parade; every boy in camp was required to attend this parade.

The first item here was personal inspection, then kit inspection. The latter, provided the weather was good, meant that all kits had to be placed outside and blankets aired. The inspection completed, all stood to attention for prayers, after which the bugler stepped forward and blew 'the General Salute', and a Senior Scout hoisted the Union Flag. This officially opened the camp activities for the day, and any orders necessary were then read out at this parade.

10.00 to 1.30 - was normally spent in rambling through the woods and nature studies. At 1.30 all were again in camp, when lunch was served, after which all had an hour's compulsory rest until 3p.m., when the boys are free until 6.30p.m. By this time the cooks had dinner prepared and after finishing this meal the boys were again free until 10.30 p.m., when every member had to be in camp. Defaulters in this direction were severely dealt with by the 'Court of Honour', which consisted of Patrol Leaders. The sentence was usually that the culprit was confined to the immediate camp for one day.

During the camp the Scout football team played two matches with Kilkeel Juniors. The first match proved to be a draw, two goals each, and the second match was also a draw of one goal each. This second match had a replay of extra time, but the result still remained a draw. On the last day of the camp sports were held and valuable prizes kindly procured by Mr W. V. Hogg, Esq., and John Weir, Esq., of Sandys Street. At the conclusion of the sports the Troop chaplain, Rev. Phineas McKee, B.A., distributed the prizes, assisted by Mrs W. V. Hogg, Mrs John Weir and Mrs. J. Briggs.

The Troop was then formed up in a circle and all joined in singing 'Auld Lang Syne' and 'God Save the King'. The flag was taken down and the camp of the 1st Newry Troop B.P. Boy Scouts was closed for another year'.

Upon commencing the new Scouting term in September, and to accommodate the expected increase in the number of recruits to the Scout Movement in Newry during the winter months, arrangements were made to find the necessary space. As a result it was decided to form the Troop into four sections and place a responsible leader in charge of each with three of the sections devoted entirely to Scouts and the fourth to Wolf Cubs. This meant that twenty five to thirty boys could attend the meetings in the Scout hall every night and receive more instruction than if the whole Troop turned up and practically packed the hall out, as had been the case in the past. It was reported that intending recruits at that time would do well to join the Movement as it was really worthwhile, and even if only one of the ten Scout Laws was kept, a boy will be much better in every way.

Scout Law (1920s)

1. A Scout's honour is to be trusted.
2. A Scout is loyal to the King, his country, his officers, his parents, his employers and to those under him.
3. A Scout's duty is to be useful and to help others.
4. A Scout is a friend to all, no matter to what social class the other belongs.
5. A Scout is courteous.
6. A Scout is a friend to animals.
7. A Scout obeys orders of his parents, Patrol Leader or Scoutmaster, without question.
8. A Scout smiles and whistles under all difficulties.
9. A Scout is thrifty.
10. A Scout is clean in thought, word and deed.

On Friday, 14 December 1923, 1st Newry Troop B.P. Boy Scouts held their annual Jamboree in the Downshire Road Lecture Hall. The large hall was filled to overflowing on the raising of the curtain at 8p.m. prompt. The Jamboree itself proved to be the greatest success of any Scout affair yet held in Newry. The programme, which is detailed below, was of intense interest from beginning to end, and at times extremely amusing. So high was the standard of performing and artists that it would be very difficult, if not dangerous, to attempt to differentiate in the matter of praise, but it was noted that the Windsor Brass and Reed Band excelled itself with a very creditable performance, especially when it is remembered that this was only a very new band. 'Mac', better known to Newry audiences as Mr John McMullan, Scoutmaster of 1st Bessbrook Troop Boy Scouts, was never before heard to better advantage, and he had to respond to numerous encore demands. Another item deserving of special mention was the sketch, 'Lucy's Lovers', a scream from start to finish, and not the least amusing was Rover Scout A. Gray as the villain of the piece. He created roars of laughter by divesting himself of his numerous vests – he was wearing ten. The other characters of the piece were ably presented by Scoutmaster M. D. Graham, Troop Leader S. Sterritt, P.L. A. McCullough and P.L. T. Graham.

At the interval a very pleasing little ceremony was performed by the Troop chaplain, Rev. Phineas McKee, and District Commissioner W. J. Sterritt, when they, on behalf of the Troop, presented Miss M. McClelland of Courtney Hill, with a Thanks Badge, as small token of their appreciation of the invaluable services rendered by her to the Cubs and Scouts in training them for that entertainment. Miss McClelland suitably acknowledged the gift with a neat little speech. The boxing bouts and drill downs were ably judged by Mr William McNeill of Trevor Hill who, at the conclusion, gave his decision as a draw, both Troops being equally good in boxing and drill. Mr McNeill's decision was received by acclamation.

Wolf Cubs from 1st Newry enjoying a swim at Mourne Park.
L-R: W. Weir, R. Allely, J. Briggs, Jack Smyth, W. V. Hogg.

The McWhirter family
W.G., R.J., G.G., and T.A. McWhirter were all members of 1st Newry Group.

The following was the programme: -

> Selections, Windsor Brass and Reed Band; Troop Chorus, 'Georgia'; The Troop, Swedish Drill; Bessbrook Boy Scouts, Snake Dance and Howl; Newry Wolf Cubs, Recitation; Cub Willie Telford, Solo 'Idaho'; S.M. John McMullan, (Mac), Recitation; Sixer S. Graham, 'Minding Baby'; Boxing; Scoutmaster Graham, Newry v Cubmaster Maginnis, Bessbrook; Solo 'Songs my Mother Sang', Miss A. Lockhart; Violin solo 'Barcarolle', Second C. Armstrong; Solo 'Vamping Rose' P.L. Mahood, Rostrevor; Nursery Rhymes, Newry Wolf Cubs; Duet 'On the River' Miss Doreen King and Cub Alan Reilly; Dialogue 'Doctor', Scouts Cowan and McCullough; Song 'Bow-wow', Scout Jim Power; Grumbling Johnny, Newry Wolf Cubs; Selection, Windsor Brass and Reed Band; Boxing, Cub Bradley, Bessbrook v Cub Graham, Newry; Chorus, 'Milestones' The Troop; Duet, 'Convent Bells' S.M. John McMullan.

On Saturday, 28 December 1923, a large contingent of 1st Newry Group was busily engaged in parcelling up the gifts for the disabled ex-servicemen and soldiers' dependents from the local branch of the British Legion. The Scout hall presented an appearance similar to a large wholesale grocery store, and the boys proved themselves no mean exponents in the art of parcelling up the goods. The boys also assisted at the end of the day in distributing the parcels to the various people concerned. Following this successful service, the Executive of the British Legion suitably acknowledged the assistance of the Scouts and also returned thanks for the loan of the Scout hall, which was admirably suited to the occasion.

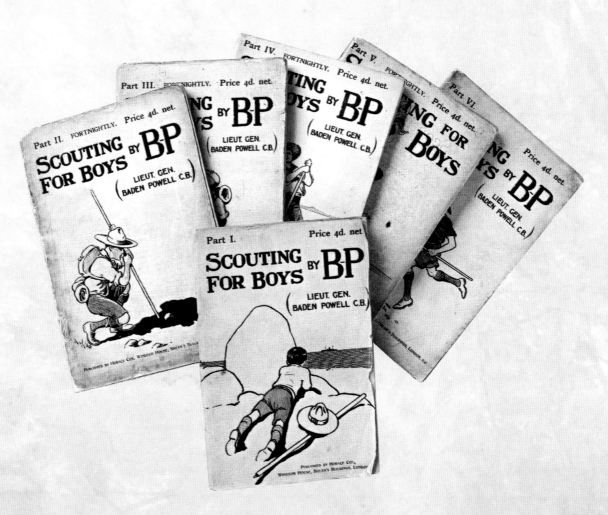

'Scouting For Boys' (first published in 1908)

1924

On the afternoon of Saturday, 24 May 1924, in the William Street school, a highly successful jumble sale was held to help raise funds for the annual summer camp of 1st Newry Boy Scout Troop. The sale, which was organised by the boys themselves, was under the capable directorship of Miss M. McClelland of Courtney Hill, ably assisted by the following band of willing workers - Mrs P. McKee, the Manse; Mrs S. Lockhart, Hill Street; Mrs J Crozier, Edward Street; Mrs Clarke, Mary Street; Mrs M McKinley, Bridge Street; Miss Gracey, Sandys Street; Miss Atwell, Canal Street; Miss Clarke, Caulfield Terrace; the Misses Mitchell, Bagot Street and Miss Lockhart, Hill Street. The total proceeds were most encouraging to all concerned with almost £20 (£20.00) being realised.

During the month of July the Troop held the most successful annual camp at Cranfield, near Kilkeel. The weather during the period of the camp turned out to be fine and all the boys taking part thoroughly enjoyed the experience. The camp was pitched in a field kindly lent for the occasion by Mr H Nicholson, and very close to the shore. The Troop was greatly indebted to the kindness of Mr Nicholson for all his help during the event. The shore and bathing facilities along Cranfield beach were ideally suited to the occasion, bathing being indulged in to the fullest extent by nearly every member of the Troop. The general health of the boys under canvas was exceptionally good and accidents, even of a minor character, were unknown. The boys themselves did all the cooking and at all times of a very high standard – two members of the Troop took it in turn to cook every day, and not once was an inferior meal served. The camp was in charge of Commissioner W. J. Sterritt, Scoutmaster D. Graham and Assistant Scoutmasters S Crozier, S. Sterritt and B. Atwell.

On 21 October 1924, it was recorded that 1st Newry B.P. Scout Group had 44 Scouts with four Leaders, W. J. Sterritt, DC, David Graham, Scoutmaster and Sam Crozier and Sydney Sterritt, Assistant Scoutmasters. There were also twenty Wolf Cubs with B.Atwell, Cubmaster.

Annual Jamboree

The annual Jamboree in connection with 1st Newry Troop B.P. Boy Scouts was held in Newry Town Hall on Friday night, 5 December 1924, with the Rev. Phineas McKee, B.A., chaplain to the Troop, presiding. The programme was of an exceptionally attractive character and the attendance was large, the body of the hall being completely filled. The arrangements were satisfactorily carried out by Mr W. J. Sterritt, District Commissioner and the Scoutmaster D. Graham, Assistant Scoutmasters S. Crozier and S. Sterritt, and Cubmaster B. Atwell. The members of the Troop attended in force and presented a neat and smart appearance in their uniform.

The chairman, in his introductory remarks, said that he thought one of the good features of the time was the increasing number of welfare organisations for boys and girls. They had often heard it said of certain persons that they had fallen into bad company. Why did they not as frequently hear the opposite remark that someone had fallen into good company? The more organisations they had would make it still easier to fall into good company. Going on to speak of the good work done for the boys by this particular organisation he said that the Boy Scout Movement was known in every civilized country of the world. Referring to the Scouts' camp life, he said he thought the funds at present being raised were intended to pay camp expenses in the future. In conclusion, he expressed hearty thanks to Mr Terence Ruddy and the members of St. Joseph's Band who had come there that night to contribute to the programme. Mr Ruddy was the best friend of all. They felt that he had brought credit and renown to the town and they were proud of him and the achievements of the band, which he so ably instructed and conducted.

The programme comprised the following, each item being well received and heartily applauded:

Overture, 'Le Domino Noir', contest piece by Auber and the march, 'Mad Major', by Alford by the St Joseph's Brass and Reed Band, Mr T. Ruddy, conductor; songs, 'Glory of the Sea' and 'Friends o' Mine', by Mr W. J. Leathem, Bessbrook (winner of the Moffat P. Clow Cup); minuet and trio by Beethoven on the piano by Miss May Cleland, L.T.C.L. and violins, Miss Vera Hardy and Scout C. Armstrong; songs, 'Arise, O Sun' and 'Star of Faith' by Mozart by Miss M. Brady; boxing displays by Scouts Stanley Graham (Newry) v. Stanley Crilly (Bessbrook), and Scoutmaster D. Graham v. Assistant Scoutmaster S. Crozier (both of Newry); songs, 'Have you paid the rent?' by Scoutmaster J. McMullan (Bessbrook); song, 'The Admiral's Broom' by Mr Bob Foster (Banbridge); song, 'The Exile's Return' by Mr Shooter (Banbridge). The two last-mentioned gentlemen, both of whom were silver medallists, also sang the duet, 'Watchman, what of the Night'; selections, 'The Old Flag' and 'The Minstrel Boy' by the Bessbrook Boy Scouts fife and drum band, conducted by Mr Magennis; clarinet solo, 'Les Alsaciennes' by Le Thiere performed by Mr Ivor Powell, with accompaniment by St Joseph's Band; physical drill display by Newry Boy Scouts; recitation, 'Petsy and I are out' by Scout Jim Cowan;

monologues', 'Kissing Cup's race', 'The Football Match' and 'Tarring the cow' by Mr W. R. King; a monologue by Scoutmaster William Johnson, B.A., LL.B., B.L., Belfast, describing Scout life and work and of the Christian principles of the Movement. The rendering of Middleton's grand selection, 'the Shamrock', a contest piece by St. Joseph's Band, concluded the programme.

The accompanists to the vocal items were Mr T. H. Reilly, Newry and Miss D. Megarrell, Bessbrook. At the close the chairman spoke in appreciative terms of the work done by Mr Sterritt, and thanked all those who had contributed to the programme.

Mr William Johnson, C.B.E., expressed thanks to the chairman, paid tribute to the labours of the District Commissioner in connection with the Boy Scout Movement, and also praised the kindness of Mr Ruddy and his band for attending the Jamboree. The playing of the National Anthem terminated a most enjoyable entertainment.

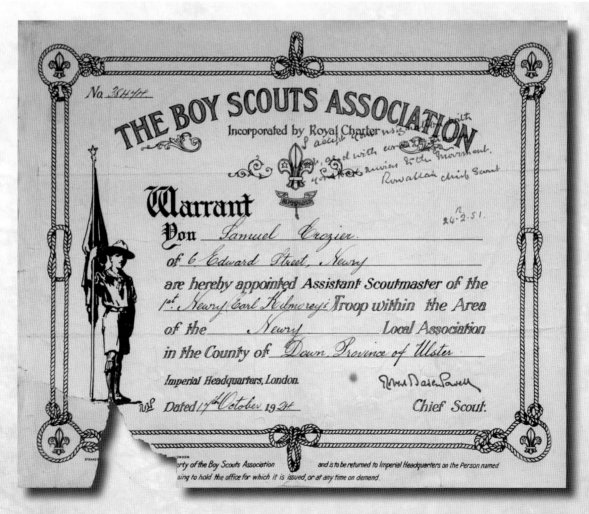

Samuel Crozier's Assistant Scoutmaster Warrant, 17 October 1924

1925

The following information was contained in the *Newry Reporter* dated 31 January 1925;

> *Parade:* On Tuesday evening last, 27 January, a parade of the 1st Newry Troop Boy Scouts was held in the Troop's newly renovated headquarters in Sandys Street. A very large number of the members of the Troop were present and the enthusiasm of the boys left nothing to be desired. Competitions were indulged in, in which every member of the Troop present took part.
>
> ### Troop Headquarters
> Extensive repairs have been recently carried out at the Scout hall by the Senior Scouts. The hall now presents a really comfortable appearance, being nicely wainscoted, and is at present being painted and generally decorated. The willing band of workers deserves great credit for the way in which they tackled, and brought to a successful finish, a difficult task.
>
> ### Recruits
> Despite the fact that 1st Newry Group is becoming quite an old organisation as Newry organisations go, new members are still enrolling, two lads presenting themselves for enrolment on the last parade. There was a grand total of sixty members of all ranks in the Newry Troop.
>
> ### Notes
> In connection with the repair work, I noticed bruised thumbs were only a mere detail, being a 'striking' illustration of the Scout Law, 'A Scout smile and whistles under all difficulties'.
>
> ### Next Parade
> The Troop will parade on Tuesday at 8p.m. sharp. A full turnout is requested'.
> The article was signed - 'Tenderfoot'.

February 1925

During the month of February 1925, the following report was given to the annual meeting of Downshire Road Presbyterian Church by Mr S. Crozier who, in the absence of Mr W. J. Sterritt, Scoutmaster and District Commissioner, read that gentleman's report as follows:

'During the past year the 1st Newry Troop of Boy Scouts under my command has made steady progress both in efficiency and numbers. The total strength of the Troop was now 60, notwithstanding the fact that during the year several of the boys left the Troop on transfer to a similar organisation in the town.

During the summer a most delightful and beneficial camp was held at Cranfield, county Down, for 10 days. 30 boys attended this camp at a cost of 10/- (50p) each. In December, a highly successful concert was held in the town hall in aid of the Troop funds. This concert was exceptionally well attended and a large sum was realised as a result. Several high-class artistes, including St. Joseph's Band, gave their services gratis.

The headquarters of the Troop, which was originally a loft belonging to the Manse, was badly in need of repair, and a special committee of

THE BOY SCOUTS

Mr S. Crozier (in the absence of Mr W. J. Sterritt, Scoutmaster and District Commissioner) read that gentleman's report as follows:—

During the past year the 1st Newry Troop of Boy Scouts under my command has made steady progress both in efficiency and numbers. The total strength of the troop is now 60, notwithstanding the fact that during the year several of the boys left the troop on transfer to a similar organisation in the town.

During the summer a most delightful and beneficial camp was held at Cranfield, Co. Down, for 10 days. 30 boys attended this camp at a cost of 10/- each. In December, a highly successful concert was held in the Town Hall in aid of the Troop funds. This concert was exceptionally well attended and a large sum was realised as a result. Several high-class artistes, including St. Joseph's Band, gave their services gratis.

The headquarters of the troop, which was originally a loft belonging to the Manse, was badly in need of repair, and a special committee of Scouts was formed in December, 1924, to have this done. The repairs effected included wainscoting, erecting presses, and painting, all done in a very creditable manner by the Scouts.

A bugle band is being formed. Some of the necessary instruments have already been obtained at a very cheap rate. It is hoped to have the band going within the next few months.

In general, I can say that the troop is progressing in a most satisfactory manner, all parades, etc., being attended well, and continued enthusiasm evinced on all occasions.

The greatest need of the troop at the moment is a new Troop Flag. The flag we have has been somewhat dilapidated through wear and tear and age; being originally presented to us by the late Countess of Kilmorey in 1910.

W. J. Sterrit, Scoutmaster and District Commissioner

Mr. Thomas Watt seconded the report, which was adopted.

Newry Reporter, February 1925

Scouts was formed in December, 1924, to have this done. The repairs affected included wainscoting, erecting presses and painting, all being done in a very creditable manner by the Scouts.

A bugle band is being formed. Some of the necessary instruments have already been obtained at a very cheap rate. It is hoped to have the band going within the next few months.

In general, I can say that the Troop is progressing in a most satisfactory manner, all parades being well attended, and continued enthusiasm evidenced on all occasions.

The greatest need of the Troop at the moment is a new Troop flag. The flag we have has been somewhat dilapidated through wear and tear and age, having been originally presented to us by the late Countess of Kilmorey in 1910'.

On Thursday, 12 February, 'Tenderfoot' once again put pen to paper and sent the following information to the *Newry Reporter*. 'Now that the 1st Newry Troop headquarters has been completed, a full parade of all ranks will be held next Tuesday evening, 12 February, at 8 o'clock sharp. Uniform will be worn. A specially large turn-out of the boys is desired. The Scout hall now presents a very neat and tasteful appearance and the various repairs and alterations effected have made an immense improvement, with the result that the Newry Scouts can boast of having the finest and best equipped headquarters in Ireland. Not a little of the credit for the wonderful improvements wrought are due to the Rover section of the Group, having left no stone unturned to bring the renovations to a successful conclusion. An opportunity will be given to all the boys' parents to visit and inspect the hall in the course of the next few days. It is hoped to arrange a parents night for this purpose'.

March 1925

'Tenderfoot' noted on 14 March that 'The usual weekly meeting of 1st Newry Troop Boy Scouts was held on Wednesday, 11 March, in the evening, when there was a very encouraging muster of the boys present.

The instruments for the bugle band had now arrived, and the first practice was to take place on Monday, 23 March, at 8p.m. The Troop was very fortunate in securing the services of Mr William Cowan as instructor to the band. Mr Cowan had a wide experience in

this connection, and in a short time the band would make its first appearance.

A district church parade had been arranged to take place very soon to Downshire Road Presbyterian Church. The Group and district chaplain, Rev. Phineas McKee, B.A., is to officiate at this event. All the Troops in the district are to be well represented, and two new flags will be dedicated at this service for 1st Bessbrook Troop.

At this service Mr J. W. Leathem, Bessbrook, will sing a solo. 1st Bessbrook Boy Scout flute band will head the parade, which is timed for 6.30p.m. The whole service and ceremony will be of an entirely Scout nature, the first of its kind ever held in Newry.

It is expected that upwards of 200 boys will be on parade at the service, and should present an imposing spectacle with their bands, flags, and neat uniforms'.

Dedication of Colours

On Sunday, 29 March, there was an exceptionally fine parade of Boy Scouts to divine service in Downshire Road Presbyterian Church, Newry. The parade was headed by the fife and drum band of the Bessbrook Troop, and comprised detachments from 1st Newry, 1st Bessbrook, 1st Rathfriland and 1st Warrenpoint Scout Groups. There was also a large turnout of Wolf Cubs from 1st Bessbrook and 1st Newry.

There was an unusually large attendance of worshippers and well wishers of the Movement in the church, which was filled to the utmost of its seating capacity.

The preacher for the evening service was the Rev. Phineas McKee, B.A., chaplain to 1st Newry Group and pastor of the church. The first part of the service was conducted by the Very Rev. W. G. Strahan, B.A., D.D., pastor of Sandys Street Presbyterian Church, Newry, with the praise items consisting of the following 'All people that on earth do dwell' (Old Hundredth), 'Onward, Christian Soldiers' and 'Stand up, Stand up for Jesus'.

Prior to the sermon, the Rev. McKee dedicated two flags to the glory of God and for the use of the 1st Bessbrook Scout Troop and Bessbrook Wolf Cub Pack. These flags, which were presented to the Troop by Mr James Bowes, Bessbrook, were received by Scoutmaster John McMullan, and Cubmaster H. Honeyford and dipped in salute as bugle bandmaster, William Cowan, Newry, sounded the 'General Salute'. The congregation then sang the National Anthem.

Mr J. W. Leathem, formerly associated with the Bessbrook Troop, rendered the tenor solo, 'The Lord is My Light', very effectively.

The Rev. McKee chose as his text some favourite words of Sir Ernest Shackleton's, 'If I take the wings of the morning and dwell in the uttermost parts of the sea; even there shall Thy hand lead me, and Thy right hand shall hold me', (Psalm 139 vv. 9-10). In an eloquent exposition, he dealt with the subject of heroism, which was beloved by all Boy Scouts. He spoke of the trials and feats of endurance which were successfully carried through by the great explorers, and explained how, after one of his famous voyages, he referred to this particular text. He compared the experience of the explorers with his two companions in the frozen icy regions to the story of Daniel, as read in the evening lesson. Throughout their voyages and struggles the three brave men had a consciousness of a fourth Great Presence, which aided and succoured them, as Daniel and his fellow sufferers were helped and protected when thrust into the burning fiery furnace. He pointed out that the greatest spur to heroism, the power which could sustain against all vicissitudes and endure all hardships and trials, was a firm reliance on the Lord and Saviour Jesus Christ. The stay of the explorer amid the icy regions was his trust in that Saviour. The strength and support of all those lads setting out on the unknown and hazardous journey of life must be the same enduring faith. They had fights and struggles ahead of them to lead a clean, pure life. The great test of courage was not death. The strong and terrible test was to live day by day a straight, upright life. He concluded with an earnest exhortation to all to place their reliance on that Saviour, and so to fulfil the promise they had made, and to honour the obligations imposed by their Scout Laws.

The singing of the hymn 'Fight the Good Fight' and the pronouncing of the Benediction concluded the service.

Miss E. McCullough capably presided at the organ.

On leaving the church, the Troops formed up and conducted the Bessbrook visitors to the outskirts of the town, being followed by a large crowd of onlookers.

The officers present were Commissioners W. J. Sterritt (Newry District) and William Johnson, B.A., B.L., LL.B. (North Belfast District), a past member of 1st Newry Troop.

Newry Scouts – Scoutmaster David Graham and Assistant Scoutmasters Sam Crozier and Sidney Sterritt.

Bessbrook Scouts – Scoutmaster John McMullan and Assistant Scoutmaster Thomas Martin.

1st Rathfriland Troop – Assistant Scoutmaster W. Brady.

1st Warrenpoint Troop – Assistant Scoutmaster Bob Haldane.

Newry Wolf Cubs – Cubmaster Ben Atwell and Assistant Cubmaster William McWhirter.

Bessbrook Wolf Cubs – Cubmaster H. Honeyford and Assistant Cubmaster J. Magennis.

April 1925

Notwithstanding the severe storm which prevailed on Saturday, 18 April 1925, county Down Scouts successfully carried out their plan to convey a sealed despatch by cyclists from Holywood to Warrenpoint. The despatch was written and sealed by Sir Robert Kennedy, K.C.M.G., D.L., and was addressed to Mr William Johnson, C.B.E., Warrenpoint, both these gentlemen being warm supporters of the Movement. The message read as follows: - 'This despatch will be delivered to you at Warrenpoint by county Down Boy Scouts relay despatch bearers, of whom the first leaves Holywood at noon to-day. The arrangement for the safe conveyance of this despatch have been made by our County Commissioner, Mr W. V. Heasley, who has under his supervision in county Down 1,100 Rovers, Scouts, and Wolf Cubs, who work together in that great Scout Brotherhood which was created in 1907 by the genius of the Chief Scout, Lieut. General Sir Robert Baden-Powell, and has since spread from Great Britain and Ireland into all the civilised countries in the world, thus forming an international brotherly league of morally, intellectually and physically trained, God-fearing and loyal citizens. I am sure that the bearers of this despatch will do credit to their training by carefully observing all the conditions of the comprehensive Scout Law to which they have pledged their obedience, and that they will overcome any obstacles with which they may be confronted in the true Scout spirit which 'smiles and whistles under all difficulties'.

Punctually at noon this message was handed over at the Maypole, Holywood, by Sir Robert Kennedy to Senior Rover Mate George Humphries, who was accompanied by Rover Scout Henry Ballagh and Patrol Leader John McKimm, the latter also receiving a verbal message from Commissioner Heasley to District Commissioner Sterritt, Newry. Both messages were to be conveyed by relays about every five miles throughout the whole of county Down, thus linking up all the Troops in the various towns and villages. Sir Robert and Lady Kennedy and the Misses Kennedy accompanied the despatch by motorcar to the first relay station at Clandeboye where it was handed over at 12.27p.m. to Bangor Scouts, the route followed being: - Bangor, Donaghadee, Millisle, Ballywalter, Kircubbin, Greyabbey, Newtownards, Comber, Ballygowan, Ballynahinch, Ballykeel Cross Roads, Dromore, Moira, Maralin, Beechpark, Waringstown, Donacloney, Tullylish, Seapatrick, Banbridge, Scarva, Goraghwood and Newry.

The scheduled time for the despatch to reach Warrenpoint was 9.50p.m. and the actual time it arrived was 10 o'clock, or only ten minutes late after a distance of 107 miles. This was a splendid performance, and reflected the greatest credit on the Scouts who took part, all of whom manfully stuck to their posts through the heavy rain and wind. The distance was said to be the longest one which any despatch had been carried by Scouts in this country and, as a feat of organisation and endurance, especially having regard to the exceedingly trying weather, will probably stand as a record for some time.

The verbal message given at Holywood was –'I hope all county Down Scouts will always play the game, and live out the Scout law and promise in their lives. Heasley, County Commissioner'. This passed by word of mouth from Scout to Scout for 107 miles and, on arrival at Warrenpoint, it was rendered as follows: - 'Mr Heasley wishes all county Down Scouts to have a good time, and live up to the Scout law'. The words 'play the game' got changed en route into 'have a good time'.

A despatch also left Warrenpoint at 11.35a.m. by the reverse route for Holywood, and reached Ballynahinch at 6.15p.m., almost an hour late. It was very hard work on the route northwards, as all the cyclists experienced the full effect of the north-easterly gale, and at times it was quite impossible to make any progress. Some of the boys were practically blown off their bicycles and had to walk considerable distances. There was a further serious delay from Ballynahinch to Comber and, as the evening was getting late, it was decided to call it off, owing to the exposed nature of the coast road, over which the despatch was to be taken. More adverse conditions could not have been experienced, but the arrangements were admirable, and the utmost credit is due to the County Commissioner who initiated the event, for the care with which he had worked out all the details.

The county Down Scouts were to be congratulated on being able to carry the despatch through to Warrenpoint, in spite of the bad weather. The test had proved to the satisfaction of all concerned that it was possible to link up all the Troops in the county, each doing his bit in a great scheme. By the combined efforts of all Scouters, Rovers, Scouts, and Cubs in the common cause of Scouting, it was hoped to make the county of Down one of the best centres in Ulster.

Patrol Leader W. Linton and Scout Jack Griffith were the members of the Bessbrook Troop who brought the Holywood despatch from Goraghwood to Newry, while the members of the Newry Troop who brought it from Newry to Warrenpoint were Assistant Scoutmaster Samuel Crozier and Cubmaster Ben Atwell.

Under the auspices of 1st Newry Troop B.P. Boy Scouts, a very successful social and parents night was held in the Scout hall on Friday evening, 24 April 1925, when there was a record attendance of parents and other supporters of the Troop. The Scouts served an enjoyable tea, accompanied by choice pastries, promptly at 8 p.m. After tea, Mr W. J. Sterritt, Scoutmaster and District Commissioner, moved that Mr Alexander McClelland occupy the chair for the evening owing to the unavoidable absence of the Troop chaplain, Rev. Phineas McKee, B.A., who was unable to be present owing to the sudden death of his brother-in-law.

Mr McClelland thanked all concerned for the honour in electing him chairman, and said that he was very glad indeed to be present and to render any assistance he could in furthering the Scout Movement in Newry. He said 1st Newry Troop had a right to be proud of their achievements, especially in regard to the very creditable way in which they had decorated and repaired the hall, and also their ability in maintaining a record Troop number with seventy boys being on the rolls.

Rev. W. Jasper Robinson, B.A., Newry Methodist minister, also made a very complimentary speech in which he said that he was more than surprised at the efficiency of the Troop and their general bearing.

A short programme was then presented to the entire enjoyment of all, the following well known ladies and gentlemen contributing: - Miss M. McClelland, Miss Jeannie Smith, Rev. H. B. Swanzy, Mr William McNeill, Scout Charles Armstrong and Scout Jim Cowan.

At the conclusion of the programme, a very hearty vote of thanks was passed by acclamation on the motion of Mr Sterritt who, on behalf of the Troop, thanked one and all for their assistance in making the evening the success it undoubtedly had been, especially to Miss M. J. Wylie for the trouble she went to in making the tea. The meeting was closed with the singing of the National Anthem.

After the event several ladies remained behind in order to discuss in what way they could help the Troop and, on the motion of Miss M. McClelland, seconded by Miss M. Gracey, it was decided to hold a jumble sale early in May, and the following committee was appointed to assist and direct: - Miss McClelland, Miss M. Gracey, Mrs Robinson (Canal Street), Mrs Smith, Miss Rainey, Miss Mitchell, Miss Wylie, Mrs Kennedy, Mrs W. J. Sterritt (Erskine Street), Mrs Armstrong, Mrs Sterritt, Mrs Dalzell and Miss E. Sterritt.

May 1925

On Saturday afternoon, 9 May 1925, in Downshire Road Church Lecture Hall, a highly successful jumble sale was held in connection with 1st Newry Troop Boy Scouts. The sale, which was organised and carried through by a willing band of lady workers, assisted by Scouts, met with unqualified success and, as a result, the handsome sum of £20 (£20.00) was added to the funds of the Troop. The following ladies acted as canvassers and saleswomen in a very creditable manner: - Mrs McKee, Miss McClelland, Miss Cooper, Miss Etta Sterritt, Mrs J. Kennedy, Mrs Smith, the Misses Smith, Mrs Truesdale, Mrs Campbell Gray, Miss Rainey, Miss Mitchell, Miss McNeil, Mrs Clarke, Miss Clarke, Mrs Hunter, Mrs Robinson, Mrs W. J. Sterritt, Miss M. J. Wylie,

Miss Gracey, Miss Atwell, Miss Magowan, Miss Flack and Miss Lily Ferris.

June 1925

At the beginning of June arrangements were well advanced for holding the annual camp, from 11 to 23 July 1925, at Cranfield, on the lands of Mr H. Nicholson, who very kindly granted the use of same for the occasion rent free. Cranfield as a camping place was considered ideally suited as all kinds of sports and bathing can be indulged in with perfect safety. It was noted that a record number of boys intended taking part in this event as already some forty members had expressed an interest and given their names to the leaders. Judging from the immense enthusiasm prevailing in the Troop at that time, it is more than probable that the actual number would be nearer sixty. In this connection it was regretted that no further recruits could be accepted until after the camp for either the Scouts or Wolf Cubs. This year it was noted that the boys attending camp would not be subjected to any irksome military training.

July 1925

Subsequently on Saturday, 11 July, 1st Newry Troop Boy Scouts left the Scout hall early in the morning for their annual summer camp at Cranfield, county Down. Over 40 Scouts and Cubs assembled for this event under the command of Mr W. J. Sterritt, District Commissioner, ably assisted by Scoutmaster David Graham and Assistant Scoutmasters Sidney Sterritt and Sam Crozier together with Cubmaster B. Atwell. Cranfield as a camping place left nothing to be desired, and was ideally situated for all kinds of sport and Scout games and sea bathing during camp. The Troop chaplain, Rev. Phineas McKee, B.A., was present during the greater part of the camp, and acted in that capacity whilst present. The total number of lads present averaged forty two and the camp was organised on the patrol system, which is that each section is complete in itself doing its own cooking, with two Scouts taking it in turn to prepare the meals for the day. The cooking throughout the period was of a very high standard, and every taste was catered for. Washing up after meals and fire lighting was also undertaken in pairs and so every Scout had the opportunity of developing their skills in these activities. Games were indulged in to the fullest possible extent, the favourites being cricket and football, and not a few availed themselves of the close proximity of the golf links and had several lessons on golf, making considerable progress during their stay. The health of the Troop whilst under canvas was excellent. With the exception of an epidemic of sunburned arms and knees, everything was normal. Arrangements had been made for a return from camp on 23 July but the camp proved so successful, and the weather conditions and scenery so delightful, that a further stay of two days was undertaken and the Troop all returned home on Saturday via charabanc, as fit as fiddles and as bronzed as copper. While 1st Newry camped at Cranfield, 1st Dungannon under the leadership of Scoutmaster W. J. Wylie, formerly Assistant Scoutmaster of 1st Newry, was encamped at Narrow Water.

October 1925

The sixth annual meeting, following the cessation of the war, of 1st Newry Troop was held on Tuesday evening, 20 October, in the Troop Headquarters, Sandys Street. Scoutmaster David Graham occupied the chair and Assistant Scoutmasters S. Crozier and S. Sterritt and Cubmaster W. McWhirter were in attendance. The meeting was addressed by District Commissioner W. J. Sterritt who, in the course of his remarks, stated that he was more than gratified with such an excellent attendance of the boys – over forty being present – which number did not include thirty Wolf Cubs, whose annual meeting would be held shortly. Such a great attendance in the sixth year after the war had ended certainly spoke volumes for the growth and popularity of the Scout Movement in Newry district. Several important items were discussed in regard to the Troop's future welfare, in which all ranks took part, amongst them being the formation of a fife and drum ban to be used in conjunction with the present bugle band. All present were heartily in support of the scheme, which it was hoped would be put into execution in about a fortnight. Owing to the existing Patrol Leaders becoming too old to hold rank, they were transferred to the Rover

Section, and the following members were appointed; James Dalzell, Robert Dougan, Lee McKinstry, Jim Cowan, William McCracken, and Robert McWhirter. These appointments were received with great enthusiasm by all present, and each individual was welcomed in his new rank according to Scout custom. Scoutmaster Graham stated that he sincerely hoped that the new leaders would put their hearts into their work and keep the flag of the old Troop flying.

The honorary secretary, Assistant Scoutmaster Crozier, in his report, stated that the number of active Scouts at present on the roll was fifty one with thirty Wolf Cubs. These figures were considered very satisfactory. This concluded the business of the meeting, which then terminated.

November 1925

The Group had planned to hold its annual Jamboree during late November but due to another organisation's event being arranged for the same date, it was decided to postpone 1st Newry's Jamboree until early December and the following notice was placed in the local press; 'We beg to draw attention to the advertisement in this issue concerning the postponement of the Jamboree to be held in connection with the Troop. This has been rendered unavoidable owing to another entertainment being arranged for the original date in connection with another organisation. The Jamboree bids fair to eclipse that of last year, which was highly successful. Prominent local artistes will appear, together with St. Joseph's Brass and Reed Band and the Frontier Pipe Band'.

December 1925

Subsequently on Friday evening, 11 December 1925, the sixth annual Jamboree under the auspices of 1st Newry Troop of B.P. (Earl Kilmorey) Boy Scouts, was held in the local town hall. There was a large attendance, the body of the hall being filled, whilst the balcony was also well occupied. A number of members of the Troop acted as stewards and programme sellers and the Wolf Cubs were in attendance. The officers who were present included District Commissioner W. J. Sterritt,

Scoutmaster David Graham and Assistant Scoutmaster Samuel Crozier.

The programme was a varied and pleasing one, and was received with enthusiasm by the audience.

St Joseph's Brass and Reed Band, Newry, which was in attendance, under the conductorship of Mr Terence Ruddy, delighted all present by the rendering of the following pieces: - March, 'Voice of the Guns'; Overture, '1001 Nights'; Grand Selection, 'Chow Chin Chow'; and Selection, 'Fantasy on American Airs'.

The Frontier Pipe Band, under Pipe Major McPherson, was also present and played two Selections, 'Irish Airs' and 'Scotch Airs', whilst Pipe Major McPherson and Band Sergeant Russell executed a duet on the pipes. Mr Thomas Anderson, baritone, Newry, effectively sang 'The Ebb Tide Flows' (Bingham) and 'Mother o' Mine' (Weatherly). In the solos 'Roses' and 'The Hymns of the Old Church Choir', Mr William McNeill, another baritone, was heard to advantage.

Mr W. R. King was greeted with loud applause which increased in vigour after he had recited the humorous monologue, 'A Newry Town Football Match'. The audience insisted on an encore and Mr King chose 'Arithmetic'. Later in the evening he renewed the laughter and applause by his recital of 'A Slight Mistake' followed as an encore by 'Tarring the Cow'.

Miss Vera Hardy, a skilful and promising violinist, was applauded for her violin playing and Scout C. Armstrong capably executed the violin solo, 'The Broken Melody'. Miss Rhoda Downey, soprano, Bessbrook, tastefully sang 'Songs My Mother Sang' (Grimshaw) and 'When the Cold Grey Dawn Breaks Silently'. The tenor solos 'She is far from the land' (Lambert) and 'Linden Lea' (R. Vaughan Williams) were pleasingly rendered by Mr R. W. McConnell.

Humorous vocal items by Mr Paul Ambrose, character comedian, were much enjoyed and he had to respond to a call for an encore. His contributions were 'Patter song', 'Sweet, Sweet Bye and Bye', 'Beware!' (an amusing parody to the air 'Asleep in the Deep') and 'That reminds me where I left my umbrella'.

Miss Elsie Strahan, L.R.A.M., played the accompaniments to the vocal items.

During an interval prior to the close of the entertainment, the Rev. Phineas McKee B.A., chaplain to the Troop, proposed a cordial vote of thanks on behalf of the Troop and of the audience, to all who had assisted in making the event a success. He thought the world had a warm corner in its heart for the Boy Scout Movement. The Chief Scout, Sir Robert Baden-Powell, did a great thing for the whole world when he founded that Association for the welfare of youth which was spreading throughout the entire world. The Boy Scouts now held a big place in the world as those who had travelled had learned. Many would remember the number of Scouts who went to Rome this year for a celebration, and would recall the very sad accident that happened on the way home, which called forth the sympathy of all Scouts to whatever church they might belong. He referred to the great gathering of Scouts at the Wembley exhibition and also said that when he visited Stockholm in August last he found many Scouts there. That the people of Newry had a warm corner in their hearts for the local Troop, was evidenced by the large audience. Mr Sterritt, the District Commissioner, deserved a great deal of credit and praise for the work done in making the arrangements for the entertainment. They wished to thank Mr Ruddy and his band for their support. Mr Ruddy required no praise from him for he was what they might term one of the monarchs in the realms of music. He and his band had brought credit to the town by their achievements. The Boy Scouts said that when Mr Ruddy was asked to assist he willingly assented without delay. They also extended a very warm welcome to the boys of the Frontier Pipe Band, a recently formed company, who had shown that evening what they could do and to whom they were looking forward for the future. Included in the vote of thanks were all others who took part in the programme but a very special word of thanks should be given to the accompanist, Miss Strahan, who had carried out a trying and difficult part of the programme in a manner that merited the very highest praise. Mr Thomas Watt, local secretary of the Boy Scout Association, seconded the motion, which was passed by acclamation. The event concluded with the National Anthem.

1926 - 1927

Remembrance Sunday 1926 at Margaret Square.
1st Newry Boy Scouts are pictured at the bottom right of this photograph.

On 2 February 1927, another annual Jamboree was held in Downshire Road Lecture Hall, when a large audience witnessed a very enjoyable programme, which was entirely performed by the members of the Troop with but one exception: - Opening Chorus – Scouts Marching Song by the Troop; Grand Howl, Bagheera dance and physical drill by the Wolf Cubs, under Cubmaster W. McWhirter; Monologue – 'Green Eye of the Little Yellow God' by Mr W. R. King; Boxing bout by Scouts S. Graham and S. Dalzell; Sketch – 'Haunted House' by Scouts N. Graham, R. Dougan and R. Donnell; Chorus – 'Swanee River' by the Wolf Cubs; Sketch – 'On the Brain' by Scouts J. McCracken, A. Gray, J. Dalzell, S. Sterritt and N. Graham; Monologue – 'Tarring the Cow' by Mr W. R. King; Sketch – 'The Black Schoolmaster' by Scouts A. McCullough, N. Sterritt, F. Dalzell, R. Dougan, W. McCracken and S. Graham; Nigger Troupe and McNamara's Band by the Boy Scouts. At the interval the chaplain, Rev. P. McKee, B.A., in the course of his remarks regarding the Troop, stated that he was proud of them and felt privileged to be their chaplain. He said the entertainment was one that everyone thoroughly enjoyed, and even though it may have lacked the finest artistry, it more than compensated for that by the mirth and amusement it provoked amongst the very large audience which he was glad to see coming to the support of the Troop. He then, on behalf of the Troop, thanked Miss Esther McCullough who acted as pianist and assisted at the training of the boys, and called upon District Commissioner W. J. Sterritt to present to her with the Thanks Badge of the Boy Scout Association. Miss McCullough suitably replied, stating that the whole affair had taken her completely by surprise, but that anything she could do for the Scouts she would only be delighted to assist.

At the conclusion of the entertainment, the Rev. McKee announced that the officers and boys of the Troop had decided to hold a repeat performance, with a slightly varied programme, on Friday, 11 February, in aid of Newry General Hospital. He hoped that everyone would endeavour to make this a success, as the Scouts had decided to hand over the complete proceeds to this very deserving local cause. The evening concluded with the singing of the National Anthem.

Entertainment in aid of Newry General Hospital - The Jamboree which was last performed by 1st Newry Troop of Boy Scouts on 2 February was, with some variations, repeated in the Downshire Road Lecture Hall on Friday, 11 February, in aid of funds for Newry General Hospital. The hall was crowded with an enthusiastic audience, and the programme was thoroughly enjoyed by all present, encores being demanded and kindly responded to in numerous instances.

Easter Monday, 12 April, saw an interesting and hard fought football match played between 1st Newry Boy Scouts and Bangor Boy Scouts in Bangor. Newry came away from Bangor victorious by 4 goals to 3. The scorers for Newry were Dougan (2), Cowan and J Crozier. The 1st Newry team was made up of - N. Sterritt, J. Crozier, S. Graham, N. Graham, H. Scott, J. McCracken, J. Cowan, J. Dalzell, S. Crozier, R. Dougan and A. Ferris. Then on the following Wednesday, 14 April, the enthusiastic 1st Newry team held a friendly match against the Church Lads' Brigade which was played on the sports ground of St Mary's Church. The match which was, by all reports, a most interesting event resulted in a well merited win for 1st Newry by 5 goals to 2. The goal getters for Newry were Scouts Crozier (2), Cowan (2) and Dougan, and for the CLB Cadets, Hughes (2).

Sunday evening, 22 May 1927, saw a united service in Downshire Road Presbyterian Church in the presence of a large congregation, when the Rev. Phineas McKee, B.A. dedicated for the use of 1st Newry (Earl Kilmorey) Troop, two sets of colours – a green Troop flag and a Union Flag. St Mary's Church Lads' Brigade, 1st Warrenpoint Scouts and 1st Bessbrook Scouts also took part in the parade, which was in charge of District Commissioner W J. Sterritt, the other officers being: - 1st Newry Troop – Scoutmaster G. F. Matson, Assistant Scoutmasters S. Crozier and S. Sterritt, with Acting Cubmaster J. Cowan in charge of the Wolf Cubs; 1st Bessbrook Troop – Patrol Leader and Acting Scoutmaster James Aulds; 1st Warrenpoint Troop – Acting Scoutmaster Alfred Cresswell and the Church Lads' Brigade was in charge of Sergeant Steele. The flags to be dedicated were presented by the members of Downshire Road congregation and the turnout of the Scouts and C.L.B. was quite imposing. The body of the church was reserved for their accommodation and, as they smartly took their places in the sacred edifice, their smartness and bearing was an eloquent testimony to the training imparted to them. The service, which was conducted throughout by the Rev. P. McKee, chaplain to 1st

Newry Troop, was of a bright and appropriate character, not the least pleasing feature being the praise service, ably led by the choir, with Mrs Adamson presiding at the organ. The solo, 'Lead Kindly Light' was given with fine effect and expression by Mr Gilbert Adamson, just prior to the sermon.

The dedication of the Colours and the Union flag was brief but impressive. The colour parties having advanced to the forefront of the Church, the Rev. McKee, as chaplain of the Troop, formally dedicated both the Troop Colour and the Union flag and handed them over to the respective bearer parties 'for safe keeping'. Mr W Cowan then sounded the 'General Salute' with the Scouts and Cadets standing to attention.

This was followed by the singing of the hymn 'Onward, Christian Soldiers', after which the Rev. P. McKee preached a sermon appropriate to the occasion, in the course of which he reminded the Scouts of some of the great figures in the Old and New Testaments who embodied in their personalities some of the chief characteristics of the Scout Movement, which stood for obedience, discipline, truthfulness and clean living. Anyone who obeyed the Scout laws was in a

1st Newry Wolf Cub Pack Registration, 4 June 1927.

fair way of becoming a Christian and, in an earnest exhortation to the boys, he appealed to them to become soldiers and followers of Christ, reminding them that the world is divided into two great camps, and it was for them to decide under which flag and Master they would serve. The service concluded with the singing of the hymn 'Stand up! Stand up for Jesus' and the pronouncing of the benediction. The collection was in aid of Newry Troop funds.

Sunday, 3 July 1927, was a red-letter day in the history of 1st Newry (Earl Kilmorey) Troop and St Mary's Church Lads' Brigade (King's Royal Rifle Cadets). In the morning the Scouts and Wolf Cubs joined the Church Lads' Brigade in a parade to St Mary's Parish Church, headed by the Frontier Pipe Band. Capt. T. W. Yarnell was in charge of the Cadets and Scoutmaster G. Matson in charge of the Scouts and Wolf Cubs, the whole presenting quite a creditable turnout. The preacher was the Rev. W. M. Taylor, curate of St Mary's, who, preaching from the text 'Fight the good fight', exhorted the boys to live clean and healthy Christian lives and prove themselves worthy members of the organisations to which they belonged.

In the evening in Downshire Road Presbyterian Church an interesting ceremony took place, when Miss Gordon, of 'Ormiston', Dublin Road, presented a Wolf Cub flag to the Wolf Cubs of 1st Newry Group. The Scouts and Cubs turned out in strength, the former in charge of Assistant Scoutmaster S. Sterritt and the latter under Assistant Cubmaster J. Cowan. The colours were received by Assistant Cubmaster Cowan and Sixers Andrews, Briggs and McWhirter and Miss Gordon, in presenting them, expressed the pleasure it gave her to do so, and said she trusted the Cubs would grow up to be loyal citizens of the King and of the Empire, and be true and faithful followers of the King of Kings. The colours were now theirs for safekeeping. The dedicatory prayer was offered by the Rev. Phineas McKee, B.A., chaplain to the Group, who afterwards delivered a very appropriate address.

Wednesday, 13 July, saw about 20 members of 1st Newry Troop leaving for their annual camp, being held this year at Lendalfoot, near Girvan, under the command of District Commissioner W. J. Sterritt. At Stranraer, a very interesting event in the history of the Troop took place when Lord Craigavon, Northern Ireland's Prime Minister, inspected the Troop, which was specially drawn up for the occasion at Stranraer harbour. The premier in the course of his remarks stated that he was very pleased to inspect 1st Newry Boy Scouts and to learn that they were bound for a holiday in bonnie Scotland, where he hoped they would have a very enjoyable time and return to the old frontier town benefitted as a result. He also complimented the boys on their smart appearance and was greatly interested in their equipment, which he thought was very complete. The Troop was then entrained for Girvan, where they arrived about 10.45pm and thence to Lendalfoot by motor, where they finally

1st Newry Boy Scouts at Lendalfoot, July 1927

Jim Dalzell, Sam Crozier, Bob McWhirter, Noel Sterritt, W. McCracken. Lendalfoot, July 1927

Jimmy Cowan with the Wolf Cub Flag, July 1927

Wolf Cubs at Cranfield, July 1927

arrived about midnight, safe and happy. The whole journey was a great adventure to the boys, who thoroughly enjoyed it to the fullest, especially the sea passage.

However not to be outdone by the Scouts having their annual camp in Scotland, 1st Newry Wolf Cubs had a most enjoyable outing to Cranfield, near Kilkeel on Monday, 25 July 1927. The boys, in charge of Assistant Cubmaster J. Cowan and Assistant Scoutmasters S. Crozier and S. Sterritt, left Newry in a large charabanc about 10 o'clock and, after a pleasant journey, reached Cranfield about 11.30, where games were immediately indulged in until one o'clock, when lunch was served. During the course of the day sports were held, and all present thoroughly enjoyed themselves. Mr R. J. McCombe, Newry, kindly presented a prize for a 5-a-side football competition. The results of the various events were: - 100 yards under 10 – W. Power; 100 yards under 14 – G. Campbell; Three-legged race – G. McWhirter and G. Campbell; Long jump – 1, B. Adamson; 2, G. Campbell; 440 yards – 1, J. Baird; 2, L. Donaldson; Tug of war – J. Kidd, W. O'Neill, G. Kennedy, H. Boyd, J. McCaigue, B. Adamson and W. McCracken and the 5-a-side football – W. Andrews, J. Kidd, H. Boyd, B. Adamson and J. Briggs. After tea, the Rev. Phineas McKee, B.A., chaplain of the Group, who was accompanied by the Rev. H. McIlroy, B.A., presented the prizes, and also gave a short address, after which the Grand Howl was given by the Cubs. The return journey from Cranfield took place about nine o'clock and the boys reached Newry, tired but happy, after a most enjoyable day. Before dispersing the boys again gave the Grand Howl and also sang the National Anthem.

Later in the year a very enjoyable social was held on the evening of Wednesday, 21 December 1927, in the Lecture Hall of the Downshire Road Presbyterian Church. There was a very large attendance of the Rovers, Scouts and Wolf Cubs, in all over 50 boys being present. After tea, which was made by the boys, a lengthy programme of games and songs was indulged in to the hearty amusement of all present. At an appropriate interval the opportunity was taken to bid farewell to Patrol Leader Robert Dougan on his impending departure to Glasgow. The Rev. P. McKee, chaplain to the Troop, made a neat little speech, in which he said that Robert's departure would be a great loss to them and that he hoped that he would be successful in his new post. 1st Newry Troop Boy Scouts is progressing by leaps and bounds at present, and the enthusiasm of the members leaves nothing to be desired.

Tuesday, 27 December, saw 1st Newry Rover football team take on Belfast Rover Scouts at Baden Park, 1st Newry Boy Scouts' sports ground, under ideal weather conditions. Mr S. Calter officiated as referee and had charge of the following teams: - Belfast – Gray, McFerran, Ivor, Semple, Frew, Bole, Johnston, Martin, Waring, Montgomery, Andrews and Newry – N. Sterritt, S. Graham, J. Crozier, F. Dalzell, W. Weir, A. Ferris, J. Cowan, C. Ferris, S. Crozier, J. Dalzell, A. Niblock. The game, which commenced at 12 noon before a large crowd, was full of vim and sparkle. Belfast opened the score through Andrews, and this had the effect of making Newry wake up, which they did in right good fashion, S. Crozier scoring from a lovely pass by Cowan. Belfast immediately retaliated by again scoring through Martin. Play continued fairly evenly for some time, Newry having the better of the exchanges. Just before half time, Dalzell equalised for Newry. The second half opened up by Newry taking the offensive, and within a few moments Niblock scored, but again Belfast broke away and scored a beauty through Andrews. Newry then appeared to take command of the game, and registered two more goals from J. Crozier and C. Ferris respectively. Both teams played well, and individually they were all good, but a special word of praise was due to S. Graham who played a magnificent game at left back for Newry.

In the late 1920s the older members of the Troop formed a Rover Crew and held meetings in the Y.M.C.I. in Hill Street. Membership grew to about 30 boys and activities included billiards, snooker and table tennis. The leader of the Rover Crew was Sam Crozier, a very dedicated member of the Scout Movement.

This is the flag from the two photos on the opposite page.

1928

The love of entertainment was shown on the evening of Thursday, 26 January 1928, when the Lecture hall of the Downshire Road Presbyterian Church played host to 1st Newry Rover Scouts' social evening, at which the Scouts, numbering about forty, were accompanied by their lady friends and other visitors. After tea had been provided by the boys, a number of toasts were honoured under the chairmanship of the Rev. Phineas McKee, B.A., chaplain to the Troop, who congratulated the Scouts on the enthusiasm they showed for the Movement. This, he said, augured well for its future in the Newry district, where already it was extremely strong and active. The usual loyal toast was honoured as well as the following: - 'Sir Robert Baden-Powell, Chief of the Scout Movement', responded to by the District Commissioner Mr W. J. Sterritt; 'The Youth of the World', responded to by the Rev. G. J. Slipper; 'Our Visitors', responded to by Miss McClelland; 'The Chairman', proposed by Mr Sterritt, was responded to by Rev. P. McKee. A cordial vote of thanks was given to the following, who were in charge of the tea arrangements: - Rover Scouts S. Crozier, R. Allely, J. Cowan, W. Gibson, J. Dalzell and J. McCracken. Thanks were also expressed to Mr and Mrs Robert Gibson for their valuable help. Rover Scout C. Armstrong rendered a number of songs. Games were played for the remainder of the evening, which was brought to a close by the singing of 'Auld Lang Syne' and the doxology.

Once again on Wednesday, 29 February 1928, an annual Jamboree (as it was then called) in connection with 1st Newry was held in the Lecture hall of Downshire Road Presbyterian Church, when the spacious building was packed to overflowing, with some unfortunate enough only to be able to obtain standing room. The chaplain of the Troop, Rev. Phineas McKee, B.A., honorary Rover Leader, presided, and the programme was under the charge of Mr W. J. Sterritt, District Commissioner, whilst Miss McClelland acted as accompanist in her usual capable style. The programme was of a highly varied character, and the humorous element – for which the Newry Scouts were well noted – was well in evidence, so much so that the audience was kept amused every minute of the two and a half hours the concert lasted. The following were the items of the programme:

> Jazz Band – The Nerots; Sketch – 'The Scout Barbers', Scouts; Solo – 'Ashore' by Miss Caldwell; Club swinging – Scouts; Recitation – 'The Fiddler' by Sixer Briggs; Pillow-fight – Scouts; Nigger Troupe – Scouts; Solo – 'Danny Boy' by Miss Caldwell; 'The Ghost' (by special request) – Scouts; Boxing – Cubs McCaigue and Clarke; Old Favourites – The Nerots; Recitation – 'The Oul' Critic' by Cub Mateer; Sketch – 'The Colonel's Consent' - Scouts.

At the conclusion of the concert Mr McKee extended the best thanks of the Troop to Miss McClelland for her assistance in helping to train the boys. This was passed by three hearty cheers.

During July the Troop held a very successful annual camp at Cranfield. W. V. Hogg provided the Scouts with transport for their gear and some of the boys to and from the camp while some of the older Scouts cycled from Newry to the camp. Whether or not it was intended but these older boys managed to arrive some time after the others and so avoided the task of erecting the tents. Everyone present had a good camp and enjoyed swimming at Cranfield beach.

On Saturday, 8 September 1928, 1st Newry B.P. Boy Scouts held a very successful jumble sale in Downshire Road Lecture Hall, which was kindly lent for the occasion by the Downshire Road committee. Commencing at 3 o'clock, the sale was soon in full swing, and by 4 o'clock the stock was cleared out, there having been a roaring trade. Operations were in charge of Scoutmaster S. Sterritt and the 'amateur salesmen' were Scouts R. Allely, J. Patterson, S. Graham, M. Andrews, J. Mateer, B. Allely, G. McWhirter, T. Caldwell, J. Cowan, J. Orr and J. Smith. A number of ladies also assisted, and the best thanks of the Troop are due to them, the Downshire Road committee, and all those who assisted in any way. Among the lady workers were Miss Gracey, Miss Wylie, Miss Donnelly, Miss McClelland, Mrs Smyth, Mrs McKee, Mrs Mitchell and Mrs Gibson.

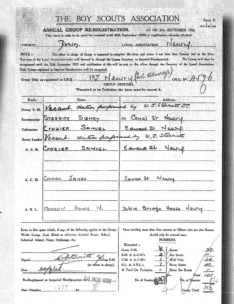

Right: 1st Newry Registration, 20 September 1928.

Above: Warrants for James Cowan (Assistant Cubmaster) and Samuel Crozier (Cubmaster)

Scout Larry Patterson serves up dinner at Cranfield annual camp

Going to Cranfield annual camp in Hogg's truck.

Albert Mateer, Jimmy Cowan, Graham Clarke, Jim Mateer (background), John McCullough

Kit inspection at Cranfield annual camp 1928. From the right Graham Clarke and Leslie Truesdale along with 3 other Boy Scouts.

Three 1st Newry Boy Scouts on their bicycles at Cranfield camp, Jimmy Cowan (right)

1929

On the night of Wednesday, 27 February 1929, the Downshire Road Lecture Hall, Newry, was filled to its utmost capacity, when 1st Newry Troop Boy Scouts presented yet another of their now famous annual Jamborees. The Newry Scouts were a very popular Troop in the district and, being well known for their sense of humour, they were well patronised by the public. A pleasing feature of the programme was the fact that most of the items were presented by the Scouts themselves, under the capable training of Scoutmaster S. Sterritt, Mr R. Graham and Mr William Inglis. As a spectator remarked, 'it was the most successful jamboree yet held by the Troop'.

The programme for the first half of the evening, which was much appreciated by the audience, was as follows:

> Chorus, 'Boys Be Prepared' by the Scouts; Songs, 'Toy Town Artillery' and 'Toy Town Parade' by James McClements, with chorus of Cubs; Club swinging, Scoutmaster S. Sterritt; Recitation, Sixer J. Briggs; Song, 'Mate o' Mine' by James McClements; Sketch, 'Lodgings to Let', Scouts; Scout Troupe, 'Tea Time To-morrow' by James McClements; 'Laughing Song' by R. Graham; Grand Howl and Drill Down, Cubs; Monologue, Assistant Cubmaster J. Cowan; Campfire song, 'Beside the Campfire' by Rover Leader H. Morrow; Gymnastic Display, Wood-Pigeon Patrol; Violin Solo, S. C. Armstrong; Sketch, 'The Black Bachelor', Scouts; Song, 'Gang Awa' Bonnie Lassie' by J. McClements; Accompanist – Mr William Inglis.

Rev. Phineas McKee, the esteemed chaplain of the Troop, and Mr William Johnson, C.B.E., spoke in reference to the Scout Movement in general.

Mr Johnson congratulated the Newry Troop on the large and enthusiastic audience they had drawn that evening, and he congratulated the audience on the excellent entertainment the boys had provided. They, like himself, must have been much impressed with the skilful display of club swinging given by the Scoutmaster, and he was very pleased at the physical drill exhibition given by the boys. He hoped the Newry Troop would start training for the forthcoming contest for the County Down Championship Flag. Mr Johnson went on to say that he always followed with interest the welfare of the Newry Troop, for his own son, when he was a small boy, joined the Pack as a Wolf Cub. He then became a member of the Newry Troop, and it speaks volumes for the early training he received in Newry that he had ever since, no matter where he resided, been continuously and actively associated with the Boy Scout Movement. Mr Johnson went on to say, 'I will always remember with pride and gratitude the services rendered by the Newry Troop during the memorable war years. When their services were required to assist with any phase of war work they most willingly responded. At the outbreak of the war the bigger boys joined up, along with Dick Scott, the Scoutmaster, Willie Scott, the Assistant Scoutmaster, and several other of their members when they reached military age but, alas, some of the Newry Scouts, like many another brave young Newry man, never came back. In Ireland we had only the voluntary method of recruitment to rely upon, and from the outbreak of the war up to the armistice, we never made an appeal in Newry for recruits for the Army or Navy without a response. The response was not confined to any one class, party or creed, for Newry's magnificent response was representative of all parties, classes and creeds in the town. In Newry there were war memorials in many churches and halls, but it was a disgrace to Newry there was no general public war memorial in the town. He suggested to the Scouters and Rovers of Newry to get in touch with the Newry Branch of the British Legion and let effective steps be initiated and taken to remove the stigma that rests on the town's good name. Although he had referred to the war, the Boy Scout Movement was no militaristic one. The foundations of the Scout organisation were sacrifice and service, and it stood for world peace and world citizenship'.

The second half of the programme included the following items:

> Jazz Band – The Nerots; Sketch – 'The Scout Barbers' - Scouts; Solo – 'Ashore' by Miss Caldwell; Pillow-fight – Scouts; Nigger Troupe – Scouts; Solo – 'Danny Boy' by Miss Caldwell; 'The Ghost' (by special request) – Scouts; Boxing – Cubs McCaigue and Clarke; Old Favourites – The Nerots; Recitation – 'The Oul' Critic' by Cub Mateer; Sketch – 'The Colonel's Consent' - Scouts. At the conclusion of the concert Mr McKee extended the best thanks of the Troop to Miss McClelland for her assistance in helping to train the boys. This was passed by three hearty cheers.

Boy Scouts' and Girl Guides' Rally

On the afternoon of Saturday, 8 June 1929, eleven thousand Boy Scouts, including a large turnout from 1st Newry Boy Scouts and Girl Guides, welcomed the Chief Scout Sir Robert Baden-Powell and Lady Baden-Powell, the Chief Guide, at the Balmoral Showgrounds, Belfast. It was the largest rally of Scouts and Guides ever seen in Ulster. The programme was conducted in eight different areas simultaneously and illustrated every aspect of the youngsters' training. In the largest area, in view of the Chiefs, an exhibition of old Irish dancing was given by Scouts and Guides, and there was also a finely contrived pageant, which included episodes from Irish legend and history. Other attractions included a handicraft exhibition, a model Irish village, a weaving and rope spinning exhibition and various Scout amusements. Rain fell heavily until a few minutes before Sir Robert and Lady Baden-Powell arrived, accompanied by the Duchess of Abercorn and the Northern Prime Minister, Viscount Craigavon. Lady Baden-Powell, in a brief address, said that she could not express how deeply touched she had been with the wonderful welcome from her 'big family – the Girl Guides'. Belfast, she said, was famous for its ships which carried messages of goodwill from Great Britain to the far distant corners of the world. Girl Guides were like ships. They sent out messages of goodwill and of hope to every corner of the globe and, like the ships, they were rendering great service to mankind. Sir Robert Baden-Powell referred to the winning of the Derby by Trigo, owned by Mr W. Barnett of Belfast. Did anyone expect Trigo to win the race?, he asked, and was answered by loud cries of 'Yes'. Belfast, said Sir Robert, expected Trigo to win the race, but all the world did not. It was thirty-three to one against them. The one was Belfast and the thirty-three were the other countries of the world. It looked an impossible job for

Trigo to win the Derby at odds of thirty-three to one, but he did not shirk it. Trigo did not say they could not do it, but said, 'I will try, I will have a go', and he won. That was what they all could do, and he wanted them to be like it. 'Every boy and girl who meets some sort of difficulty or disappointment on a job that they might think they could not tackle, should remember Trigo and have a go, and they would come out successful in the end'. The Duchess of Abercorn then presented Sir Robert and Lady Baden-Powell with a parcel of Ulster table linen. 1st Newry Scouts, under the command of Scoutmaster S. Sterritt, attended the rally in force.

At the beginning of August 1929 W. J. Wylie had the honour of officially representing 1st Newry (Earl Kilmorey) Scout Troop at the World Jamboree held at Arrowe Park, Birkenhead. However on Tuesday, 6 August, another eleven members of 1st Newry Troop along with Scouts from Warrenpoint, assembled at Newry train station where they embarked on the train to Belfast for the onward journey by boat, *Ulster Monarch*, to Liverpool to experience camping during the second week of the Jamboree and, from all accounts, everyone had a wonderful time. Following their return from this amazing adventure, a member of the Troop took time to send an article to the editor of the *Newry Reporter* entitled 'How a week was spent' giving a detailed description of his experiences at the Jamboree.

Later in the year, on the morning of 10 November, during the Remembrance service held in Downshire Road Presbyterian Church, Scoutmaster W. J. Sterritt placed a wreath at the War Memorial in the church on behalf of 1st Newry Troop in remembrance of those members who had paid the supreme sacrifice during the 1st World War. Large numbers of Scouts and Wolf Cubs under the command of Scoutmaster Sydney Sterritt and Cubmaster James Cowan attended the evening service in the church.

A former member of the Troop, Judge William Johnson, who became the first Chief Commissioner for Northern Ireland and D. O. Mahood, one of the first King's Scouts in Ireland, also belonged to the 1st Newry Troop.

Newry Boy Scout Tom McWhirter is seen here with back to us at Troop annual camp, Arrowe Park Jamboree

Newry Reporter: How a week was spent

Contributed by a member of 1st Newry Troop

Eleven Newry and eighteen Warrenpoint Scouts were amongst the Ulster Troops that were present at the great Jamboree at Arrowe Park, Birkenhead, for the second week. The Newry Scouts were under the command of Scoutmaster S. Sterritt and Warrenpoint under Assistant Scoutmaster Crosswell.

We left Newry on Tuesday 6 August 1929 on the 4.20 pm train to Belfast, where we assembled at the Queen's Bridge Trans-Atlantic shed. After having partaken of tea, we rambled about until the time to board arrived, and we got on the *Ulster Monarch*. It is a fine vessel and we were all greatly pleased with our comfortable quarters. Altogether there were about 300 Ulster Scouts on board, so that there was not much room for anyone else. Some of us went below, while the majority congregated on the deck, and the heavens did re-echo to their singing.

We had an excellent crossing, and arrived in Liverpool at 6.15 a.m. on Wednesday morning, 7 August. We crossed from Liverpool to Birkenhead on the ferryboat, and thence to Arrowe Park on special buses.

And what a spectacle on entering the Park! Hundreds of tents, some white, some brown, some green, gently flapping in the slight breeze that was blowing, while the sound of chopping and the rattle of billy-cans as the cooks prepared the breakfast, echoed in harmony.

First day in camp

We soon arrived at our own sub-camp (No.1) and, having been sorted out into different patrols, we adjourned to our tents to have a rest before breakfast; but not for long, as we learned from County Commissioner W. V. Heasley, who was in charge of County Down Scouts, that we were the first patrol on duty, as orderlies. The first day passed uneventfully, and when night came we were getting into form for camp life. Lights-out was at 10.15 p.m.; reveille at 7.30 a.m.; breakfast at 8 a.m.; kit inspection at 9.15 a.m. and prayers at 9.30 a.m. After that we were free until 12.30, when lunch was served out. Dinner was at 6.30 p.m. and supper at 9.30 p.m.

Our first thought on wakening on Thursday would be hard to tell, but we were all eagerness to be up and see some of the wonderful sights in and around the camp. After the formalities of the morning were over, we proceeded on a tour of the camp.

Interesting visits

The first place of interest was the Hungarians' camp. They had a magnificent collection of pictures and flags in a marquee for the purpose. It was a typical art gallery. Among the most interesting of the articles exhibited was a footprint of the Chief Scout (Sir Robert Baden-Powell) embedded in a slab of brass, an excellent souvenir. We spent quite a long time in the camp of the Hungarians. They are a very friendly crowd. Next we came upon the Swedish Scouts, but few of them could speak the English language. They had some quaint articles of 'furniture', including two chairs made from the trunks of trees, very excellent handiwork.

Among the other various camps we visited were the Chinese, Spanish, American, Scottish, Irish Free State, Norwegian, Canadian, Australian, African, New Zealand and several other foreign countries. The camp was indeed so enormous that it would have taken a much longer period than a week to go through it thoroughly.

Day in Liverpool

Friday came and we devoted it to visiting Birkenhead and Liverpool and seeing the various places of interest, including the museum, where you can see very interesting specimens of bird and animal life. Saturday brought with it the realisation of a trip to New Brighton, which is a beautiful seaside resort a few miles from Birkenhead. We spent a most enjoyable time there – boating, bathing and patronising the various amusements. One of our chaps, while boating, took a liking to the water and capsized the boat. Doubtless he felt a bit soggy afterwards. However we all returned to camp in the best of spirits.

Sunday was recognised as a day of rest. In the afternoon a Scouts' Own was held in the large arena, conducted by the Rev. F. Douglas Morley, D.D., Scout Chaplain, Free Church. There was a wonderful assemblage of Scouts present, and the service was a most impressive one.

On Monday Ulster had yet another trip to Chester, that ancient and famous cathedral city on the River Dee. Here we saw many interesting historical places, including the tower where King Charles stood and saw his army defeated. We had a trip on the River Dee on a pleasure boat and enjoyed the magnificent scenery.

Tuesday morning presented a scene of hustle-bustle, with the various contingents getting ready for departure. We left Arrowe Park with regret at 1.45 p.m. and spent the remainder of the day in Liverpool. At 10 p.m. we departed for old Erin, amid the farewells of our English friends who had assembled at the landing stage to wish us bon voyage.

In due time we reached Ireland and carried with us the memories of the greatest, most interesting, educative, and wonderful holiday we had ever enjoyed or, in a patriotic sense, ever will enjoy. May our Chief be ever happy in the thought that 2,000,000 boys are trying to live up to his ideals and manners, which could not be excelled.

1st Newry football team 1929

L-R: Harry Morrow, Reg Grogan, Albert Ferris, Noel Sterritt, Alan Niblock, Jim White, Willie Hamilton, Robert Allely, Sam Crozier, Jim Dalzell, Jim Chambers, Stanley Graham

1930s

Boy Scouts with lay helpers ready to leave for Aberystwyth, 1936

1930

During the 1920s and 1930s an annual Scout concert, locally called a Jamboree, of which you have read about and no doubt will read a lot more of later in this book, was first held in Downshire Road Church Lecture Hall, later moving to the town hall, due to the great demand and support from the public for this very popular event. However, the concerts stopped in the late 1930s, just before the Second World War, and were never resumed.

By 1930, the Scout uniform was modified to khaki shorts and shirt with a green scarf, Cubs wore a red scarf and blue uniform while the Rovers had khaki shirts and blue shorts. To meet increasing costs, the weekly subscription was raised to the grand sum of 2d. (1p)

On Wednesday, 26 February 1930, in Downshire Road Lecture Hall, 1st Newry Troop B.P. Boy Scouts, held their annual Jamboree. The hall, as usual, was packed to its utmost capacity, testifying to the popularity of the local Troop's concerts. For months past the Scouts had been hard at it, training to make this year's Jamboree a record one in the history of the Group. In this they succeeded and their untiring efforts were generously rewarded on Wednesday night. A tribute was due to Scoutmaster Sidney Sterritt and Mr G. Clarke, late of the Moore and Burgess Minstrels, for the efficient manner in which they had trained the boys.

The first part of the programme commenced with the singing of the Scout's marching song, 'Boys, Be Prepared', sung by the entire Troop of fifty boys, which was followed by a violin solo by Cub Tommy Magowan which was pleasingly rendered as was the encore. 'Land of Hope and Glory' was sung by Scoutmaster W. J. Wylie of Dungannon and formerly of Newry, the singer acquitting himself with credit and responding to a merited encore. A humorous song entitled 'Digging up the Road' by Rover Scouts Noel Sterritt and A. Ferris delighted the audience and the item was accorded rapturous applause. A sketch, 'Found a Peanut', was accomplished by Patrol Leader J. Gracey, Scout McWhirter and Scout J. Mateer, and provided much enjoyment. The most popular item in the programme was the jazz band. Mr Stanley Graham was excellent as 'Kelly's Mule' and kept the entire audience in fits of laughter. Undoubtedly, he was the success of the night. The boxing was supplied by Patrol Leaders J. Smith and W. Weir. Patrol Leaders J. Gracey and J. Smith and Seconds T. Adamson and R. Allely showed their prowess as club swingers, a novel feature being the illumination of the clubs. The first part concluded with the Cub campfire and the singing of 'The End of the Road' and other popular pieces.

During the interval the chairman, Rev. Phineas McKee, B.A., on behalf of the Troop, returned thanks to all who had assisted with the concert in any way and complimented the Troop on their fine performance. The statue dance and the nigger troupe composed of Scouts were much appreciated. Rover C. Armstrong gave a rendering of 'Erin's Wreath' which he had to repeat as an encore. 'Black Justice', a very humorous sketch, created roars of laughter. Mr S. Graham was again to the fore with his witty remarks. The singing of 'Auld Lang Syne' and the National Anthem was the finale of an excellent programme. Miss S. Lockhart provided the accompaniment during the entire evening.

This event was closely followed by a social evening, again in Downshire Road Lecture Hall, and attended by Wolf Cubs, Scout and Rover Scouts during which Miss S. A. Lockhart was introduced as Cubmaster and Mr G. H. Clarke as Group Scoutmaster.

1st Newry Troop of Boy Scouts was making plans to host a sports and athletic meeting under N.I.A.A.C. and C.A.A. rules at the Newry Showgrounds on Wednesday, 18 June 1930. A very representative committee had been formed and the arrangements were well advanced. The following had been appointed to act as judges: - District Inspector Cooke and Messrs H. J. McConville, D.L., J.P., W. V. Hogg, A. Shiells, J. Orr, G. Rowland, S. Lockhart, J. McClean, G. W. Holt, J.P., J. Fleming, J. Boland, J.P., B. Meeke, S. Hanratty, B. Adams, Bertie Thompson and E. Thompson. The big programme of events was to include flat, obstacle, egg and spoon and cycle races, long and high jumps, and tug of war competitions. In addition there would be a 5-a-side football match and a pushball contest between Newry and Bessbrook Scouts, while several sideshows and attractions had been arranged.

The entry fee would be 1/- (5p) for the first event and 6d (2½p) for any additional event. Boys and ladies races would be 6d (2½p) each. The closing date for entries was to be 10 June and entry forms could be had from Mr S. Sterritt, 111 Canal Street, Newry and Mr G. H. Clarke, Hon. Secretary, 33 North Street, Newry.

Valuable prizes were being offered and the event promised to be a most successful and entertaining one. The entry prospects were already very encouraging and each event was sure to draw a large number of competitors.

An Empire Day parade of Scouts, Rovers, Wolf Cubs, Girl Guides and Brownies took place in Newry on the evening of Sunday, 25 May 1930, when the members of the following organisations attended a service in Downshire Road Presbyterian Church. A number of Boy Scout Groups took part in the parade, under the command of Group Scoutmaster G. H. Clarke, Newry: - 1st Bessbrook Group, in charge of Scoutmaster T. Martin and Assistant Scoutmaster S. McMinn; 1st Jerrettspass Troop, in charge of Scoutmaster H. Barton; 1st Newry Troop – Scoutmaster S. Sterritt; Newry Wolf Cubs – Cubmasters Miss S. McClelland and Miss L Lockhart; Newry Company of Girl Guides, under the command of Captain Miss A. Sterritt and Lieutenant Miss Berry and Newry Brownies, in charge of Brown Owl, Miss Coleman. The parade went from the Scout hall, Sandys Street, to the church, with each Troop of Scouts and Company of Guides being preceded by their colours. This made an imposing display and was witnessed by a very large crowd of spectators who lined the route.

Sunday was also Children's Day in connection with Downshire Road Presbyterian Church, which gave increased interest in the service, and the spacious building was filled in every part. An impressive touch of beauty was given to the interior of the church by the magnificent display of flowers, evergreens and plants, arranged with artistic taste. The services, both morning and evening, were conducted by Rev Phineas McKee, B.A., who delivered helpful, inspiring and encouraging addresses to the young people. The musical portion of the services was specially arranged, the choir being under the conductorship of Mr Gilbert Adamson, with Mrs Adamson presiding at the organ.

Following the decision taken during the previous month by 1st Newry Group of Boy Scouts, an athletic sports event was held in the Newry Showgrounds on Wednesday 18 June 1930. Beautiful summer weather favoured the event, but the attendance was disappointingly small. A splendid programme was arranged and a large number of competitors took part, and close contests were witnessed.

The patron for this event was the Earl Kilmorey, D.L., while the Judges were Messrs H. J. McConville, D.L., J. Boland, J.P., W.V. Hogg, A. Shiells, J. Orr, G. Rowland, S. Lockhart, J. McClean, G.W. Holt, J. Fleming, Ben Meeke, S. Hanratty, D.I. Cooke, B. Adams, B. Thompson, E. Thompson, A. Smyth, Isaac Long and W. F. Osbourne. The handicapper was J.W. Jefferson and the organiser and honorary secretary, G.H. Clarke, with assistant secretaries, W.J. Sterritt and S. Sterritt.

For all those not taking part in the various events, St. Catherine's Brass and Reed Band, St. Joseph's Brass and Reed Band and the Frontier Pipe Band were in attendance and played selections during the evening.

The results of the various events were as follows: Fancy dress cycle parade – 1, Gene Cochrane, Newry; 2, V. Lockhart, Newry; 3, Jack Smyth, Newry; 100 yards handicap (confined to Scouts only) – 1, J. McCallum, Waringstown; 2, William Moorhead, Newry; 3, R.J. Orr, Newry; One mile cycle – First Heat: 1, W. Livingstone, Leapough (140); 2, D. J. Corr, Portadown Wheelers (8); 3, P. M. McClinton, Belfast (150); Second Heat – 1, W. J. Crane, Leapough (70); 2, A. Magee, Caledon (90); 3, S. Thompson, Leapough (70); Final – 1, D. J. Corr (80); 2, W. J. Crane (70); 3, W. Livingstone (140) - time 2 min 53 1/5 sec; 100 yards flat open handicap – First heat: 1, S. D. Foreman, Bangor (11 ½); 2, W. McNally, Portadown (12); Second heat: 1, E. H. Jones, Belfast R.U.C. (12); 2, W. T. Hayes, Trinity (10). Third heat: 1, J. Hill, Portadown (10); 2, T. L. Millar, Duncairn (12); Final – 1, J. Hill (10); 2, S. Foreman (11 ½); 3, W. McNally (12) - time 10 1/5 sec.

Putting the Shot – 1, A. L. Colhoun, R.U.C., Belfast (Irish Champion) (2), 43 ft. 10 ins (his longest official distance); 2, T. L. Mills, Duncairn (6), 37 ft.; 3, E. H. Jones, R.U.C., Belfast (6), 36 ft. 5 ½ ins; 220 yards flat – First Heat: 1, W. McNally, Portadown (20); 2, E. H. Jones, R.U.C., Belfast (20); 3, W. T. Hayes, Trinity (14 ½) - time 24 4/5 sec.; Second heat: 1, R. Wilkinson, Duncairn (20); 2, T. McCormick, county Antrim (17); 3, J. Hill, Portadown (20) - time 25 2/5 sec.; Final; 220 Yards flat open handicap – 1, T. McCormick, county Antrim (17); 2, W. T. Hayes, Trinity (14½); 3, W. McNally, Portadown (20) - time 25 sec.; Pushball match – Newry R.U.C. beat Newry Scouts by 2 goals to nil; Two mile cycle – 1, W. J. Crane, Leapough (180); 2, D. J. Corr, Portadown; 3, A. Magee, Caledon - time 5 min 59 3/5 sec.; Veterans' race, 220 yards – A. L. Calhoun; Long jump – 1, J. R. Matchett, Portadown (4), 23ft 5 ½ ins.; 2, H. Francis, Dromore (4), 22 ft 3 ins, 3, T. McCormick, county Antrim (4), 21 ft. 8½ ins; Exhibition 5-a-side football match – 'Hasbeens', Newry beat Armstrong Siddeley depot, Belfast by 4 goals to 3 goals; Five mile cycle – S. Thompson (350) and W J. Crane (350), both of Leapough dead-heated for first place. On a toss-up, Thompson was declared the winner. 3, D. J. Corr, Portadown (300); 440 yards flat open handicap – 1, J. R. Matchett, Portadown (30); 2, J. D. McVeigh, Portadown (24); 3, T. McCormick, county Antrim (30); Boot and jacket race – 1, J. McCullough, Newry; 2, G. Clarke, Newry; 3, J. McAleavey, Newry; Egg and spoon race for ladies – 1, Miss E. Hogg; 2, Miss Eileen Hogg; 3, Miss Burnett.

'Deil Tak' the Hindmost' – 1, W. J. Crane, Leapough; 2, W. Livingstone, Leapough; Tug of war – Newry R.U.C. beat A. Shiells and Co., Newry by 2 pulls to nil; Obstacle race – 1, W. T. Hayes, Trinity; 2, J. Turkington, county Antrim; 3, M. McArdle, Newry; Sack race (Junior) – 1, W. V. Hogg, Newry; 2, Miss E. Hogg, Newry; Sack race (Senior) – 1, B. Walsh, Leapough; Musical chairs – 1, M. McArdle, Newry; 2, J. Kane, Newry; Pushball match – Newry Guides and Scouts beat Newry Town Ladies and Scouts by 1 goal to nil; Relay race – county Antrim (Hayes, McCormick, Turkington and McVeigh) beat Newry easily; The Daily Mail push-ball which for the first time took place in Newry was between Warrenpoint Wolf Cubs and Newry Wolf Cubs and resulted in a scoreless draw. Following the end of the various events, the prizes were presented by Mrs J. Boland.

1st Newry football team, 1930
L-R: A. Ferris, J. Chambers, A. Niblock, R. Alleley, N. Sterritt, S. Crozier, R. Grogan, J. Dalzell, W. Hamilton, S. Graham, J. White

1st Newry football team captain, Sam Crozier

The Troop annual camp, under the command of Scoutmaster Sidney Sterritt, this year was held closer to home at Cranfield, near Kilkeel with 18 Wolf Cubs present for one week and 12 Scouts for two weeks. The venue was most suitable for the various activities such as swimming, beach combing, hiking and pioneering which took place during the two-week camp. Each patrol had the responsibility of cooking their own meals, washing up and ensuring that their kitchen areas and tents were kept both clean and tidy as inspection took place each morning. Everyone returned home safely but tired and looking forward to future camps.

In November an excellent turnout of Scouts, Cubs and Rover Scouts accompanied by their leaders took part in the Remembrance Day parade and wreath laying ceremony in Newry.

1st Newry Scoutmaster Sidney Sterritt (left) at Cranfield camp

Top: Scoutmaster Sidney Sterritt (right) helps out at meal time with the Wolf Cubs at Cranfield camp.
Above: Camp at Cranfield.

1st Newry Boy Scouts at Cranfield camp

Above: The pots and pans are all clean for these Boy Scouts at Cranfield camp.

Middle: 1st Newry Boy Scouts at Cranfield.

Left: Sidney Sterritt, S. Graham, Walter Scott, H. McWilliams, Godfrey McWhirter

1931

Once again early in 1931 the talent and training of 1st Newry came to the fore when the Group held its now famous annual concert (Jamboree) in Downshire Road Presbyterian Church Lecture Hall on Tuesday 24 February, under Scoutmaster Sydney Sterritt. A large and enthusiastic audience was enthralled with the enterprise and ability of all those who took part in this event.

One of the features of an excellent programme was the music supplied by the Scouts' mouth organ band, under the conductorship of Mr T. Giles.

The programme for the evening was as follows: -

Chorus 'Scouts of All the World', the Group; mouth organ band, Scouts; Wolf Cub marching song; Wolf Cubs trio; 'Only To See Your Face Again', Group Scoutmaster Clarke, P.L. Gracey and Scout Caldwell; Monologue, Scout Anderson; Violin solo, Wolf Cub Mateer; Sketch 'White Lies' by Wolf Cubs Truesdale, McWhirter and B. Truesdale; Mouth organ solo, P.L. J. Orr; Physical drill display, the Scouts; Wolf Cub campfire scene, the Cubs; Chorus 'Boys, Be Prepared', the Group; Mouth organ band, Scouts; Wolf Cub song 'Twelve Little Wolf Cubs; Illuminated club swinging, Scoutmaster Sterritt; Sketch 'Baby Elephant', the Scouts; Mouth organ solo, P.L. G. McWhirter; Duet, humorous, Scouts G. McWhirter and T. Caldwell; Statue dance, Scouts; Scout camp fire scene, Scouts; 'Home, Sweet Home', the Band. The concert concluded with the singing of 'God Save the King'.

During the evening Cubmaster Miss S. Lockhart and Miss M. Lockhart capably presided at the piano. During the interval, Rev. P. McKee, B.A., presented Cubmaster Miss S. Lockhart with a Thanks Badge on behalf of the Group.

1st Newry Assistant Scoutmaster,
Jimmy Cowan

1st Newry Scoutmaster, S. Sterritt

1st Newry Boy Scouts at camp in
Bray, county Wicklow

In presenting the annual report for 1931 of 1st Newry Boy Scouts, attached to the church since its formation in 1909, to the annual meeting of Downshire Road Presbyterian Church, Mr Sydney Sterritt said 'the Group, which was composed of Wolf Cubs and Scouts, was in a very flourishing position and at present they had on the roll 50 boys, 20 of whom are Wolf Cubs and 30 Scouts'. Mr Sterritt went on to say that 'The Group was in charge of Group Scoutmaster G H Clarke; the Wolf Cubs under the capable leadership of Cubmaster Miss S. A. Lockhart and Assistant Cubmaster Miss M. Lockhart; the Scouts in charge of Scoutmaster S. Sterritt and Assistant Scoutmaster James Cowan. During the past year the Scouts and Wolf Cubs had been well up to standard in Scouting. On 17 December, in the small schoolroom, we had an enrolment ceremony, 12 boys being enrolled as Scouts and 6 boys as Wolf Cubs. During the year a number of church parades were held at which they had a splendid turnout of all the members. The committee of 1st Newry Boy Scouts would like to take this opportunity of thanking those who gave them such valuable assistance during the past year, and also for the use of the Scout hall in Sandys Street. The Wolf Cubs held their weekly parades on Thursdays and the Scouts on Tuesdays. Other nights of the week were taken up with games. The annual camp was held in Bray, county Wicklow from 11 to 21 July. Every boy had enjoyed himself to the utmost. On 4 November we had a sale of work in the Lecture Hall which was a great success'.

1932

1st Newry Group Baden-Powell Boy Scouts once again held their most successful 12th annual Jamboree on Wednesday, 9 March 1932, in the Lecture Hall, Downshire Road. Year after year this event of the Scout world was becoming more interesting and enjoyable, both from the point of view of variety of programmes and a steadily improving standard of presentation. This was due in no small measure to the efforts of Messrs G. H. Clarke, Group Scoutmaster, S. Sterritt, Scoutmaster, and J. Cowan, Assistant Scoutmaster, who in collaboration with the Misses Susie Lockhart, Cubmaster and May Lockhart, Assistant Cubmaster, were mainly responsible for the success of the entertainment.

Rev. P. McKee, B.A., chaplain of the Group who presided, heartily congratulated the Scouts on this, another and perhaps the most successful Jamboree yet promoted. He gave well-deserved praise to the enthusiasm that marked the delivery of every item on the programme. This, he said, augured well for the success of the Group in all its other different lines of endeavour. In conclusion, he wished specially to express his appreciation, speaking as chaplain, of the support provided by the large audience who had come to show their appreciation of the Scouts and their work.

The varied programme which was submitted included: - 'Be Prepared', Scouts' marching song; 'Broadcasting', a humorous sketch; Cubs' Scena, based on Kipling's jungle story, 'Kaa's Hunting' and 'Lamuel's Ghost'; Song Scena, 'Guards and Sailors'; Quartet, 'Eleven more months and ten more days'; Violin solo, Albert Mateer; Duo, S. Graham and J. Gracey; Songs, Walter Scott; 'Furnished Apartments', a sketch and a campfire scene. The manner in which the different phases of this presentation were performed to the audience made it one of the most popular and enjoyable items of the evening. Miss Susie Lockhart provided the piano accompaniments.

1st Newry Wolf Cub Pack spent a very pleasant time on Saturday, 25 June 1932, in the grounds of Mourne Park, Kilkeel, kindly granted by the Earl Kilmorey. Early in the day a large number of boys left Newry by motor bus, the party being under Cubmaster Miss S. Lockhart, Assistant Cubmaster Miss M. Lockhart, Group Scoutmaster G. Clarke, Assistant Scoutmaster J. Cowan and a number of the senior members of the Boy Scouts.

On arrival at the Park, a substantial dinner was cooked in the open and served to the boys, after which the Rev. Phineas McKee, Newry, Group chaplain, joined the party. Some members of the party, accompanied by Rev. McKee, made the journey up Knockchree, a mountain peak on the estate. Even the younger members managed to make their way through the heather and gorse, and at last everyone reached the summit in the best of spirits.

The remainder of the party, under Assistant Scoutmaster J. Cowan, went bathing in the river which flows through the estate.

When the boys re-assembled, tea was served, after which Rev. McKee, who had to leave, received three hearty cheers.

A splendid sports programme brought the day's activities to a close. Details: -

50 yard race (under 10) – 1, H. Tighe; 2, W. Gray; 3, H. Cochrane.

50 yard race (over 10) – 1, W. Mitchell; 2, F. Truesdale; 3, B. Truesdale.

Boot race -1, J. Kennedy; 2, B. Truesdale and V. McClean, tied; 4, N. McClean.

Knot race (junior) – 1, W. McMinn; 2, H. Hegan; 3, J. Gibson.

Knot race (senior) – 1, D. Hamilton; 2, W. Harbison; 3, N. McClean.

Obstacle race, winners of heats – F. Truesdale, W. Beggs, S. Cowan, W. Mitchell, J. Gibson and L. McConnell.

The prizes were presented by Mr W. Morrison, gamekeeper on the estate.

Newry Scouts Rally

Encouraging co-operation of various troops - South Down and South Armagh districts represented

A grand rally of Scouts and Wolf Cubs from Banbridge, Bessbrook, Donacloney, Kilkeel, Newry and Warrenpoint was held in the Showgrounds, Newry on Saturday, 2 July 1932, and was a huge success in every way.

The rally was organised by the Newry and District Scouters with a view to furthering Scouting activities, and to encourage the co-operation of the various Troops in the district.

The Troops and Packs assembled at the Scout hall, Sandys Street, at 2.30 p.m. and marched in a body to the Showgrounds which had been kindly lent for the occasion by the Committee of Newry Town Football Club.

The parade was in charge of District Commissioner W. J. Sterritt, and was over 200 strong.

The following officers were in charge of their respective groups: -
Group Scoutmaster Wilson Emerson, 1st Banbridge.
District Commissioner W. Liddell, 1st Donaghcloney.
Scoutmaster T. McGonigle, 1st Kilkeel.
Group Scoutmaster G. H. Clarke, 1st Newry.
Group Scoutmaster J. R. Corkhill, 2nd Newry.
Group Scoutmaster Robert M. Haldane, 1st Warrenpoint.

On arrival at the Showgrounds a series of Scouting tests was carried out before a representative attendance of the general public.

The first test comprised a march past of all Troops and Packs, which included drill with staves. County Commissioner W. V. Heasley of Holywood took the salute. Scoutmasters T. E. Saunders and T. Watson of the 44th and 77th Belfast Troops, who kindly consented to act as judges for the competitions, then inspected the parade. The various Troops then gave a series of Troop calls and yells.

Wolf Cubs Circle
Cubmaster Miss M. V. Ryan of Warrenpoint Pack formed a grand circle of all Wolf Cubs under their respective officers – Cubmasters Miss Watts, Miss Bittles and the Misses Lockhart, and gave a very impressive rendering of the Wolf Cub howl, which was much appreciated by the large audience.

Each Scout Troop in turn gave a display of ambulance work, which included imaginary accidents and the administering of the necessary first aid in the circumstances. The last of the Scouts' tests was a verbal despatch relay race, comprised of teams of four from each Troop, and a very keen race took place.

Owing to the inclemency of the weather, the foregoing tests had been carried through under great difficulties and, before continuing the sports programme which was to include flat races, high and long jumps, tug of war and 5-a-side football competitions, it was decided to adjourn for tea, which was prepared and served in a very efficient manner by 1st Newry Company Girl Guides under Captain A. Smartt and her officers.

Sports Event Postponed
After tea, as the weather showed no sign of improvement, it was decided to postpone the sports events to a later date, to be held in Banbridge. The Troops and Packs were then formed into a hollow square and were addressed by Commissioner Heasley who, in the course of remarks, complimented the various bodies participating on their exceptionally smart appearance and the high standard of the tests. He emphasised the importance of the co-operation of the Troops in districts and he hoped that the rally would be carried out annually.

Commissioner Heasley also intimated that he was pleased to announce that he had appointed Group Scoutmaster Robert M. Haldane as Assistant District Commissioner for the area. This announcement was received with great applause by all the Scouts, which testified to the popularity of the Scouter in question. Mr Heasley then called upon Mrs A. Shiells of Warrenpoint to present the beautiful flag so kindly given by her husband, Mr Archie Shiells, to the Local Association for annual competition for the Scout championship of South Down and South Armagh. The winning Troop on this occasion was 1st Warrenpoint Troop and Pack under Group Scoutmaster R. M. Haldane, Assistant Scoutmaster J. C. Crosswell and Cubmaster M. V. Ryan. Mrs Shiells, in presenting the flag to Patrol Leader A. Toombs, said it gave her great pleasure in presenting the flag to Warrenpoint, and she hoped it would be an incentive to work hard to keep up the standard of Scouting. The meeting then concluded with the singing of the National Anthem.

In 1932, under the leadership of Scoutmaster G. Clarke and Assistant Scoutmaster James Cowan, fifteen Scouts went to Maidencombe, Newton Abbot in Devon for their annual camp from 9 to 23 July. The visiting District Commissioner from Torquay made very favourable comments on their visit.

Group Scoutmaster G. H. Clarke, of 1st Newry Troop, writing from Court Farm, Maidencombe, South Devon, commented: -

'Here we are, all merry and bright, having a glorious time in sunny Devon. The visitors, of whom there are a great number to this beauty spot of Devon, know that the 1st Newry Scouts are here, and that they are Irish, and there is a danger of the Troop being spoiled by the kindness and friendliness they show to all. Some of the Home Fleet is expected to be in Torbay next week, when arrangements will be made for a visit by the Troop. All are unanimous in voting this to be the finest camp in the history of the Troop, and not a single complaint has been heard, especially in the grub line, as the appetites are quite up to Scout standard, and when that unwished-for time comes and they return home, it will take the Troop colours to be very much in evidence for them to be recognised as 1st Newry'.

Annual Report for 1932 - Scouting Activities

This is the 24th year of 1st Newry Group of B.P. Boy Scouts, and in many ways has proved a record one. First of all I would like to say on behalf of the Scouts, that we deeply regret losing the services of Mr Sydney Sterritt as Scoutmaster, who resigned during the year owing to business reasons.

I am glad to be able to report an increased membership, the total of the Group being 69, comprising 39 Scouts and 30 Wolf Cubs. The officers are myself as Group Scoutmaster and Mr Sam Crozier as Scoutmaster, who has already shown his ability as an experienced Scouter, and is capably assisted by his two Assistants, James Cowan and Jack Smyth.

The Cubmistress is Miss Susan Lockhart and Miss May Lockhart, Assistant Cubmistress, both of whom are doing really splendid work in the training of these embryo Scouts.

During the winter our chaplain, the Rev. P. McKee, B.A., read to us some interesting lectures on character, which I am sure will bear good fruit in the future. I may mention that, though we have a Local Association comprised of the committee of this church, our working interests are vested in the hands of a committee comprised of the officers and patrol leaders of the Group.

We would once again like to place on record our indebtedness to the Downshire Road Church committee for the use of the Scout hall in Sandys Street, and the Lecture Hall on many occasions and also for their kind assistance which is always forthcoming at any time required.

G. H. CLARKE, Group Scoutmaster

1st Newry Boy Scouts arriving at Torquay, Devon
Scouts known to be in the photo are: T. Clarke, W. Scrimgeour, Jack Smyth, B. Mitchell, Noel Graham, Jim Cowan, Albert Mateer, John McCullough, Trevor Kennedy, B. Truesdale, H. Tighe.

John McCullough (left) and Albert Mateer (right) along with Boy Scouts at camp in Devon

1933 - 1934

Jack Smyth (left) and Jimmy Cowan with pheasant at Mourne Park in 1933. Above right is a feather from the captured bird.

During the early part of 1934 it was reported that 1st Newry Group was in the process of forming a Rover Crew but had unfortunately not yet been able to secure the services of a Rover Scoutmaster. However Group Scoutmaster George H. Clarke and Rover Mate James Locke were holding the fort until such time as a suitable leader could be found. The Scout Troop, under its recently appointed executive of Scoutmaster Jack Smyth and Assistant Scoutmasters J. Gracey and Stanley Graham, had been working smoothly and to good purpose during the last few months.

The Scouts had been working very hard for their first and second class badges under the capable leadership of Scoutmaster Jack Smyth. The Troop had recently paid a visit to Armagh and, after an enjoyable game of soccer with the Armagh Rover Scouts in which they were defeated by 3 goals to 2, they were entertained to tea, having had a very pleasant outing. The Cubs held their usual day outing in June, proceeding by bus to Mourne Park and spending a most enjoyable day there. They also participated in a grand county rally held in Banbridge and worthily upheld the traditions of the Pack. The District Commissioner particularly congratulated them on their splendid marching through the town.

The Troop held a very successful and enjoyable annual camp from 14 to 28 July at Vrom Farm, near Colwyn Bay, north Wales, under the care of G. H. Clarke, Group Scoutmaster, along with Scoutmaster Jack Smyth, Assistant Scoutmaster Stanley Graham, Cubmaster Jim Cowan, and Assistant Cubmaster Jim Mateer, where the eighteen Scouts and six Cubs took part and spent a most enjoyable fortnight. An innovative venture was the inclusion of the six Cubs who had been invited to join the Scouts at camp and this experiment met with great success. The Cubs gave no trouble and, in fact, happily undertook their share of camp work, even to the extent of trying their hand at cooking. A feature of our camps is that every boy took his turn at cooking, under the guidance of a senior, to ensure that food was well cooked, and that there was plenty of variety. Dinners usually consisted of roast or stewed meat, two or three vegetables with a pudding of rice, farola, cornflour, plum duff, or even, as on one memorable occasion, raspberry fritters to follow. Tinned food was absolutely barred.

Two cricket matched were played – one against Colwyn Bay Secondary School and the other against the Co-operative Society. A football match was also played against a Liverpool Scout Group. Newry won all three games. During his visit to the camp, the visiting District Commissioner for Colwyn Bay gave a very satisfactory report.

Later in the year the Wolf Cub Pack, although somewhat reduced in numbers due to boys moving up to the Scouts, had been working hard to raise the general standard of the Pack, under that very efficient veteran in Newry Scouting circles, Cubmaster James Cowan, assisted by Assistant Cubmaster James Mateer. In October the Group Scoutmaster, George H. Clarke, was pleased to report that a Rover Crew had now been formed despite earlier difficulties in finding a leader.

Their first meeting had been held on top of Camlough Mountain during the month of October 1934, an altogether auspicious event and one which would long be remembered. The Rovers had already proved very useful by taking on lots of other tasks previously undertaken by the other leaders and Senior Scouts.

Above
Graham Clarke (second from left) pictured at the Colwyn Bay camp.

Right
Top: Boy Scouts arriving for camp at Colwyn Bay railway station. Known to be in the photo are Noel Graham, Trevor Kennedy, Jack Smyth, George Kennedy, Jack Gracey, Bertie Truesdale, Stanley Graham, Jim Mateer, Graham Clarke, Albert Mateer, John McCullough, W. Scrimgeour, H. Mitchell, Billy Mitchell, Leslie Truesdale, Sam Holt, Jack Mitchell.

Middle: Boy Scouts enjoying camp.

Bottom: The Colwyn Bay camp.

1935

A grand rally, staged by 1st Newry Wolf Cubs and Boy Scouts, was held in the Downshire Road Lecture Hall on 25 January 1935. Other Groups from the district were also in attendance, clearly showing to all those who attended the display the remarkable revival of interest in the Movement in the Newry area. The audience thoroughly enjoyed the contributions made by all the Packs and Troops and congratulated the leaders for all their dedication and hard work. The County Commissioner, who requested the general support of the public in forming a new Local Association, delivered an address. The Group was practising for their forthcoming Jamboree, which will include a number of new and original items specifically written by some of the Scouts for the occasion. The Troop once again placed on record its thanks to the church committee for their kindness in giving the free use of the Scout hall as well as the Lecture Hall which was also used on many occasions.

1st Newry Boy Scouts held their annual concert in Downshire Road Lecture Hall on Friday, 29 March 1935, and once again attracted a large audience. The comedy and musical element was particularly well enjoyed.

The Rev. P. McKee, B.A., presided.

The programme was as follows: -

Opening Chorus, 'Where are the Boys of the Old Brigade'? - the Group.

Piano solo, selection - Scout F. McWhirter.

Boxing – the Scouts.

Duo - Scouts Graham and Gracey.

Scena -'The Cub Pack' - under the direction of Cubmasters J. Cowan and J. Mateer.

Song - 'Love's Old Sweet Song' - Rover T. McWhirter.

Sketch - 'Border Blunders' – the Rovers.

Recitation - Scout E. Thornberry.

Stave drill – the Scouts under Scoutmaster J. Smyth.

Step dance - Rover W. Graham.

Sketch - 'Fooling the Press," – the Rovers.

Song - Cubmaster J. Mateer.

Campfire sing-song by the Group.

National Anthem.

This 17th annual concert was a great success, both financially and as a stage performance.

Outstanding Features of the Jubilee Beacons, May 1935

The Jubilee weekend was one of great activity for the Boy Scouts of Newry and district.

Members of 1st Newry Boy Scouts spent the weekend, 3 and 4 May, collecting materials to build the official beacon in a field kindly lent by Mr John McCullough at Lisdrumgullion on the Armagh Road, Newry. This was the beacon that was sponsored by the Newry District Boy Scout Association in conjunction with the Newry Branch of the British Legion. The latter provided the finance, while the Scouts built the beacon, under the direction of Mr W.J. Sterritt, District Commissioner.

Approximately five tons of fuel was built into the beacon which stood about 20 feet high when complete. The structure was then liberally saturated with 20 gallons of oil and a same quantity of tar. Promptly on the stroke of 10.45 p.m. on Monday, 6 May, the fire was set alight and the signal rocket discharged amid great enthusiasm to the strains of the National Anthem sung by the great crowd present. The huge bonfire, when set alight, formed a link in the chain of similar Scout fires around the Ulster coast. The flames of the beacon rose to tremendous heights and were easily visible for miles around the district. A grand display of fireworks was also given which lasted over an hour and was much enjoyed and appreciated by the spectators.

The whole proceedings ended with the Scouts leading in singing 'Land of Hope and Glory', 'Auld Lang Syne' and 'God Save the King'.

The thanks of the Scouts and the Legion are due to the following who helped with materials for the beacon – Messrs. Joseph Fisher & Sons, J.S. Fisher Ltd., Magowan and McCullough, Edward McAlinden, Rowland & Harris Ltd., G.W. Holt, S. Lockhart & Co., S. Connor & Sons and Sidney Sterritt, as well as to Rover Scout Noel Graham for his invaluable assistance in collecting the materials.

In June the Group regretfully accepted the resignation of Mr G. Clarke as Group Scoutmaster but it was hoped that Mr Clarke would still be able to assist the Group in some way or perhaps play a role in the district. The Group placed on record its appreciation of the good work done for the Group by Mr Clarke during his years in office. He had also rendered valuable assistance in the lighting and stage effects during our annual concert which followed shortly after his retirement.

Mourne Park Outing

1st Newry Group of Boy Scouts had been very busy. On Saturday, 15 June, the Cub Pack held their annual outing to Mourne Park, and in spite of the inclement weather, it was a joyful party which set out from the Scout hall at 10 a.m. An enjoyable day was spent with sports, which included 5-a-side football and Cub games, after which prizes were awarded. After a hearty tea, the party returned somewhat damp in body but not in spirit.

Two Scouts who accompanied the party stayed over the weekend and carried out part of their first-class test. Later in the month an investiture ceremony for Scouts and Cubs was held in the Scout hall, Sandys Street. The old Group colours of 1st Newry Group were handed

King's Jubilee beacon, 6 May 1935.
Scouts from top right: Noel Graham, Jim Mateer, James Cowan, Jack Smyth, J. McConnell

over for safe keeping to Mr W.J. Sterritt, for many years Scoutmaster of this Group and now District Commissioner. Mr Sterritt expressed the wish that the flag be installed in the Downshire Road Presbyterian Church Hall. Musical items and tea concluded the evening.

Armistice Day at Newry Cenotaph, 1935
From second left: Marine Percy Fleming, Boy Scout Bertie Truesdale, Wolf Cub Leslie Truesdale

Camping Arrangements: The annual camp this year was held at Dane's Dyke near Bridlington, Yorkshire, and was attended by 21 members of our Group. The sun played its part to the utmost and everyone had a very enjoyable camp. Much of the time at camp was occupied by patrols visiting the interesting places that surrounded our campsite. One favourite spot was the famous Flamborough Lighthouse, a few miles from the camp. A section of the Troop visited Leeds to witness a day's cricket in a test match being played at Headingley. The *Newry Reporter* of 27 July 1935 reported that 1st Newry Troop Boy Scouts had safely returned from their very enjoyable camp at Bridlington.

Work started as soon as they returned home from camp to prepare the Troop for the South Down Challenge Flag competition in Bessbrook. The boys were not successful in bringing home the Flag, but their keenness and the desire to do better next time made it most worthwhile.

The Ulster Scout bazaar next claimed their attention, and apart from money raised in selling the official badges, the contribution to this bazaar amounted to £5 (£5.00).

The Rover Section was still at the experimental stage but, under the leadership of S. Graham, hoped to make good headway.

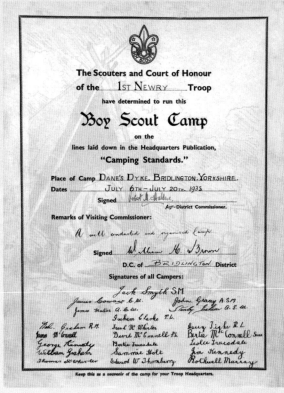

Camp Standard, Bridlington, July 1935

Troop photograph taken while at annual camp, Bridlington, 1935
Back: Frank McWhirter, D. McConnell, J. Smyth, Billy Graham, George Kennedy, G. Clarke, S. Holt, B. Truesdale.
Middle: J. McConnell, James Cowan, Stanley Graham, Jack Gracey, Jim Mateer, Noel Graham.
Front: H. Tighe, B. McConnell, Edward Thornberry, L. Truesdale, Rothwell Murray, J. Kennedy.

1936

The Group's annual Jamboree was organised by 1st Newry Group Boy Scouts and took place on 4 April 1936 in the Lecture Hall, Downshire Road and proved to be an outstanding success. Rev. P. McKee, B.A., presided. The following was the programme presented:

Opening chorus – 'Keep Right on to the End of the Road' by the Group; Piano Solo – Selection – Patrol Leader F. McWhirter; Patrol competition – Blindfold Boxing, and Greasy Pole by the Scouts; Trio – Rover Scoutmaster S. Graham and Rovers N. Graham and J. McConnell; Scena by the Cub Pack; Song – 'Little Grey Home in the West' by Rover T. McWhirter and some of the boys under Rover Scoutmaster S. Graham; Sketch – 'The Laurel Crown' by the Scouts; Song – 'There's a Little Dash o' Dublin' by Rover Scout W. Power; Step Dance by Rover Scout B. Graham; Violin Solo – 'Cradle Song' by Scout B. Gordon; Sketch – 'Doh and Dough' by the Rovers.

Miss Esther McCullough was the accompanist. The entertainment concluded with the singing of the National Anthem.

Unfortunately at the beginning of May the Group experienced the sad loss of James Kennedy, one of the younger members of the Group. It was indeed a tragic event in the life of the Wolf Cub Pack, of which James had been a very popular member.

On Tuesday, 14 May 1936, youth joined with youth to pay a final tribute of respect to the memory of one of the most popular of Newry's younger generation on the occasion of the funeral of Mr Jack Gracey, Sandys Street, Newry, to St Patrick's churchyard. Members of 1st Newry Group of Boy Scouts, under Mr Jack Smith, Scoutmaster, and the Wolf Cubs under Mr J. Cowan, Cubmaster, marched on either side of the hearse. The coffin, draped with the Union Jack and covered with a profusion of beautiful floral tributes, along with his Scout hat and thumb stick, was carried the entire distance to the churchyard by relays of relatives, Scouts, and members of Newry Olympic Hockey Club, who followed immediately behind the chief mourners in an impressive funeral procession. Besides his work on behalf of 1st Newry Troop of Boy Scouts as a keen member of 1st Newry Troop for fifteen years and Assistant Scoutmaster and Group Treasurer for six years previous to his death, the late Jack Gracey was prominently identified with the Newry Olympic Hockey Club and was a member of the team which brought the Irish Junior Cup to Newry for the first time.

On Tuesday evening, 23 May 1936, a very enjoyable social function took place in 1st Newry Group Scout hall, Sandys Street. About 50 members of the various sections of the Group were gathered to bid farewell, and express in a tangible form, their admiration and esteem for Mr Stanley Graham, who was leaving the district to take up a business appointment in New Zealand. After an enjoyable meal and games, the Rev. P. McKee, B.A., chaplain to the Group, Jack Smyth, Group Scoutmaster and James Cowan, Cubmaster, spoke eloquently on the long record of service Mr Graham had with 1st Newry Group. For a period of 15 years he had always been a loyal and willing worker in the various activities of the Group, and they extended to him their heartiest good wishes in his venture to new lands. Mr Graham carried with him the best wishes of all Scouts in the district for his success in his business career in New Zealand.

In June 1936 the Group, under Cubmaster James Cowan, attended the Louth and District rally, where they succeeded in carrying off some first and second prizes.

In July the annual camp was held in Aberystwyth, Wales, and in spite of the inclement weather, those who attended gained much experience in outdoor Scouting life. After the camp, the Group settled down to its winter programme of Scout work and the training of new recruits.

The following were the current office-bearers of the Group: - Scoutmaster, Jack Smyth; Assistant Scoutmasters, George Kennedy and Albert Mateer; Cubmaster, James Cowan; Assistant Cubmaster, James Mateer; honorary secretary, Tom McWhirter; and honorary treasurer, Albert Mateer.

Dates July 11th — July 25th 1936
1st Newry Annual camp, Aberystwyth.

1937

On Saturday, 19 June, Scouts from various parts of South Down and South Armagh took part in a rally at a field kindly lent by the Misses Moorhead, Downshire Road, Newry.

The principal event on a comprehensive programme of sports was the competition for the South Down Challenge Flag. Mr William Johnson, B.L., Scoutmaster, Belfast, and formerly a member of 1st Newry, acted as judge. Two Troops, Newry and Warrenpoint, tied for first place; Bessbrook were runners-up and Newtownhamilton came next in the placing.

The events which made up the competition were: - inspection, knotting test, ambulance test, verbal dispatch relay race and physical culture test. The sports, which included races for Scouts, Cubs, Girl Guides, Brownies and Rover Scouts, were greatly enjoyed by the spectators as well as those taking part, and competition was keen. The weather held good throughout the afternoon and the event proved most successful.

Messrs. W. Halliday, W. Heather, W. G. McWhirter and B. Allely acted as stewards, and 1st Newry Girl Guides, under Miss Jean Smyth, served refreshments. Mrs McKee, wife of Rev. Phineas McKee, B.A. distributed the prizes.

Assistant District Commissioner R. Haldane (Warrenpoint) voiced hearty thanks to Mrs McKee, Mr Johnson and the Misses Moorhead, and all who had in any way assisted to make the event a success.

The Hunter Moore Memorial Flute Band headed the parade from Edward Street Railway Station, where the Newry Troop met the visitors, to the field.

The following were the officials: -

Field Arrangements – Scoutmaster J. Smith.
Starter – G. McWhirter.
Judges – W. Sterritt, W. Halliday, R. Hamilton and W. Heather.
Teas – Miss Gracey, Miss J. Smith and 1st Newry Guide Company.
Gate – T. McWhirter and A. Mateer.
Stewards – Rev. John McCleery, B.A., Rover Scoutmaster J. Toombs and R. Wilson, Warrenpoint Rover Crew.
The rally was brought to a close by the singing of the National Anthem.

The coronation of our beloved King was a time of great happiness and service for our members.

No annual camp was held this year although a number of training weekend camps were held in Mourne Park during the months of July and August instead.

The Earl of Buckinghamshire, the travelling commissioner from Imperial Scout Headquarters, visited Newry on Friday, 26 November, when he addressed members of 1st Newry Boy Scouts. The Earl arrived in Ulster on Saturday, 30 October, and stayed over the weekend with Mr Henry H. Dobbs, Cushendall, who was honorary secretary of the Ulster Boy Scout Association. The Earl met supporters and friends and the boys greatly appreciated his cordial manner and enjoyed the games and songs he taught them. During his stay he also visited Scout Groups in Magherafelt, Portstewart, Coleraine, Limavady, Londonderry, Larne, Carrickfergus and Ballymena.

Membership had increased, with almost 50 boys in the three sections of the Group. During the winter months the boys enthusiastically participated in the 'Fitter Britain' campaign.

1938

This year the Group had a larger membership than for many years and it was most encouraging to find so many young men of Rover Scout age coming into the Group for the first time. The annual concert was an outstanding success. A patrol from the Troop participated in the South Down Challenge Flag competition held in Bessbrook but were unfortunate not to win this coveted award which went to 1st Kilkeel Troop.

The Troop camp was held once again at Dane's Dyke, Bridlington, Yorkshire, and was voted by the boys to have been one of the best ever held. All enjoyed a happy fortnight and the friendships made there were a lasting memory of a splendid holiday. The National Crisis was a time of great activity in Scouting and the Group had been asked by Headquarters to keep the boys aware of National Service and to encourage them to work for badges which would serve a useful purpose in this connection. At the close of the year the Troop leaders were re-warranted, the following receiving warrants: - G. Clarke, T. McWhirter, A. Mateer, D. McConnell and J. Cowan.

It is hoped that the Troop, under these newly appointed leaders, would go on and prosper and become a really successful Group in the district.

The Troop, as in previous years, placed on record its thanks to the session and committee for placing the Scout hall at its disposal and for use of the Lecture hall when requested.

Boy Scouts enjoying camp at Bridlington

Fetching water during annual camp, Bridlington

Boy Scout Leslie Truesdale being tossed in the blanket

1939

The 21st annual Jamboree, organised by 1st Newry Group of Boy Scouts, was held in Downshire Road Presbyterian Church Lecture hall on Thursday, 6 April 1939. The function, which took the form of a variety entertainment, was an overwhelming success. An appreciative audience filled the hall to capacity and every item on the well-conceived programme was thoroughly enjoyed. Rev. Phineas McKee, B.A. presided and the programme was given a good send off with the singing of the chorus 'Land of our Birth' by the Troop.

Songs were rendered by Rover Scouts T. McWhirter, W. Power and H. Mitchell; a duo by Rover Scouts Gibson and Jess; a pianoforte medley by Rover Scout B. Mann; a recitation by Scout Bram Baird; 'Romeo and Juliet (revised version) by Assistant Scoutmasters M. Mateer and Rover Scout Graham; a Cub scene by the Pack under Cubmaster Graham Clarke and Assistant Cubmaster Frank McWhirter; physical jerks by the Scouts; a duet by Rover Scouts Graham and McWhirter; a mouth organ trio by Rover Scouts Graham and Jess and Scout W. Cowan. Three amusing sketches were presented – 'Paddy's Mistakes' by Rover Scouts H. Tighe, R. Copeland, W. Mitchell, H. Mitchell and Assistant Scoutmaster T. McWhirter; 'The Ghost House' by Scoutmaster J. Cowan, Assistant Scoutmaster A. Mateer and Rover Scout Graham; 'Matrimonial Agency' by Scoutmaster J. Cowan, Assistant Scoutmaster A. Mateer and Rover Scouts J. McConnell, S Noble, N. McMinn and Assistant Cubmaster F. McWhirter, Miss Jean Smyth and Rover Scout Bruce Mann ably played the accompaniments. An enjoyable programme was concluded with the singing of the National Anthem.

During the latter part of the year the Group began the task of collecting waste paper in aid of the war with their efforts being well supported by members of the public although transport and weather conditions proved somewhat difficult to handle.

1939-1945 War Memorial

With the outbreak of the Second World War, the numbers in the Troop decreased since many members went to serve their country. They were: -

Scoutmasters: J. Cowan, S. Graham.
Assistant Scoutmasters: D. McConnell, A. E. Truesdale
Assistant Cubmasters: A. R. Hunter, B. Baird.
Bugle Major: I. Smith.
Rover Mates: W. Graham, G. Kennedy.
Rovers: J. McConnell, H. Caldwell, W. Truesdale, W. Power.
Patrol Leaders: L.P. Nicholl, F. Truesdale, J. Mitchell.
Scouts: B. McConnell, H. Tighe, W. R. King, R. Copeland, T. Burnett, D. Graham, E. Thornberry

Photos from annual camps during the 1930s

1940s

Mourne Park, 1944
Known to be in the photo are Leslie Truesdale, Jim McClean, James McConnell,
Godfrey McWhirter, Kenny Cowan, Ernest Ferris, Billy McAlpine, Maurice Graham,
Stanley Ferris, Kenneth Weir

1940

Early in the year James Cowan, Scoutmaster, along with other members of the Group, left to join the armed services and play their part in serving their King and country during the 2nd World War. The role of Scoutmaster was taken over by Frank McWhirter.

This year, although many Rover Scouts had left the Group to join the armed services, the Rover Crew continued to flourish. The Troop continued to be very active during the year and entered a number of patrols under Scoutmaster Frank McWhirter and Assistant Fred Jess for the annual South Down Challenge Flag competition which was held in June with glorious weather prevailing in Warrenpoint. However on this occasion the patrols were not successful in bringing home the flag but the keenness and interest aroused in the boys and the desire to do better next time made it all worthwhile. The members of the Group have been busily engaged in the collection of waste paper with the proceeds from the sale of which being handed over to the Red Cross fund. During the year the Troop lost a valuable member in the death of Jackie O'Neill after a long illness. Owing to the ongoing international situation this year there was no annual camp held. There are now 25 Cubs, 35 Scouts and 12 Rover Scouts along with the following leaders on the roll: Group Scoutmaster Jack Smith, Cubmaster Graham Clarke, Assistant Cubmaster Norman McMinn, Scoutmaster Frank McWhirter, Assistant Scoutmasters Albert Mateer and Fred Jess, Rover Leader W. J. Gibson.

Young Wolf Cub Billy McAlpine saluting. Billy had just joined and had yet to receive his badges.

1941

On Sunday evening, 12 January 1941, a memorial service took place in Downshire Road Presbyterian Church in tribute to the memory of the Chief Scout, Lord Baden-Powell who died on 8 January. The event was attended by all the members of 1st Newry (Earl Kilmorey) Scout Group who wore black armbands as a remark of respect to their esteemed leader. The Group was under the command of Scoutmaster F. McWhirter, Assistant Scoutmaster A. Mateer while the Cubs were supervised by Cubmaster G. Clarke and Assistant Cubmaster N. McMinn. There was a large congregation for the service which included a contingent from 1st Newry Girl Guides under their leaders Miss I. Orr and Miss R. Campbell. The service was conducted by the Group's chaplain Rev. Phineas McKee, B.A. who alluded to the work of Lord Baden-Powell, the founder of the Scouting Movement, and our Chief for many years and stated that his death would be a sad loss to this great Movement. During the course of the service both the Scouts and Guides renewed their Promise and Laws and the service concluded with the 'Dead march'. The organist was Mrs G. Adamson.

During the year the membership of the Group had remained fairly constant with all the members taking a keen interest and working very hard for their proficiency badges. The Cubs have been doing their bit in the National effort assisting the Scouts in the collection of waste paper which by the end of the year had reached a staggering forty tons. The proceeds of their collections have been handed over to the Red Cross. Owing to wartime restrictions camping was on a smaller scale this year but nearly all the Scouts spent at least a week under canvas at Mourne Park and Ballyedmond where much experience in outdoor scouting life was gained by all those who attended.

1st Newry Boy Scouts on the Upper Damolly Road, Newry.
Back row L-R: R. McCullough, W. Erskine, S. Ferris, W. Cowan
Middle row: R. Patterson, R. Hodgett, E. Ferris, R. O'Donoghue
Front row: Not known, S. Jones, H. Rowland

1st Newry Wolf Cubs. Left to right: Jimmy Jones, Billy Turkington, Eric Moorehead, David Lynas.

1st Newry Wolf Cubs on the Upper Damolly Road Newry.
1. Billy Turkington, 2. David Lynas, 3. Jimmy Jones.

1942

Throughout the year the Group worked hard for proficiency badges and quite a number were earned. The annual camp was held at Mourne Park where lots of Scouting activities were shared with a Belfast Troop which was also in camp at the same time. Membership of the Group continued to remain constant and attendance at the weekly meetings remained good.

The drive for more waste paper continued and the Cubs, Scouts and Rover Scouts all worked hard on this venture. A great deal of paper had already been collected and the leaders asked anyone who had waste paper to give their names and addresses to any of the Scouters. Rover Scout Robert McCullough, along with his colleagues, excelled in these paper collections and was presented with a service award for all their hard work. Robert and all the Rovers were rightly proud of their endeavours. Early in the year a social was held in aid of the Prisoners of War Fund, and the Troop was able to forward a substantial sum to this worthy cause. A further sum of £13/13/0 (£13.65) had also been forwarded to the Baden-Powell Memorial Fund as the result of a special effort in the drive for salvage.

1st Newry Wolf Cubs, 1942
Back row L-R: G. McVicker, R. James, J. McKee, W. J. Wylie, D. Baker, R. Kennedy
Middle row: Not known, J. Dalzell, Not known, W. Boyd, E. Barton, J. Trimble
Front row: G. Agnew, R. Baker, A. McLeod, D. McKee, Not known, Not known, J. Kimberly

1943 - 1944

1943

Two camps were held during the summer at Dundalk, and many Scouting activities and friendships were exchanged with the Dundalk Troop. These camps were thoroughly enjoyed by all the boys who were able to attend. During the summer the boys also undertook several interesting and enjoyable hikes and cycle runs.

It was with profound sorrow that the death of the Group's beloved chaplain, the Rt. Rev. Phineas McKee, B.A., D.D., in November 1943, was recorded. Dr McKee had devoted much of his time and energy to Scouting in Newry and district and was a friend and brother to all. His death robbed the boys of their most popular and prominent member and they joined with the congregation of Downshire Road Church in mourning the loss of their beloved minister.

Membership had again held up well and high standards of Scout work had been maintained by the boys under the leadership of their dedicated leaders. Both Scouts and Cubs showed their keen interest in badge work, and a number of proficiency badges were gained.

1944

The annual report for the year 1944 given by F. McWhirter, Scoutmaster, recorded that a high standard of Scouting had been attained. This had been due mainly to the help and encouragement given during the year by the Field Commissioner, Mr D. Irvine, who visited the Troop on a number of occasions.

During the month of July the Scouts held a very successful ten-day camp in Mourne Park, from which the boys returned with a renewed zeal for true Scouting.

The Group had been able in some small measure to assist in the working of many great causes. They assisted in the collection of about £36 (£36.00) for the Royal Victoria Hospital, and were also engaged in helping to raise money for the Ulster Light Anti-Aircraft Regiment Comforts' Fund.

Later in the year the Group was pleased to install as chaplain the Rev. N. Small, B.A., whose interest in youth work was widely known.

The Scouters had been forced, owing to lack of accommodation, to reduce their numbers slightly, although membership in both Cubs and Scouts had remained at a steady level. Once again the Group put on record its thanks to the session and committee of Downshire Road Presbyterian Church for the use of our hall, and for the way in which they had facilitated them on every occasion.

1st Newry Troop at Mourne Park, 1944

1. Maurice Graham
2. Kenny Cowan
3. Billy McAlpine,
4. Stanley Ferris
5. Frank McWhirter (SM)
6. Leslie Truesdale
7. Freddy Jess
8. Billy Blair
9. James McConnell
10. 'Darky' Sloan

1945

After more than thirty six years of Scouting activities, 1945 had proved to have been one of the Group's most successful years.

In April they revived their old custom of running a Scout Jamboree concert in Downshire Road hall. This was their first concert since 1939, and it turned out to be a tremendous success. After a second night's performance of the show, the proceeds were donated to help the Boys' Residential Hostel, Malone Road, Belfast.

On 26 April 1945 the Group was saddened and shocked to hear of the death of one of their former and beloved members, Flying Officer A.E. (Bertie) Truesdale, R.A.F.V.R., who had been killed in action. His parents, Mr and Mrs A. E. Truesdale, 1A Edward Street, Newry, had received a letter from Buckingham Palace which read as follows:

> *The Queen and I offer you our heartfelt sympathy in your great sorrow. We pray that your country's gratitude for a life so nobly given in its service may bring you some measure of consolation. – George, R.I.*

Flying Officer Truesdale, or Bertie as he was known to a host of friends, joined the R.A.F. very shortly after the outbreak of war and took part in many bombing raids over Germany and German-occupied territory. By sheer courage and skill he rose to the rank of Flying Officer, much to the admiration of all his friends. He was reported missing in May 1944, with the official news of his death in December 1944 which came as a terrible shock to all who had known him.

Bertie had been a very active and much liked member of the Group prior to volunteering for active service. Both Bertie and his younger brother, Leslie, who was also a Rover Scout with the Group, took very active roles within the Group and Bertie would be sadly missed. The Group's heartfelt sympathy was extended to all the family. Two of Bertie's brothers also served in HM Forces, William in the Royal Navy, and Fred in the R.A.F. Their father had been an ex-serviceman of the last Great War.

The month of June was most successful for the Rover Crew when they formed a bugle band under the very capable directorship of Mr P. Campbell. There were also 30 Scouts and 25-30 Cubs in the Group at this time.

The South Down Flag competition was held in Mourne Park during the weekend 6 – 8 July 1945, with Troops from Bessbrook, Newry, Kilkeel and Warrenpoint taking part. The competition included tenderfoot and first and second class tests as well as opportunities to participate in pioneering, woodcraft, signalling, first aid, cooking and camp craft. The standard of camping was high despite the inclement weather and all who took part voted the competition as being one of the best ever arranged by the Local Association. Warrenpoint were declared the winners with 92 marks, with Newry coming second with 89 marks.

The judging was carried out by Mr D. Irvine, Field Commissioner for Ulster, H.R. Scott, county secretary for Down, with the assistance of District Commissioner R. Haldane, and Miss Ryan, District Cubmaster from Warrenpoint.

In the summer months many enjoyable camps were spent in the district. The annual Troop camp was held, during the month of July, in Mourne Park under the leadership of Assistant Rover Scoutmaster James Lawson and Rover Mates Truesdale and Meeke. The camp was attended by more than twenty Scouts, who did much to improve their Scout work as well as having a most enjoyable holiday at the same time. During camp the boys had climbed Knockcree and had spent time swimming in the Whitewater river. It was hoped that in future some camps might be held in England.

On Tuesday, 7 August, in the Scout hall, Sandys Street, members of 1st Newry Rover Crew honoured three of their former comrades who had served with H.M. Forces. Rev. Wm. McAdam, M.A. presided and the honoured guests were W/O Fred Truesdale, R.A.F., Air Transport Command; Cpl. R. Copeland, R.A.F. and Sgt. James Cowan, R.A.F.

1st Newry Rover Scouts Teddy Cowan and Robert McCullough c.1945

Scoutmaster Frank McWhirter welcomed the guests and visitors and introduced Rev. McAdam, M.A., who in the course of a short address said they were meeting to show their gratitude to those members of 1st Newry Group who had served in H.M. Forces. He thought it wonderful to reflect for a moment upon the map of the world and consider such places as Hong Kong in the East, or the banana and orange plantations of the West Indies or the beauties of the Coral Isles, and to realise that their friends had been to all these wondrous places and had returned to tell their story.

He then called for three hearty cheers from the Rover Crew for the guests. Rover Mate R. McCullough, on behalf of the Group, then presented the servicemen with tokens of their esteem, amidst applause.

Sgt. James Cowan, R.A.F. replying, recalled his many memories of his association with the Scout hall. Looking back ten years he could remember, when they had been among them, some of the greatest boys ever to stand in the hall. A good many of them had passed out into the world and one or two had died, but were with them in spirit. They could never again return to their hall, although the boys of 1st Newry would keep their memory fresh.

He congratulated those Scouts who has stayed at home for their magnificent asset to the war effort in salvage work and the Home Guard. Every one of them had been touched by the war and had done his job well. They should never forget their comrades who had made the supreme sacrifice. W/O Truesdale and Cpl. Copeland also spoke, returning thanks. A moment's silence was observed for the members who had given their lives in the services.

A musical programme followed to which the following contributed: - Scout K. Cowan, Cub J. Jones, Rover Scout R. Jess, Rover Scout Meeke, Rover Mate McCullough, Assistant Scoutmasters Jess and Truesdale, Cub Dalzell and Rover Scout T. Cowan.

1st Newry Troop of Boy Scouts, at a pleasant social evening on Friday, 5 October, in the Scout hall, honoured their Troop chaplain, Rev. N. Small, B.A., and Group Scoutmaster, Frank McWhirter, on their recent marriages. Assistant Scoutmaster, Fred Jess, presided and, apologising for the absence of Rev. Wm. McAdam, M.A., gave a hearty welcome to Mrs Small and Mrs McWhirter.

Welcoming the Group Scoutmaster, Mr Jess paid tribute to his long and active association with the Troop extending over sixteen years, during which time he had progressed through the various ranks to his present position of Group Scoutmaster. Welcoming the chaplain, the Assistant Scoutmaster said he was a man who took a very great interest in the Newry Troop. In conclusion he welcomed Mr and Mrs Small and Mr and Mrs McWhirter, and extended his best wishes for their future happiness. P.L. S. Jones made the presentation on behalf of the Group. The recipients suitably replied.

The following Cubs, Scouts, Rover Scouts and Leaders contributed to the entertainment: - Fred Jess, K. Cowan, R. McCullough, W. Meeke, L. Truesdale, R. Jess, D. O'Donoghue, R. James, R. O'Donoghue, H. Linton and T. Dalzell. The evening terminated with the National Anthem.

Sporting activities within the Group attained a high standard, with the football team playing many enjoyable matches. During the year the Group again welcomed many regular visits from the Field Commissioner, Mr D. Irvine.

For the Group's special Christmas good turn, the boys gave a Christmas party for over three hundred children of the various churches and entertained the residents of Newry Workhouse to a variety concert. It was hoped to make this an annual event.

The boys were now working hard to raise enough money to build a new Scout HQ as the existing one is becoming too small for their increasing numbers.

Many changes had taken place in the various ranks and during the year Mr F. McWhirter filled the office of Group Scoutmaster. Scoutmaster Fred Jess was leaving to take up residence in England and Mr L. Truesdale had filled his position. The Scouters welcomed into the Group Mr Walter Hammond who is now temporarily in charge of the Rover Crew.

With the war over, many of the Group's old and most valued members were returning and were welcomed home. Some forty members of 1st Newry Group had served and eight of these had made the supreme sacrifice. They would always be remembered as King's Scouts who had died that others might live.

1946

The Chief Scout, Lord Rowallan, made a visit to the Province which also took him to Portadown where he met Cubs, Scouts and Senior Scouts with their leaders. 1st Newry, under the leadership of Scoutmaster F. McWhirter, was well represented at this event.

Once again the Troop decided to hold annual camp at one of their favourite camping grounds, Mourne Park. Those attending took part in a range of outdoor pursuits including swimming, the usual climb to the top of Knockcree, compass and mapping as well as having a number of late night campfires.

Later in the year, as a result of an appeal from the county, members of the Troop took part in the first ever Scout Job week. The purpose was to raise funds to ensure the proper functioning of the county. The amount of money raised was not recorded but it was likely that 1st Newry performed well.

THE BOY SCOUTS.

The Scouts' Job Week
21st - 28th September, 1946.

"BE PREPARED"

To meet running expenses the Scout Group finds its own funds, but our County needs money to help meet the increasing demands. The County helps the Scout Districts in their necessary work, and growing leadership means more activity.

Funds are needed to maintain the flow of support — the training, the organisation, the Headquarters.

Please assist by giving a JOB and PAY.

The Money raised by the efforts of the Scouts, Wolf Cubs, Rovers, will be devoted to Scout Funds. PAY AS WE EARN !! We ask for Work and Pay on this occasion. Every Scout wants to earn at least **2/6** in JOB WEEK. Give what you think the job is worth.

If you have a job that needs doing please let me know at :—

(ADDRESS)..

(SIGNED)...

THANK YOU.

The Scouts' Job Week poster from September 1946

1947

The District had been allocated one place for a Scout to represent Scouting from the district at the World Jamboree in France and Samuel Boyd, 1st Kilkeel Group, was nominated with Patrol Leader W. J. Wylie to fill a second place if one became available.

A large contingent of Cubs, Scouts and Rover Scouts from 1st Newry Troop accompanied by their leaders took part in the first district St George's Day parade and service which was held in Warrenpoint Parish Church on Sunday, 20 April. During the service, one of the lessons was read by Seconder Roy Kennedy and the offertory, which was in aid of the fund for distressed children of Europe, was taken up by 1st Newry Rover Scouts Leslie Neill, Harry Crawford, John Power and Karl Gordon.

During the months of April and May the Rover Scouts held a number of weekend camps at Mourne Park. On a few occasions they were accompanied by fellow Rovers from Dundalk.

In July the District Commissioner presented warrants to Mr F. McWhirter, Group Scoutmaster of 1st Newry Group and W. Smith, Assistant Scoutmaster.

1st Newry Rover Scout Crew held their annual camp on the Annesley estate at Castlewellan. From all reports everyone had a wonderful time with lots of Scouting skills put into practice. The Troop held annual camp at Mourne Park where all who attended took part in the many Scouting activities arranged by their leaders. As in previous camps the great attraction was swimming in the Whitewater river and climbing Knockcree as well as mapping, compass, cooking and pioneering. Everyone returned home tired and weary but very happy after a very successful ten days.

On 1 July the Newry Wolf Cub football team travelled to Bessbrook to play against the local Pack. The match was evenly matched, resulting in a 1-1 draw.

On Saturday, 5 July, the Cub Pack travelled to Belfast for their annual outing where they spent the evening at Bellevue Zoo.

On Saturday, 16 August, St. Mary's Parish Church, Newry was the scene of a pretty wedding when Miss Violet Harkness, Cowan St., Newry, married Mr Fred Jess, St. Mary's Terrace, Newry. As the happy couple left the church, they passed through a guard of honour formed by the members of 1st Newry Troop of Boy Scouts of which the bridegroom was Assistant Scoutmaster.

Some of the signatures of the Rover Scouts who camped at Mourne Park during the months of April and May.

1948

The District Flag competition was held at Mourne Park during the weekend 11 to 13 June. Ideal weather favoured the event which was voted one of the most enjoyable since its inception. There were various tests including signalling, cooking and first-aid which helped the patrols taking part to be self-supporting and self-sustaining from Saturday afternoon until Sunday evening. One particularly exciting activity was transporting a lighted fire across the Whitewater river which all patrols succeeded in undertaking successfully. The adjudicators were District Commissioner W. J. Radcliffe of Banbridge District, and District Commissioner Robert Jones of Newry District.

The result of the competition was - first place: 1st Newry; runners up: 1st Kilkeel. This was a popular result.

The members of the winning Newry Bulldog patrol were: P.L. Robert Aiken, Second W. McVicker and Scouts J. Dalzell, J. Jones, J. McVicker and J. Wylie.

A campfire on the Saturday night under the direction of Rover leaders Truesdale and McLean of Newry was thoroughly enjoyed by all the boys.

1948 District Flag winners   1st Newry Boy Scouts at Mourne Park

1948 Bulldog Patrol, winners of the South Down Challenge Flag competition, 13th June, Mourne Park.
L-R: R. Aiken, W. J. Wylie, J. Dalzell, W. McVicker, J. Jones, J. McVicker

During July 1948 the Troop held annual camp at Silver Strand, county Wicklow, and all who attended came home with fond memories of the camp and looking forward to future events.

L-R Front row: J. Aiken, D. McClean, D. McClean, G. McCullough. 2nd row: A. McLeod, J. Dalzell, H. Crawford, W. Blair. 3rd row: R. McCullough, W.J. Wylie, Not known. 4th row: D. Crozier, R. Aiken. L. Dalzell.

Rover Scout Kenneth McClean at Silver Strand

Top of page and above: Annual camp, Silver Strand, county Wicklow

Rover Scout Harry Crawford and William Smith at Silver Strand

The Rev. Nathaniel Small, B.A., in the presence of a large congregation in Downshire Road Presbyterian Church on Sunday, 3 November, dedicated four Colours presented to 1st Newry Group Boy Scouts by their Group committee. He addressed the Scouts in particular on their motto, 'Be Prepared', and urged them to be faithful to it both by precept and example. He concluded by saying that the boys should 'Go out into a world to serve the Master and the flags you have had dedicated today'.

As well as the dedication of the Colours, a specially hand drawn plaque by former Scout J. A. Craig which bore the Roll of Honour of Newry Scouts who had made the supreme sacrifice and those who had served in World War Two, was also dedicated. During the service, Miss Alice Adgey, of Toronto, Canada, sang 'The Lord's Prayer'.

The Frontier Pipe Band headed the parade to the church, and participating in it were B.P. Boy Scouts, Wolf Cubs, Girl Guides and Sea Rangers from Newry, Bessbrook, Kilkeel, Tandragee, Warrenpoint, Mullavilly, Portadown, Newcastle and other centres. At the march past, Mrs M. A. Lockhart, County Commissioner and Mr Robert Jones, District Commissioner took the salute.

Signatures of the Troop members who took part in the Newry District Flag competition.

Signatures of the winning Bulldog patrol.

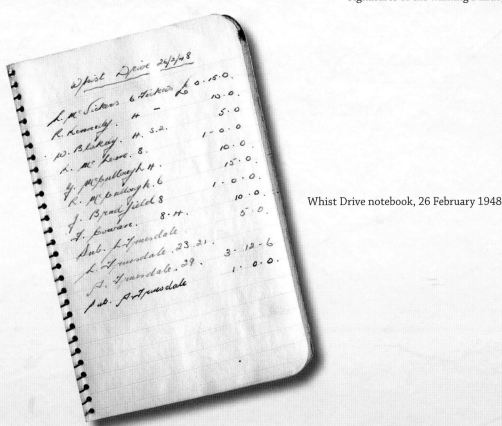

Whist Drive notebook, 26 February 1948

1949

Bob-a-job week launched

On Thursday, 7 April 1949, the following article appeared in the pages of the *Newry Reporter*:

To the Editor, *Newry Reporter*

Sir,

The Chief Scout, Lord Rowallan, has called upon every Wolf Cub, Scout, Senior Scout, Rover Scout and Scouter in Great Britain and Northern Ireland to earn the sum of at least 1/- (5p) for Scout funds during the week April 18 to April 23.

This step has been made necessary due to the reduction of investment income during recent years, and by the expenses incurred in the rebuilding of Scouting since the war. Our Movement, with membership in the United Kingdom alone of nearly half a million, has won the support of your readers in the past, and it is with confidence that I appeal to them to find jobs for the Scouts during next week. Any odd jobs they consider to be within the capabilities of boys will be welcomed – household or gardening work such as chopping wood, cleaning brass, tree felling, hedge clipping, weeding, creosoting fences, cleaning cars, running errands and bathing the dog – these are but a few examples of the great variety of jobs which can be undertaken.

It is a principle of Scouting that, as far as possible, the boys shall earn their own funds, and I have no hesitation in asking the public through your columns to support their efforts. In these days when there is a great danger of the rising generation growing up with the idea that some mysterious 'they' will hand everything to them on a plate, it is of the utmost importance that young people be taught the satisfaction of achieving something through honest labour.

Each Scout will be in possession of a card authorising him to work on behalf of the Movement. On this card the 'employer' is asked to enter the nature of the work carried out by the boy and the amount paid to him.

You will be doing Scouting a very good turn, Sir, if you will be good enough to publish this letter.

Yours, etc.,
R. Jones
District Commissioner
10 Slieve Foy Place,
Warrenpoint,
2 April 1949.

All the members of the Group then took part for the first time in Scout Bob-a-job week which had just been inaugurated by Headquarters this year. However there is no record of what amount was raised or the types of jobs undertaken.

St George's Day in Newry was marked on 24 April by a parade of B.P. Boy Scouts and Cubs, headed by the Newry Rover Crew bugle band, to Downshire Road Presbyterian Church. The parade was under the auspices of Newry and District Boy Scout Association, and there was a fine turnout of Scouts from Newry, Kilkeel, Warrenpoint, and Bessbrook.

The Rev. J. N. Goulden, B.A., curate of Warrenpoint and Clonallon and Scoutmaster of the Warrenpoint Scouts, was the special preacher, and the Rev. N. Small, B.A., minister of Downshire Road Church, and chaplain to 1st Newry Scout Group conducted the service. The Male Voice Choir of the local Guild of Boy Scouts, with Mr J. Harry Heather, L.L.C.M., at the organ, led the singing. Mr Anson Chapman sang the Boy Scout hymn, while others taking part in the service were Cubmaster Thomas Glass, who read the Cub Law, and Scout Jackie Dalzell, who read the Scout Law.

Rover Crew Bugle Band, St George's Day Parade, April 1949

Officers in the parade also included – District Commissioner Robert Jones, Assistant District Commissioner William Gardiner, Scoutmaster R. McCullough, 1st Newry, Miss T. Hamilton, Assistant Cubmaster. 1st Newry, and Group Scoutmaster A. McKnight, Bessbrook.

Changes in Scout uniform, which took effect from October 1949, were announced in the Boy Scout Association's weekly news bulletin. The present world famous hat, adopted by Lord Baden-Powell over 40 years ago, is retained but members of the Movement over 15 years of age will be allowed to wear a beret for camps, hikes and other informal occasions. For Scouts over 15, Senior Scouts and Scouters in charge of Senior Scouts, the colour of the berets will be maroon. For Rover Scouts, all other Scouters, including Lady Cubmasters, Commissioners and non-executive and honorary ranks, the colour will be 'scout green'.

During the month of November the patrol system within the Scout section of the Group had been reformed and all the Scouts were settling down to a winter of hard work under their Group Scoutmaster Bryson and Scoutmaster A. Storey. The Wolf Cubs, under Cubmaster D. Manderson and Assistants Dalzell and McKee, held a very successful 'Tramps supper' which was attended by the chaplain Rev. N. Small and the parents of the Cubs who entered into the fun of the evening with zest.

Between late 1949 and early 1950 there was a decline in the number of Scouts and the Troop almost came to an end but for the efforts of Sam Cassidy who became Scoutmaster in 1950 and who took a very keen interest in the Group and built up the Scout section again. However the Group during this period was well served by the Wolf Cubs whose numbers remained fairly constant.

1st Newry football team 1949. Back row L-R: Billy Kernaghan, Jack Dalzell, Bob Aiken, Billy Blakely, Derek Foster, Leslie Dalzell
Front row: Derek Gamble, Billy McVicker, Kenny Cowan, John Wylie and Godfrey McWhirter

1950s

Scouts on the boat to Isle of Man on their way to annual camp, 1959
L-R: S. Poots, R. Allely, L. Girvan, J. Mateer, M. McConnell, N. McCullough,
R. Baird, Roland Torrens. Back: M. Matier (1st Kilmore), Derek Ball

1950 - 1951

1950

On Thursday, 22 June 1950, an evening meeting was held in the Scout hall with a view to reforming the Group Committee which had declined in numbers and had not been working effectively for some time. The minutes of the meeting record the election of Mr Sidney Sterritt, a former leader, as chairman, Miss O. Manderson as secretary and Mrs S. Sterritt as treasurer. This committee's responsibility was to look after the financial affairs and general welfare of the Group. It was also recorded that discussion took place concerning the various ways of helping the Troop with uniforms. It was agreed that Mr McCleery, manager of Fosters Department Store, Hill Street, be approached with regard to stocking the Scout uniform. This would facilitate the parents by purchasing locally and would ensure some degree of uniformity. However, at a subsequent meeting on 31 August, it was reported that discussions with Fosters had proved unsuccessful. The Scouts had redecorated the Scout hall and it was decided to repair the door and floor as soon as possible. The chairman agreed to get an estimate for the job and M. Bryson, Group Scoutmaster, was to apply for a permit for the wood. A jumble sale was arranged to take place on the last Saturday in September or the first Saturday of October. Due to the financial situation and the current economic situation, the Troop held their annual camp at Ashgrove, Newry. A guest tea, held in November by the Group and the Ranger Guides, was quite a success with the sum of £19/9/1 (£19.45) being raised and, after expenses, the balance was divided equally between the Scout Group and the Rangers. Also in 1950 John Wylie joined the Group as an Assistant Scoutmaster.

1951

Discussions took place in 1951 concerning the replacement of the floor in the Scout hall. It was agreed that, instead of removing the floor, a new floor be laid on top of the existing one. It was also agreed that the Group Scoutmaster Sam Cassidy be empowered to purchase a suitable tent for weekend camping. The Cubmistress sought funding of £4 (£4.00) from the Group to take sixteen Cubs to the Scout Gang Show in Belfast in place of the annual Cub outing. During Bob-a-job week in April the Scouts and Cubs worked very hard to earn much needed finances for the Group and succeeded in raising the sum of £26/18/1 £26.90) with first prize going to Scout Norman McAlpine and David Kay receiving second prize. During the months of May and June the Group attended the Children's Day services in the Presbyterian churches in Downshire Road and Sandys Street as well as the Methodist Church.

A most successful and thoroughly enjoyable Troop annual camp was held at Mourne Park, Kilkeel. During the camp the boys had to make their own meals as well as tidying up afterwards as the leaders carried out snap inspections to ensure that everything was spick and span. The Scouts took part in swimming in the river as well as the usual camp craft skills, pioneering, river walk, compass and mapping as well as climbing Knockcree mountain. The parents and friends were invited to attend on 'visitors' day' which was held on Wednesday, 18 July, with the Cubs also going down for the whole day under the care of Assistant Cubmaster K. Cowan. At the end of camp everyone returned home tired but having had a wonderful time at camp. The expenses for this camp came to the grand total of £35/18/9 (£35.94). During the year the Group Committee held a number of events such as a social, a jumble sale and a whist drive to raise funds for the Group.

Easter camp at Mourne Park, 1951

1952

The year commenced with plans for a sale and sporting competition in Downshire Road Church Hall on 12 March. The sale included a cake stall, pound stall, the sale of ice cream and minerals, bean board, darts, shooting and an aunt Sally. Miss I. Foster carried out the official opening of the sale and from all reports the event proved to be a great success. It is recorded in the minutes of the Group's annual meeting that the balance of cash in hand at 31 March was £84/12/10 (£84.64). The Troop held a very successful weekend camp at Mourne Park where, under the care of Assistant Scout Leader John Wylie, ably assisted by Cub Leader Tommy McCullough, the members of the Troop gained valuable camping knowledge and experience which was to prove most useful over the following months. Once again this year the Cubs and Scouts took part in Bob-a-job week and raised the princely sum of £26/10/6 (£26.53). With the experience gained from the weekend camp at Mourne Park, a patrol of six Scouts from the Troop put these talents to good use when taking part in the South Down Challenge Flag competition and were successful in winning this event. Following their success, and as a reward for the marvellous effort achieved, the patrol was granted the princely sum of £2 (£2.00) towards the cost of an outing to the Belfast Air Display. A grant of £5 (£5.00) was given to the Cubmistress to cover the expenses of a Cub outing to Dundalk.

For ten days during the month of July a contingent of Scouts from the Troop headed off from Edward Street railway station via Belfast to the Isle of Man where they held their annual camp at Quayles Orchard, Ballasalla. The overall cost of this event came to the magnificent sum of £71/9/4 (£71.47).

A parents night which was arranged to take place on Tuesday, 2 December, in Downshire Road Church Hall proved to be a great success with a good attendance of parents and friends being entertained with sketches, demonstrations and campfire songs from the Cubs and Scouts.

Weekend camp at Mourne Park, 1952. Above left: Godfrey Ferris. Above middle: Jim Dalzell, Mervyn Ferris.

Annual camp, Quayles Orchard, Isle of Man, 1952
L-R Front row: J. Cowan, A. Jones, B. McCullough, N. McAlpine, J. Dalzell, E. Farquhar, M. Ferris, W. Baines, J. Wilson.
2nd row: N. McCormick, D. McClean. Back row: S. Cassidy SM, T. Bradfield, S. McMinn, G. Ferris, W. McAlpine, J. Wylie,
T. McCullough, D. McClean, J. Dalzell, W. Holmes

Below L-R: B. McCullough,
N. McAlpine, T. Bradfield,
J. Wilson, J. Dalzell, A. Jones,
D. McClean, M. Ferris (front)

1953

In 1953 Noel Hodgett joined the Group as Assistant Scoutmaster and, with this dedicated trio of Sam Cassidy, John Wylie and Noel, the Troop and indeed the Group moved from strength to strength. This year the Troop annual camp was held at Peter's Hill, Newcastle, county Down. Unfortunately the weather during the camp proved to be extremely wet and the Leaders and Senior Scouts were forced to brave the elements and dig trenches around the patrol tents in order to allow the water flowing though the site to drain away from the tents. Despite the bad weather the camp proved to be a great success and did not deter anyone from looking forward to next year's event.

Discussions took place during the year regarding the renovations to the downstairs part of the Scout hall and it was agreed to seek permission from Downshire Road Church to allow work to progress. The Scout hall in Sandys Street was a two-storey outhouse before being taken over by the Group although only the top half had been used. Bob-a-job week which took place in April brought in the sum of £22/8/10 (£22.44). The annual St George's Day parade and service was held in Newry starting from The Mall, past Newell's shop, up Hill Street, along Kildare Street and hence to Downshire Road Church. On the return journey the parade marched from the church along Downshire Road, Trevor Hill, Kildare Street, down Hill Street and around the green clock in Margaret Square before being dismissed at the Institute in Hill Street. There was a magnificent attendance at this event and all visiting Groups were entertained to tea and refreshments in the Institute following the event. Later in the year it was noted that permission had been received from Downshire Road Church agreeing to the alterations to the Scout hall. This allowed planning to go ahead to have the work commenced during the latter part of 1953 and into the following year.

1st Newry at annual camp, Peter's Hill, Newcastle

Annual camp patrol, Peter's Hill, Newcastle.
Back row L-R: Jim Henning, Norman McAlpine, T. McCullough CM, W. McAlpine ACM
Front row: Mervyn Ferris, Not known, Edmund Farquhar.

2nd class badge, 1953

1954

The renovations to the hall were completed in March 1954 under the leadership of Sam Cassidy and Noel Hodgett with help from the Senior Scouts. New windows were installed along with a new floor, ceiling and relocation of the door. This work allowed downstairs to be brought into use by the Group for its various activities. The opening ceremony was performed in April by W. V. Heasley, the County Commissioner for Down. The ladies of the Group Committee provided a variety of mouth-watering refreshments following the opening ceremony. Everyone in attendance showed their appreciation not only for the excellent changes to the building but for the refreshments provided by the ladies. The treasurer's report at the annual general meeting showed the Group with a balance of £67/5/8 (£67.28) in the bank.

This year the Troop annual camp was held at Tawd Vale, near Liverpool under the leadership of Scoutmaster Noel Hodgett, assisted by Assistant Scoutmaster Godfrey Ferris and Assistant Cubmaster Billy McAlpine. During the camp those attending took part in the usual camping activities such as pioneering, mapping and compass, games and variety of activities including swimming and raft building in the quarry adjacent to the campsite. The Cubs were now playing in a football league and a grant of £5 (£5.00) was given towards travel and entertaining visiting teams. Once again a patrol from the Troop had won the South Down Challenge Flag. Permission was given for the Hunter Moore Memorial Flute Band to have the use of the Scout hall for practice on evenings when no Scout meetings were being held. The chairman remarked that, as the band had always turned out for any Scout function, the Group would like to show its appreciation and support by facilitating the band in any way possible. The treasurer informed the Group committee that the bank balance now stood at £25/9/0 (£25.45). Following a voluntary collection, as part of the Christmas good turn from the boys within the Scout Troop, the sum of £2/10/0 (£2.50) had been forwarded to Rev. T.G. Eakins towards the Spastic Fund.

Wolf Cubs, c.1954

Wolf Cub Pack. Leaders (L-R): Tommy McCullough, Mrs Dover, Madge Dalzell, Billy McAlpine.

1st Newry Troop annual Camp to Tawd Vale, Liverpool
L-R Front: E. Mitchell, N. Girvan, J. Girvan, K. Atkinson, W. Baines, W. Graham, W. Holmes. Back: G. Ferris, N. Hodgett SM, W. Pollock, M. Whitehead, D. McClean, N. McAlpine, W. McAlpine ACM, J. Wylie ASM, S. Whitehead.

1955

On 8 January 1955 a dance was held in Newry Town Hall which raised the sum of £29/3/2 (£29.16) towards Group funds. A very successful parents night was held on 24 March. The annual general meeting of the Group council, which was attended by Rev. N. Small and Rev. E. Shaw, President of the Methodist Church, received reports from the Group Scoutmaster, Scoutmaster and Cubmaster on the various activities throughout the year. The treasurer reported that, due to the funds from the dance and jumble sale, our balance now stood at £78/13/2 (£78.66). Bob-a-job week, which took place over the Easter period, raised the sum of £44/7/2 (£44.36) and the chairman congratulated two Scouts and one Cub who earned £4/5/0 (£4.25), £4 (£4.00) and £2/5/0 (£2.25) respectively.

The Troop annual camp was held at Powerscourt, county Wicklow from 9 to 16 July. The camp was a most successful one and held in ideal weather conditions. Billy McAlpine received his warrant as Assistant Cubmaster. Mr Sam Cassidy, who was in attendance at the meeting in September, informed everyone that he had resigned as Group Scoutmaster and handed over a list of all equipment held by the Group. The Rev. N. Small spoke of the amount of work which he had done for the Group and of his influence with the boys. Mr N. Hodgett, Scoutmaster, also spoke of all that Sam had done and the hard work which he had put into the renovations of the Scout hall. He hoped that Mr Cassidy would remain as a member of the Group Committee. A donation toward Group funds was received from Newry District Motor Club in appreciation of assistance given at their race meeting at Cranfield on Saturday 3 September. During the year a jumble sale and social/dance had raised the sum of £25/12/4 (£25.62) and £5/14/8 (£5.73) respectively.

Annual camp at Powerscourt

1st Newry Scouts at Goraghwood Station en-route to camp at Powerscourt

L-R Front: L. Girvan, R. Mears, W. Steele, J. Rcid. Middle: W. Baines, N. Girvan, H. McAlpine, E. Mitchell, I. Ferris (hidden), W. McCullough, K. Atkinson. Back: J. Dalzell, N. McAlpine, T. Bradfield, J. Wolsley, S. Whitehead, M. Whitehead, S. Cassidy GSM, N. Hodgett SM, G. Ferris ASM.

1956

At the beginning of 1956 a new Romesse stove was installed in the hall and everyone was now most satisfied with the warmth of the building. A whist drive held in April raised the sum of £16/12/1 (£16.60) and this, together with Bob-a-job week (£32/2/7) (£32.13) helped, after the payment of accounts, to swell the finances of the Group to £66/5/8 (£66.28). The annual general meeting of the Group held on 17 April was opened with a prayer by Rev. N. Small. The Scouters reported that the Group now had sixty members and the programme of activities was working well. Assistant Scoutmaster Godfrey Ferris reported that there were now two patrols of Senior Scouts totalling 12 boys. The chairman, Mrs C. McAlpine, commented on the flourishing condition of the Group and endorsed the Scoutmaster's appeal for greater interest by parents. The Rev. N. Small proposed the adoption of the various reports. Three Cubs, Jim Baines, Tom Mears and Alan O'Donoghue, had gained the Leaping Wolf Badge, the highest award available to Cubs.

Cubs, Scouts and Senior Scouts along with their leaders attended the District St George's day parade and service which was held in Rostrevor. Also in attendance were Scout Groups from Dundalk and Monaghan. A team of Cubs won the District football competition and were awarded the District cup for their achievement. The Scoutmaster was granted the sum of £30 (£30.00) towards the cost of annual camp which was held in Colwyn Bay, north Wales, and a further £10 (£10.00) for additional cooking equipment. Twenty six Scouts attended the annual camp from 6 to 18 July. It was reported that the camp was a great success with good weather during the period and many activities enjoyed by all. Mr Cassidy, former Group Scoutmaster was also in attendance and during the camp taught a number of the Scouts who were previously unable to swim to do so before the local swimming pool was closed due to a polio scare. During the camp the leader of the local youth club, Mr. W. Hollywood, who was originally from Belfast, arranged a number of events, football and cricket, with some of the club members. Everyone left Colwyn Bay at the end of the camp happy and contented but some sadly had to say goodbye to a few of the young local girls with whom they had become good friends.

Once again the Newry Motor Club recognised the services of the Scouts at their race meeting and donated £2 (£2.00) to Group funds. All the members of the Group travelled to Dundalk on Sunday, 16 September, to take part in a parade and service in the parish church. It was agreed that the Group would meet the expenses of a Scout from the Troop if he was chosen to attend the Golden Jubilee Jamboree from 10 to 21 August in Coventry next year. As in previous years the Group took part in the remembrance parade to the Cenotaph when the Group wreath was laid in memory of those past members of the Group who had given their lives in service to their country. Later in the afternoon Cubs, Scouts, Senior Scouts and leaders attended the service held in the Unitarian Church, Hill Street.

Colwyn Bay annual camp, 1956

1st Newry leaders at Crawfordsburn, 1956.
L-R: H. Crawford, W. J. Wylie, T. McCullough, T. N. Hodgett, W. McAlpine.

1st Newry Wolf Cubs, winners of the 1956 District football competition.
Back: W. McAlpine CM
Middle row L-R: N. McCullough, M. McConnell, Not known, N. Mears, D. Bradfield, R. Kynes
Front row: J. Grant, J. Getty, M. Towers, D. Armstrong, V. Chambers

Wolf Cubs getting ready for football.
Back L-R: W. Andrews, N. Mears,
R. Moorehead, J. Nichol, D. Armstrong, P. Shellard,
V. Chambers, J. Grant, D. Bradfield
Front: M. Towers, M. McConnell, Not known,
R. Kynes, I. Lockington.

1956 1st Newry Senior Scouts
Front row L-R: Norman Girvan, Mervyn Ferris.
Middle row: Martin Whitehead, Billy Pollock, Kenny Atkinson.
Back: Geoffrey Hosford.

Below: Colwyn Bay annual camp 1956, day out at Llandudno.
Front: Jim Dalzell.
Middle row L-R: William Holmes, Norman Girvan,
Mervyn Ferris, Billy McCullough.
Back row: Harry Crawford SSM, Martin Whitehead,
Jim Henning.

Mervyn Ferris

Mervyn Ferris,
Godfrey Ferris

1957

The Troop sent a representative, Scout Jim Dalzell, to the Jubilee Jamboree held in Coventry, England and 1st Newry Guild of Old Scouts provided the funding to allow Jim to go to this major event. The Group made a donation of £3 (£3.00) towards the cost of erecting an outdoor Chapel at Crawfordsburn in honour of the County Commissioner, Mr W. V. Heasley. The Senior Scouts undertook to provide cleaning services at the Institute, Hill Street, and a cheque for £4 (£4.00) was handed over to the Group in recognition of their services. The annual meeting of the Group was informed that, following the payment of expenses, the financial situation of the Group now stood at £41/11/7 (£41.58), somewhat reduced from previous years. The Group now had a membership of seventy one. The Cubmaster Tom McCullough reported that there was a waiting list for the Cub section and, due to the number of Cubs, it had been decided to divide the Cub Pack into two sections. In reporting on the Senior Scout Section, Mr H. Crawford stated that Jim Dalzell had qualified for the Queen Scout Award, the highest award possible for any Scout in the Movement and that Senior Scout Joe Cowan had been presented with a certificate for being among the first ten 1st Class Scouts in this Scouting's Jubilee Year.

Senior Scouts at Crawfordsburn, 1957.
Front row L-R: Mervyn Ferris, Jim Dalzell, Norman Girvan, Billy Graham
Back row: Billy Pollock, Martin Whitehead, Jim Henning

A grant of £70 (£70.00) was approved for the Troop annual camp which took place from 26 July to 9 August at Rough Close, Coventry, close by the Jamboree. During the camp the Scouts paid a number of visits to the Jamboree site where some thirty five thousand people attended this magnificent event. Our Scouts were impressed by the site and especially the great number of Scouts from many countries throughout the world, who were camping there. One of the memorable events, which took place during the camp, was when one of our Scouts, while preparing dinner, accidentally dropped the meat for the Irish Stew on the ground. Rather annoyed with himself he approached the Scoutmaster, Noel Hodgett, seeking advice as to what he should do. The reply was 'just give it a wash and everything will be alright, it only fell on the grass'. Taking the Scoutmaster literally, the Scout then proceeded to place the stewing meat in a basin, add some well known washing powder, reputed to make your whites whiter than white, and give the meat a thoroughly good wash. The comments made following this escapade were many and varied with some suggesting that this popular product had indeed done its job extremely well. Rumour has it, however, that the stew was prepared and everyone ate a hearty meal with no adverse affects. Some time later in the camp, Jim Baines, then a Scout and now our Honorary Treasurer, recalled that early one morning prior to inspection the Senior Scouts got hold of Scout Leader Noel Hodgett's pyjamas, wrapped them in the flag and then waited. Following prayers one of the Patrol Leaders dutifully approached the flagpole and carried out flag break only to see a pair of pyjama bottoms come floating down to earth. There was much hilarity on seeing 'skip's' PJs floating to the ground.

The wedding of our Cubmaster, Tom McCullough, took place in Scotland the day following the Troop's return from annual camp. Scoutmaster Noel Hodgett and Cubmaster William McAlpine had just time to change before crossing over to Scotland to attend the wedding.

Later in the year a further payment was received from the Institute in respect of services provided by the Senior Scouts to the Club. Estimates were received for replacement of the wooden steps to the upstairs of the Scout hall but, as these were quite high, it was decided to leave the matter for further discussion at a later meeting. Once again the Scouts had assisted at Newry Motor Club Race and the Club generously donated the sum of £3/3/0 (£3.15) for Group funds. Mr T. Girvan offered his services to the Group in relation to replacement of the wooden steps with a more substantial concrete structure. A very successful parents night had been held during the month of November and all who attended had a most enjoyable evening. A dance in Newry Town Hall was arranged for Saturday, 14 December. A letter expressing a speedy recovery from his illness was sent to Rev. N. Small who had recently been admitted to hospital. In December it is recorded that the net proceeds of a whist drive held on 24 October amounted to £15 (£15.00) and a further payment had been received from the Institute of £9 (£9.00).

The Troop at Edward Street Railway Station on their way to 1957 Jubilee Jamboree at Sutton Coldfield, England
L-R Front: J. Pollock, J. Baines, R. Miskimmons, I. McKee, B. Taylor, J. Reid, M. Forsythe, A. Hewitson, W. Ewing, M. Towers. Middle: Not known, I. Ferris, E. Moorehead, W. Steele, J. Wylie ASM. Back: S. Cassidy, GSM, D. Hamilton, W. Pollock, G. Hosford, J. Henning, N. Girvan, M. Ferris, H. Crawford SSM, N. Hodgett SM, S. Whitehead.

Scouts at the 1957 Jubilee Jamboree gate, Sutton Coldfield. 1st Newry representative is Jim Dalzell, back row, 3rd from left

1958

The year opened with the announcement that Mr William McAlpine had taken over the role of Cubmaster in place of Tom McCullough who had gone to reside in England following his marriage. The dance held in Newry Town Hall on 14 December had made a net profit of £29/6/0 (£29.30). During the year the Institute donated the sum of £27 (£27.00) to Group funds for work done by the Senior Scouts. The Senior Scouts attended the Scout Gang Show in Belfast where everyone thoroughly enjoyed the show. The annual general meeting of the Group Committee recorded that there were now fifty Cubs in the Cub Pack and William McAlpine stated that he had the help of Agnes and Marjory Porter, Elizabeth Wylie, John Aiken and Albert Jones in running the Pack. Reports from the Scout Master Noel Hodgett showed the Troop in a flourishing condition and Senior Scoutmaster Harry Crawford spoke of the work within the Senior Scout Section.

The Group's financial position had improved and a balance of £122/7/5 (£122.37) was now in hand. Bob-a-job Week raised the princely sum of £62/7/0 (£62.35). The Group attended the Annual St George's Day parade and service which was held in Kilkeel. The Group Committee agreed to pay part of the cost of the hire of the bus. It was announced that the Chief Scout, Lord Rowallan, would be visiting Lurgan on 28 June and the leaders wished to take all the Cubs and Scouts to the rally. The Group agreed to pay the balance of the cost of the bus for this event. The Northern Ireland contribution for the Baden-Powell Memorial House Fund would be presented to the Chief Scout on his visit and the Group was pleased to learn that the BP Guild of Old Scouts had forwarded the grand sum of £37/10/0 (£37.50) in the name of 1st Newry to Headquarters. Once again a patrol of Scouts from the Troop had won the South Down Challenge Flag.

The Troop held its annual camp at Tollymore Forest Park with thirty one boys taking part. Although the site was not of the best, being under the trees and with rain every day, the programme was carried through and all had an enjoyable camp. A donation was received from a Troop of Scouts from Liverpool thanking 1st Newry for the loan of equipment during their annual camp at Mourne Park in July. At the end of October Mervyn Ferris volunteered to take on the role of Assistant Scoutmaster. A very successful parents night was held on 5 December with the ladies of the Group Committee preparing the tea and sandwiches. The Cubs and Scouts once again sent toys to the children of Manor House and a letter was received thanking everyone for their kindness to the children.

Embroidery by J. Dalzell and T. McCullough in the 1950s

1959

During Bob-a-job week in 1959 the Group was grateful to the manager of Fosters Department Store, Hill Street for allowing the use of one of their windows for a Scouting display. Bob-a-job week raised the sum of £82/8/3 (£82.41). The annual general meeting, held on Monday, 13 April, was opened in prayer by Rev. N. Small, with Mr D. Lockington presiding. The leaders reported that the Group was progressing well with numbers on the increase and enthusiasm very high. The treasurer, Mrs McConnell, reported that the balance in the bank now stood at £174/10/0 (£174.50). The adoption of the reports was proposed by Rev. N. Small and seconded by Mr Baird. Mr Sterritt, a special guest and a past Scoutmaster, thanked the chairman for his very kind invitation and congratulated the Group on its continued progress. He said that in his opinion it was mainly due to the use of the Scout hall, which was invaluable. He wished to put on record the generosity of Downshire Road Presbyterian Church and the support of the Rev. N. Small. This year the annual St George's Day parade and service was held in Newry and once again the Institute was used for refreshments following the event.

Accident

On 7 May 1959, the Troop experienced one of its worst accidents for many years when Mervyn Ferris, Assistant Scoutmaster, was seriously injured while on a hike in the Mourne Mountains with a number of other members of the Senior Scout section.

However the Scoutmaster, Noel Hodgett, reacted quickly and took charge of the situation. Painfully, Mervyn managed to walk from the Hare's Gap down to the road where Noel then transported him to Daisy Hill Hospital for treatment. But for Noel's quick action, the situation could have been more serious and everyone was brought off the mountains safely, if somewhat shocked.

Mervyn remained in hospital for some seven months before being discharged later that year just before Christmas.

A patrol from the Troop had attended the County Down Challenge Flag competition and was placed second in this event.

County Flag competition, Ballynahinch, May 1959
L-R: A. Allely, R. Niblock, T. Bradfield, M. McConnell, J. Baines, J. Mateer

Senior Scouts at Mourne Park Warden's hut.
Back row: Rodney Mears, Jack Girvan, Ivan Ferris.
Front row: Eric Moorehead, John Wylie.

Ballasalla in the Isle of Man was the location for the Troop annual camp which was well attended with twenty five boys and two leaders taking part. The weather was ideal, the standard of camping fairly high and a good report was received from the visiting Commissioner.

Above left: Scouts at Douglas, Isle of Man. L-R: Jim Baines, Jim Pollock, Leslie Girvan, M. Matier (1st Kilmore).

Above L-R: Roland Torrens, Norman Moore, Hector Robb.

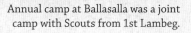
Annual camp at Ballasalla was a joint camp with Scouts from 1st Lambeg.

Scouts at camp, Isle of Man. Back row L-R: Ian McCullough, William McAlpine CM, Jim Mateer. Front row: Derek Ball, Hector Robb, Norman Moore, Roland Torrens.

The Cubmaster reported that the Cubs had won the shield at the sports held in Dundalk and the winning six would be taken on an outing to Belfast as a prize.

September saw the Group boarding a bus for Dundalk to attend a church parade there along with Scouts from Dundalk. The work being carried out by the Senior Scouts for the Institute was being discontinued because of the unavailability of the boys. Once again the boys did their usual good turn at Christmas by sending toys to the children at Manor House. The Group Committee organised a jumble sale to take place on 4 December.

Cub Sixers outing to Botanic Gardens Belfast. With Assistant Leader Agnes Porter are Gilbert McWilliams, Joe Wylie, Sammy Weir, Tom Weir.

The Senior Scouts held a very successful Christmas party in the Scout hall to which they invited their girlfriends and leaders. The Senior Scouts ended the year with a weekend stay in the Warden's hut at Mourne Park and although the weather was very cold everyone enjoyed the short break.

1st Newry Senior Scouts Christmas party in the old Scout hall

1960s

Easter camp Mourne Park, 16-17 April 1960
L-R Front: T. Bradfield, D. Anketell, L. Girvan, M. McConnell.
Back: W. McAlpine CM, M. Ferris, J. Reid, K.Frame, E. Moorehead, R. Mears, I. Ferris,
A. Wylie ASM, J. Wylie ASM.

1960

The year began with the announcement in the recent Honours List of the award of the MBE to two very good friends of 1st Newry, Mr T. Grills, a former member, and Mr R. Jones, the former District Commissioner. Congratulations on behalf of the Group were sent to both recipients. The Group Committee welcomed the return of Mervyn Ferris after his long stay in hospital and wished him a full recovery. It was worth noting that the approval of the committee was given to purchase a football at the meeting of 28 March 1960. At the Group's annual meeting it was noted that Mr O. Mahood, chairman of the BP Guild of Old Scouts, a former member and a King's Scout, had been awarded The Gold Medal, the highest award of the British Legion. A suitable letter of congratulations was sent to Mr Mahood. The AGM ended with supper provided by the ladies and a film show presented by Mr Gowdy from Banbridge. The boys of the Group contributed the sum of £4 (£4.00) from their pocket money to the local appeal for World Refugee Year. The proceeds from Bob-a-job week this year amounted to £71/12/3 (£71.61).

Over the Easter weekend, 15 to 17 April, the Troop held a very successful camp at Mourne Park in glorious weather conditions. Also during the summer months a number of Senior Scouts took part in overnight hikes in the Mourne mountains during which they were visited by Alex Wylie and Mervyn Ferris. Two Cubs won prizes at the recent county sports.

Mervyn Ferris (left) and Alex Wylie checking on hikers on one of the overnight hikes.

The Troop annual camp, which was attended by fifteen Scouts from 1st Newry, two from Rathfriland, one from Coleraine and one from 1st Warrenpoint, was held at Powerscourt, county Wicklow. Everyone had a most enjoyable time and all returned home safely. The Cub Pack held a weekend camp at Mourne Park where the Cubs had a wonderful time with many splendid

L-R: Malcolm McWhirter, Joe Wylie, Colin McWhirter, John Wylie, George McWhirter, July 1960

1st Newry Wolf Cubs at the old Scout hall.
L-R: Derek Torrens, Ronnie Baird, J. Wylie, Nigel McCullough, J. Wylie.

activities taking place. Members of the Cub Pack and Scout Troop paraded to St Patrick's church for the harvest service and were inspected by the Bishop of Meath. Cubmaster W. McAlpine completed all the requirements for the Wood Badge which is an essential requirement for all leaders in the Movement.

A tragic accident occurred on 3 December 1960 when Scout Ian McCullough was struck by a hockey ball during a schools match in Belfast and died. His funeral was attended by many leaders and boys from 1st Newry. A memorial cup was subsequently presented in Ian's memory.

1960 Annual camp at Lacey's Bank, Powerscourt, county Wicklow

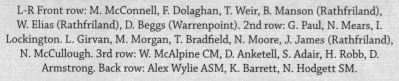

L-R Front row: M. McConnell, F. Dolaghan, T. Weir, B. Manson (Rathfriland), W. Elias (Rathfriland), D. Beggs (Warrenpoint). 2nd row: G. Paul, N. Mears, I. Lockington. L. Girvan, M. Morgan, T. Bradfield, N. Moore, J. James (Rathfriland), N. McCullough. 3rd row: W. McAlpine CM, D. Anketell, S. Adair, H. Robb, D. Armstrong. Back row: Alex Wylie ASM, K. Barrett, N. Hodgett SM.

Leaders and 'old Wolves', 22 May 1960

Scout sports, Newry, 11 June 1960

Group preparing for harvest service.

Wolf Cubs going up to troop, November 1960.

Wolf Cubs Christmas party, 19 December 1960.

1961

At the beginning of the year Scouts took part in a number of midnight hikes in the countryside around Warrenpoint and Rathfriland. The Group celebrated their Golden Jubilee with a week's display in the Scout hall and a thanksgiving service in Downshire Road church. All our 'Old Boys' were invited to come along and take part in the parade and service. The passing of one of our 'Old Boys', William L. Craig, was noted in the minutes of the annual meeting of the Group. William Craig had been a member of the Group for some years and also a very active member of the BP Guild of Old Scouts. He took a very keen interest in the Group and will be greatly missed. Bob-a-job week raised the sum of £62/11/6 (£62.58).

A patrol from the Troop won the County Down Challenge Flag competition for the Junior section. This was followed in July by the annual camp at Noirmont farm, Portelet Bay, Jersey. This camp will always be remembered because of a great storm which commenced on 12 July, creating havoc among the tents and lasting for three days. During this trying time the Troop had an unexpected visit from the District Commissioner whose role it was to inspect the camp. He was most surprised to see so many tents down but, after a good strong mug of tea, scrambled egg and toast, he went away a lot happier. At the same camp one of our Scouts accidentally set fire to some of the whin bushes alongside the kitchen area but everyone managed to control the flames and eventually quench the fire.

At the Group Committee meeting held on 2 November 1961, the secretary was requested to make an application to the rating authorities to have the Scout hall de-rated. Mr T. Girvan had completed the building of the new steps up to the first floor of the hall with the help of some of the Senior Scouts. The committee expressed their appreciation for all the hard work which he had put into the project. The meeting ended with a film show of the annual camp at Jersey, which was enjoyed by all in attendance. The Group held a very successful parents night in the church hall during which Cub Sixer Charles Adair was presented with his Leaping Wolf badge by the Commissioner for county Down, Robert Jones. The programme consisted of a number of sketches by the Cubs and Scouts, individual acts and ended with a selection of campfire songs. As part of the Christmas good turn the boys sent a parcel of toys to Dr. Barnardo's home and received a letter of thanks from the home for their kindness.

1st Newry parents night. Newry Cub Sixer Charlie Adair received the Leaping Wolf Badge from County Commissioner Robert Jones (ex Warrenpoint); pictured with them are L-R David Paul (CM 1st Bessbrook), Billy McAlpine (CM), Agnes Porter (ACM) and Elizabeth Wylie (CM)

Midnight hike.

50th anniversary exhibition in the old Scout hall, February 1961.

Judge Wm Johnson, Chief Commissioner for Northern Ireland (top left), opened the exhibition.

L-R Front row: M. Shellard, N. McCullough, M. McConnell, T. Weir, I. Lockington.
2nd row: D. Bradfield, P. Shellard, J. McWhirter, L.Girvan, M. Morgan, T. Black.
3rd row: W. McAlpine CM, G. Paul, R. Baird, D. Anketell, T. Mears, J. Pollock, N. McCullough, N. Mears, N. Hodgett SM,
N. Moore, M. Ferris ASM.

Annual camp, Jersey, Channel Islands, 1961.

Gale force winds wreaked
havoc on the tents, 12 July
1961.

1962

The 1962 annual general meeting of the Group Committee took place on 11 April in the Scout hall with Mr D. I. Lockington in the chair. The Rev. J. J. Harrison opened the meeting with prayer and it was recorded that a good number of parents and members of committee were present. The various reports from Cubs and Scouts were read and adopted by the committee. The treasurer reported the bank balance to be £165/19/5 (£165.97). After the election of office bearers, the meeting finished with a film show given by Mr Jack Neilson, Scoutmaster of 1st Nendrum Scout Group, of his Troop's tour of Europe the previous year. It was with much sadness that the Group learnt of the tragic death of one of its former members, Jim Pollock, during the Easter holidays in a car accident near Newry. Jim, who had been in training with London Metropolitan Police, had been a very enthusiastic and loyal member of the Group and his death at such a young age was a great shock to all who had known him throughout his young life. The Troop held a weekend camp at Castlewellan over the Easter weekend but, due to the death of Jim, the joy and excitement of camp was somewhat muted after hearing the bad news. Mervyn Ferris took part in a training weekend held at Crawfordsburn to complete all the requirements for the Wood Badge training award. The Cubmaster took thirty two Cubs to Mourne Park for a day outing. A profit of £21/10/0 (£21.50) had been made from the stall selling hot dogs and minerals on 12 July. Donations totalling £35 (£35.00) were received from four former members who were now residing in New Zealand. The financial situation at 31 March was greatly improved with the income of £78/19/0 (£78.95) from Bob-a-job week this year.

The Troop's annual camp at Mourne Park was attended by twenty two Scouts and Senior Scouts along with four leaders. During the camp the boys took part in a variety of activities such as pioneering, compass and mapping and climbing Knockcree as well as rafting on and swimming in the Whitewater river. Each Patrol was encouraged to build a camp oven with the result being very favourable and a variety of scones, cakes etc. being provided for all to sample. The patrol system was once again in place and well organised with each patrol looking after their own cooking and cleaning up. All agreed that the camp was a great success.

A sale was held in Downshire Road Church Hall on 12 October which raised the sum of £107/18/6 (£107.93). A beetle drive, organised by Mr Black, was also held to raise funds for the Group with the following prizes; two of 10/- (50p) each, socks, a box of chocolates, a pair of nylons, fifty cigarettes and two booby prizes. This event made the grand sum of £12/12/0 (£12.60).

L-R: Irwin Lockington, Noel Mears, Rodney McCullough

Wood Badge weekend, Crawfordsburn

District sports at Warrenpoint with Lord Roden.

1962 Annual camp at Mourne Park

L-R front row: J. Ferris, S. Weir, W. Brown, R. Weir,
R. Anketell, I. Halliday, M. McWilliams, J. Stevenson.
2nd row: M. McConnell, P. Shellard, M. Shellard, R. Baird.
rd row: N. Mears, G. Paul, D. Bradfield, T. Black, L. Girvan,
D. Anketell, N. McCullough, I. Lockington, J. McWhirter,
R. McCullough. Back row: W. McAlpine CM, N. Hodgett
SM, J. Wylie ASM, M. Ferris ASM.

Boy Scouts Sammy Weir (front) and John Stevenson.

Leslie Girvan baking a cake.

121

1963

The year began with proposals to hold a teenage social, a beetle drive and a jumble sale during the months of February and March. The teenage social, which was held in the Scriptural School on 1 February, was quite successful even though the profit from this event only came to £6/0/11 (£6.05). It was agreed to make a donation to St Patrick's church of 10/- (50p) for the use of the Scriptural School. Arrangements were made for the beetle drive to be held in Downshire Road Church Hall with the prizes being donated by the men of the Group Committee and with the ladies providing the tea. The Group's equipment was insured for the sum of 12/- (60p). The leaders reported that they had travelled to Holywood in a severe snowstorm to attend the memorial service for the late County Commissioner, W. V. Heasley. The treasurer reported that the Group's financial status had improved and now stood at the princely sum of £371/18/5 (£371.92). The Cubmaster, William McAlpine, was delighted to report that four Cubs had gained the Leaping Wolf badge which was the highest award available to Cubs. On 2 April the District Commissioner, Mr Noel Hodgett, had the pleasure of presenting Thanks Badges on behalf of the Group to the chairman, Mr Douglas Lockington, secretary, Mrs F. Wylie, and treasurer, Mrs S. McConnell, in recognition of their valuable services to the Group over many years. The Scoutmaster outlined arrangements for holding the Troop annual camp at Wiltz in Luxemburg from 29 June to 16 July. He informed everyone that the Troop would spend two nights at Baden-Powell House in London during the journey and asked parents to assist with return transport to Belfast. He further advised the Group committee that it was the intention to subsidise the boys at the rate of £10 (£10.00) and asked the committee for the sum of £290 (£290.00) with an emergency float of £60 (£60.00) in case of unforeseen circumstances. Bob-a-job week this year made the sum of £72/18/10 (£72.94). In May 1963 the Drake Patrol of the Senior Scouts took part in the County Down Challenge Flag competition at Seaforde where their Scouting skills were put to the test over the weekend and, on the final day, they turned out to be the winners. This was a very proud moment for all who took part.

Cub county sports

1st Newry parents at Cub county sports day. These ladies provided the catering for the event which was held in the field adjacent to the Scout hall and belonging to the Newry Grammar school. The field commonly known as the 'cut field' is now the location of Windsor Hill Primary School.

L-R front row: Mrs P. Morgan, Mrs E. J. Ferris, Mrs W. Wylie, Mrs C. McAlpine, Mrs H. Cowan
2nd row: Mrs S. McConnell, Mrs G. Ferris, Mrs Lynas, Mrs Stevenson
Back row: Billy McAlpine (CSM), Mervyn Ferris (ASM), Noel Hodgett (SM), Alex Wylie (ASM)

Bicycle expedition in the Mournes, December 1963
L-R: David Bradfield, Peter Shellard, Leslie Girvan, John McWhirter, Michael Shellard.

At the end of June the Troop set off for their annual camp at Wiltz in Luxembourg. 35 Scouts attended this camp with four Scouters and during their camp they presented an illuminated address from the Newry Urban District Council to the Burgomeister of Wiltz. In return he presented them with with an inscribed photograph of the old castle of Wiltz, which was subsequently presented to the Newry District Council and now hangs in the City Hall. This camp will be remembered by all because of a number of incidents which took place while going to, camping at and returning home from Wiltz. One of our Scouts had to be left in the care of the nurse in Baden-Powell House whilst on the way to Wiltz because he was suffering from a severe influenza attack. After some days he was fit enough to return home to Newry but unfortunately missed the camp. On arriving at Wiltz the boys were amazed with the cleanliness of the town which was in great contrast with our home town of Newry. During our stay the boys stayed in Chalet Jitz for a week and then moved to one of the newer chalets which had been recently built for the rest of their stay. We visited the city of Luxemburg, Vianden and also the area around the village of Diekirch where the Battle of the Bulge took place during World War Two. However once again the dreaded virus came to the fore when a number of Scouts and one of the leaders were confined to bed for a few days before making a full recovery. Near the end of our stay in Wiltz the Burgomeister arranged for us to collect a gift of some of the local bread and other delicacies for our Scouts to sample. On the day before we left for home another drama unfolded as Scout Leslie Girvan took ill, was diagnosed with acute appendicitis and subsequently admitted to the local hospital for the emergency removal of his appendix. Leslie remained in hospital for some days and Assistant Scoutmaster Mervyn Ferris stayed to accompany him on the flight home about a week later. While Leslie and Mervyn remained in Wiltz, the drama continued when yet another of the Scouts became ill in London on the homeward journey and had to remain in Baden-Powell House for a few days, as it was unsafe for him to travel directly home. Cubmaster William McAlpine remained with him to see him safely home later in the week. However eventually everyone arrived back in Newry with many happy memories and stories to tell. At the commencement of the autumn session for the Group and during the Group Committee meeting the Assistant Scoutmaster, John Wylie, reported that the overall cost of the camp was £185/15/3 (£185.76).

The Cubmaster informed all that there were now forty Cubs on the roll and they had spent a day out in Mourne Park where they cooked their own food. The meeting ended with a film show of the activities and places visited during the Troop annual camp at Wiltz. In the run up to the end of the year the Troop once again held a number of midnight hikes this time around the Kilkeel and Cranfield areas. These events proved very popular with the boys although not a lot of sleep was had and everyone went home tired in the morning.

Copy of inscribed photograph presented to the Troop by the Burgomeister of Wiltz for the town of Newry.

The original now hangs in the City Hall.

1963 Annual camp at Wiltz, Luxembourg

L-R: M. McWilliams, N. Lockington, D. Bodel,
L. Morgan, B. Dilworth.

Scouts at Chalet Jitz.

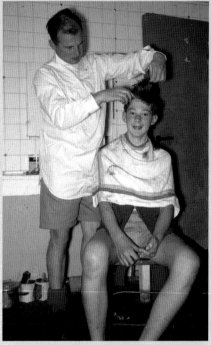

John Wylie ASM gives Peter
Shellard a haircut.

Noel Hodgett SM presents Burgomeister of Wiltz with an illuminated address.

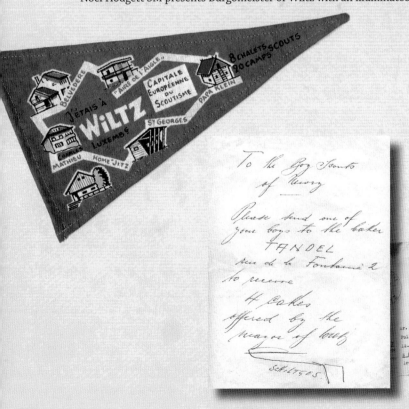

The documents above are from Leslie
Givan's stay in hospital.

On the left is a letter from the
Burgomeister of Wiltz.

1964

The year began with the welcoming into the Group of Mr Jacob Gamble as Assistant Scoutmaster. The minutes of the Group indicated that some discussion took place on proposed alterations to the Scout hall and John Wylie stated that both he and Noel Hodgett had been in contact with the Ministry of Education with regard to an application for grant aid toward these changes. A sub-committee of Mr Lockington, Mr John Wylie and Mr Noel Hodgett was appointed to take the matter forward. Following the proposal by Mrs Ferris, seconded by Mrs Morgan, this was passed unanimously by all. A donation of £2/2/0 (£2.10) towards the building of their new hall was forwarded to the Hunter Moore Memorial Flute Band which had faithfully supported the Group and the District in turning out for local parades over the years. Senior Scout Marshall McConnell, son of the treasurer, Mrs S. McConnell, gained the much-coveted Queen's Scout Award which was presented to him by former Scoutmaster of the Group, Mr Frank McWhirter. Bob-a-job week managed to raise the sum of £88/15/9 (£88.78).

Annual camp this year was held at Ely Lodge, the estate of the Duke of Westminster, near Enniskillen, on the beautiful shores of Lough Erne. A wonderful time was had by all with the weather being very warm and quite dry for all of the camp. Many adventurous activities took place along with a visit to Enniskillen and a boat trip along Lough Erne. The Troop also built a number of large scale pioneering projects with the many small saplings which they were allowed to cut down from the small plantation adjacent to the camp site. The estate was keen to have a small area cleared as electricity power lines were very close to the trees in the vicinity. The camp was held in a marvellous setting and, combined with great weather throughout, everyone returned home from a wonderful camp with many tales to tell. Also during the summer months some of our Scouts took part in a BBC programme from Mourne Park. A sale of work was held on 2 October, Lady Roden, wife of Lord Roden, County Commissioner, carrying out the official opening of this event. The proceeds from the sale amounted to £133/1/10 (£133.09).

Members of the Drake Patrol of Senior Scouts, 1st Newry, winners of the County Down Senior Challenge Flag at Seaforde, last week-end May 1964

Winners of the County Challenge Flag, May 1964
L-R: David Bradfield, Leslie Girvan, Michael Shellard, Irwin Lockington, Marshall McConnell.

Seeonee pack at Warrenpoint, December 1964

1964 Annual camp at Ely Lodge, Eniskillen

Pictured in the life ring are Ronald Baird, Tom Weir,
Jim Ferris and John McWhirter.
Standing is Peter Shellard.

L-R: R. Anketell, G. McWhirter, F. Martin, C. Massey,
J. McGrath, W. Cully, L.Campbell.

1965

As the old stove in the Scout hall had now worn out, a new Romesse stove was installed at the princely sum of £10/16/6 (£10.83). Insurance of the equipment was noted as 15/- (75p) and the electricity account £1/19/9 (£1.98). Sketch plans for the hall improvements were almost complete and the request to the district valuer for the de-rating of the hall was likely to be successful. Mervyn Ferris reported that the Senior Scouts had held a dance in the Orange Hall and a profit of around £7 (£7.00) had been made. This year saw the departure of Scoutmaster John Wylie to Belfast as his employment had now forced him to move from the area. Mervyn Ferris, Senior Scoutmaster, congratulated Senior Scout, John McWhirter, on gaining the Queen's Scout Award indicating that John had put a great deal of effort and hard work into gaining this badge which was very well deserved. John would be attending Gilwell Park later in the year to receive this much-coveted award. The Cubmaster, William McAlpine, reported that the Cubs had won the District Sports Shield.

Forty Scouts and four leaders took part in annual camp during July which once again was held in Mourne Park, one of our favourite camp sites. This was one of the largest camps the Troop had held for a number of years and all attending made the most of the wonderful natural amenities of the site. Each Patrol was responsible for looking after themselves, preparing meals, cleaning up and keeping their tents in order. During the camp everyone climbed Knockcree, swam in the river, built towers and generally took part in all the activities. The Senior Scouts built a 'toll' bridge across the Whitewater river to allow the parents to gain access to the site on parents open day. This proved to be a great attraction with the parents with many favourable comments being made on the quality of the

Scouts at the top of Knockcree
L-R front row: E. Clydesdale, M. McCaigue, G. Anketell, N. Browne, G. Holmes, T. Holmes, D. Little, D. Robinson.
2nd row: M. Brown, D. Gamble, L. Morgan, M. McWhirter, P. Shellard, I. Gamble, C. Hamilton, V. Wright, T. Auterson.
3rd row: R. Weir, L. Campbell, H. Andrews, P. Browne, C. McWhirter, J. Thompson, D. Bodel.
Back row: W. McAlpine CM, J. Gamble SM, N. Lockington, W. Brown, B. McCullough, W. Cully, G. McWhirter.

Annual camp, Mourne Park

1st Newry with German Scouts in
Newry Scout hall

German Scouts in Mourne Park

build and the sum of £3/6/9 (£3.33) toll charge being collected during the afternoon. At the end of camp everyone went home well pleased but rather tired.

Following annual camp twenty two German Scouts arrived to camp at Mourne Park and a few of our Senior Scouts were invited to camp along with them for a few days. On ending their stay at 'The Park', the German Scouts were given hospitality in the homes of some of our Scouts and entertained by the Group during their stay in Newry. Everyone was sad to say goodbye when it came time for them to depart, as many friendships had been made. As a thank you for all the kindness shown to them by the Scouts, their parents and helpers during their stay in Newry, the German Scouts presented the Troop with one of their special black tents.

The Group had a site under consideration in relation to building a new hall and Mr Gamble had ascertained that the cost of purchase from St. Mary's Church would be somewhere in the region of £350 (£350.00). Mr Lockington agreed to complete the necessary forms for the grant towards a new build if the Ministry approved the site. It was agreed that if this happened the Group should go ahead with the purchase. The Cubmaster, William McAlpine, and the Cubs were entertained to an evening of activities by the Newry Catholic Cub Scouts. Later in the month of November the Group held a very entertaining parents evening, which was extremely well attended, in Downshire Road Church Hall. During the evening the parents were entertained with a number of sketches by Cubs and Scouts as well as a pioneering display by the Senior Scouts. The event ended with campfire songs and refreshments provided by the ladies of the Group committee. Once again the Group had a fine turnout when it paraded to the harvest service in St Patrick's church. During the year Mr Alex Wylie was appointed Assistant District Commissioner for Scouts. Just before Christmas the Cub Pack held a very successful Christmas party to which they invited 1st Dromore CBSI Cubs along. The evening went with a swing with all the Cubs having a wonderful time.

Cubs, June 1965

Parents night in Downshire Road Church Hall.

1st Newry Cubs Christmas party with 1st Dromore CBSI Cubs.

Leaders at parents night.
Front row: Douglas Lockington (Chairman), John Wylie, Agnes W
Noel Hodgett, Billy McAlpine
Back row: Jacob Gamble, Alex Wylie, Marshall McConnell, Mervyn Ferris, J
McWhirter (Queen's Scout).

1966

This was a notable year in the history of the Group. The Cubs were celebrating their Golden Jubilee and, as 1st Newry Cubs had actually been in existence from 1915, the year before the official recognition of this junior section, this was a truly unique situation as our Cub Pack was also genuinely more than fifty years old. Senior Scout Tom Weir was chosen as a representative of Scouting in Northern Ireland to attend a thanksgiving service marking the 900th anniversary of Westminster Abbey.

Patrick Moore

The annual meeting of the Group Committee was held on 23 March in the Methodist Church Hall with the very special guest being none other than the famous astronomer, Mr Patrick Moore. Very favourable reports were received from all the office bearers with the treasurer reporting that the Group's finances were in a very healthy state with a balance of £482/9/3 (£482.46) in the bank. William McAlpine, Cubmaster, reported that there were now 52 Cubs on the roll, the highest number for many years, and mentioned the fact that Newry Cub Pack was one of the first Packs to be formed. He had plans for special celebrations for the Pack this year. Mervyn Ferris, in reporting on the activities of the Senior Scouts, congratulated Senior Scouts Ronald Baird and Tom Weir on gaining the coveted Queen's Scout Award and wished them both good luck in the future. A presentation of a Thanks Badge, in recognition of very valuable services given to the Group over many years, was made to Mr R. Baird by the chairman, Mr Douglas Lockington. Mr Patrick Moore then give all those present a most interesting and exciting talk on astronomy explaining about life, or the lack of such, on the various planets in our universe. At the conclusion of his talk, Mr Moore was given a big thank you by the chairman, this being followed by acclamation from the audience.

L-R: Jacob Gamble, Douglas Lockington (Chairman of the Parents Committee), Patrick Moore F.R.A.S. (Director of Armagh Planetarium), Mr Baird (Principal Windsor Hill PS), Mervyn Ferris, Billy McAlpine

Later in May the chairman also presented a Thanks Badge to the Rev. N. Small. In making the presentation, Mr Lockington stated that the Rev. Small, and indeed Downshire Road church, had been a tower of strength to the Group and thanked Rev. Small for all his help over the years. A patrol of Senior Scouts, Jim Ferris, John McWhirter, Samuel Weir, Ronald Baird and Tom Weir attended the County Down Camp competition where they put in a wonderful effort over the weekend and won the Senior Challenge Flag. Scouts and Cubs took part in and successfully completed the 10 mile

Flagstaff Walk during Civic Week in June. During the month of June the Scouts and Cubs along with Guides, Brownies and Ranger Guides attended Children's Day services in Downshire Road and Sandys Street Presbyterian churches as well as Newry Methodist Church as had been the custom now for many years.

In July, as a result of an invitation from the German Scouts who had camped at Mourne Park the previous year, the Senior Scouts travelled to Germany where they toured the Rhine Valley as well as camping along side the Rhine at a number of very interesting places. The party visited many places of interest including Frankfurt and Cologne as well as taking a boat trip up the Rhine with their German hosts. During the visit to Germany, the Senior Scouts and leaders were given hospitality in the homes of the German Scouts and everyone watched with great excitement the final of the World Cup when England played Germany. All those who took part in this trip had a truly magnificent time and this was the first time the Group had travelled by air.

Senior Scouts in Germany, July 1966

Annual camp at Bray, county Wicklow

Getting ready for camp at Mourne Park

Cubs in Mourne Park.

Cubs Alan Auterson and Philip Parker during Bob-a-job week.

Scout leaders in Mourne Park.

1966 County Flag winners Jim Ferris, John McWhirter,
Sammy Weir, Ronnie Baird, Tom Weir.

William McAlpine

Newry District Sports winners 1966
L-R: A. Weir, G. McIlwaine, M. Parker, D. Caldwell, R. Massey.

Mrs McConnell, the treasurer, reported that the Group's bank balance now stood at £401/7/3 (£401.36). The Cubs had a very enjoyable day at the County Sports held at Ballykinlar and the Sixers and Seconders had spent a day with the Scouts at Mourne Park. The Troop annual camp was held at Bray, county Wicklow, where they all had a great camp with fine weather throughout the period. During camp a film company was filming scenes for the film, *Viking Queen*. Everyone had a close up of how the various shots were filmed and saw many of the stars on the set. A very successful sale of work, held on 21 October, brought in the sum of £150/4/0 (£150.20), the sale of Christmas trees raised £11/10/0 (£11.50) and the jumble sale £48/7/2 (£48.36).

A scheme was set up to enable the Scouts to save on a weekly basis in order to allow them to purchase the new Scout uniform when it became available early in 1967 as a result of the Advanced Party Report. One of the Group Committee members, Mrs Bodel, agreed to collect the savings each week and lodge them in the bank until the uniforms arrived at the Scout Shop. This report brought many changes to Scouting with changes in uniforms for both Cubs and Scouts, revision of Scout Promise and Laws and change of name for Senior Scouts to that of Venture Scouts, to mention but a few. December saw the Cub Pack celebrate their 50th anniversary with a birthday party, at which the guest of honour was Mr Sydney Sterritt, a founder member of the Pack. The Group was most disappointed that the search for a suitable site for the proposed new hall had proved unsuccessful due to a number of reasons.

Honour for Newry Scouts

At a Queen's Scout reception held in City Hall, Belfast, two 1st Newry Senior Scouts were presented with their Queen's Scout Certificates by the Chief Scout for Northern Ireland, W. Brennan, F.R.C.S.

This badge is the highest award obtainable in Scouting and was awarded to Thomas Weir and Ronald Baird. Both Tom and Ronald joined the Scouts when they were 11 years old, Ronald having been in the Cubs for three years and Tom for about one year.

In October, 1965, Tom Weir was presented with his Queen's Scout badge at a local Association meeting in Rathfriland by Mr W. J. Wylie, an old Scout of 1st Newry.

Ronald Baird soon finished his other badges and thus in due course made his Bushman's Thong and was presented with his Queen's Scout badge at the Senior Scouts Annual Dinner in December by D.C., Mr T. N. Hodgett.

Both these Senior Scouts were presented with a Royal Certificate by the Chief Scout for N.I. in the presence of the Lord Mayor of Belfast, Sir Wm. Jenkins.

After the presentation the Queen's Scouts were guests of the Mayor for lunch and then went on a tour of Carrickfergus Castle.

Although Tom Weir was greatly honoured by gaining his Queen's Badge, there was also one more great honour to be bestowed upon him as he was selected as one of the three representatives from Northern Ireland to attend a Thanksgiving service in connection with the celebration to mark the 900th Anniversary of Westminster Abbey.

Cubs celebrate the 50th Anniversary of Cub Scouts with founder member, Sidney Sterritt.

1967

A team of four Scouts won the County Down Home Safety Cup and then proceeded to the semi-finals of the Northern Ireland competition. However the team was disappointed to lose by only one point in the semi finals in the competition to the ladies group from Finaghy. The members of the team were presented with book tokens by the Group Committee for the wonderful effort in getting to the semi finals. The Group welcomed John Reid into its ranks as an Assistant Cubmaster. Also during the year the Advanced Party Report came into being resulting in a change of uniform, from shorts and short-sleeved shirts to a green long-sleeved shirt with mushroom long trousers. This also meant changing Group scarves from the original green colour to red and white. Venture Scout Leader Mervyn Ferris took part in a week long Wood Badge training camp held at Gilwell Park, London in order to complete training for the Venture Scout section. For the first time in its history the Group was able to apply for a grant, available to all youth groups throughout Northern Ireland, which became available from the Department of Education on a 'one off' basis and was successful in their application.

With the grant the Group was able to purchase six new Icelandic patrol tents at a cost of £168 (£168.00) in anticipation of their annual camp which was held in Troon, Scotland, from 15 to 22 July. Forty Scouts and Venture Scouts along with four leaders took part in this camp which was held in fine weather. This was one of the largest numbers attending annual camp for a number of years. Many and varied activities along with visits to places of local history were undertaken during the event and everyone enjoyed the experience. Transportation to and from the ferry at Belfast was provided by some of the parents. Previous to receiving this 'one off' grant, the Group, since its formation, had to rely on its own resources to raise funds in order to meet Group activities. It has been the perception of some people in the area that 1st Newry Group had everything and received funding from government departments at Stormont. However nothing could have been further from the truth as the Group had always found it very difficult to raise the necessary funds to meet its ever increasing expenditure. A sale of work was held on 13 October which was opened by the new District Commissioner's wife, Mrs Jones. November saw the Scouts heading off from the Scout hall late at night for another midnight hike which took place in the hinterland around Newry and ending in Rathfriland where they stayed overnight.

Troop at annual camp in Troon, Ayrshire.
L-R front row: R. Weir, M. Little, M.Parker, T. Andrews, D. McAlpine, J. Halliday, W. Porter, D. Boyd, M. McCaigue, N. Browne.
2nd row: W. McConnell, K. McGaffin, R. Little, D. Thompson, R. Massey, B. Malone, W. Kingston, D. Robinson, G. McIlwaine.
3rd row: C. Massey, D. Gamble, T. Auterson, T. Holmes, J. Ferris, M. McWhirter, I. Gamble, B. Hamilton, M. Baillie, E. Martin, D. Caldwell, G. McWhirter (head turned), V. Wright, E. Clydesdale, W. McWilliams, H. Andrews, C. McWhirter, P. Shellard.
Back row: J. Gamble SM, N. Hodgett GSM, N. Lockington, W. McAlpine CM, J. Reid ACM.

Scouts in Mourne Park

1967 Annual camp in Troon, Ayrshire.

Jacob Gamble DC and Cantrell and Cochrane's manager presents Cub Ala...
McGaffin with the C&C Cub Sports Shield.

Snipe Patrol at annual camp, Troon
L-R: David Robinson, Walter Porter, Michael Parker, Brian Malone, William McWilliams, Colin McWhirter

1968

During the annual meeting held on 23 April, the chairman, Mr Douglas Lockington, presented a Thanks Badge to the Rev. Moore Graham. Mr Lockington paid tribute to Rev. Graham for his interest in the Group during his stay in Newry and wished him all the best on his retirement. Following the secretary's tribute to Mrs Graham, Cub Gary McGaffin presented her with a bouquet of flowers. The secretary reported the failure of the sub committee to procure the ground to the rear of the Scriptural Schools for a new Scout hall. A letter from the secretary of St Patrick's Select Vestry regretting this decision was read and noted.

In July one of the largest camps in the Group's history was held in Mourne Park with forty five members taking part. This was the opportunity for all involved to take part in many outdoor activities such as pioneering, orienteering, canoeing, hill walking and to show off their camping skills in the wonderful setting which is Mourne Park. This year the Cubs gained a number of district and county awards including the County Down Sports Shield. The Venture Scout Unit was formed in the latter half of the year. A jumble sale which raised £51/11/0 (£51.55) was held on 25 October. The annual sale of work, which was held on 6 December, was opened by a former member of 1st Newry, Judge William Johnson, and his sister, Miss Mabel Johnson. The sale proved to be a great success raising the sum of £123/2/6 (£123.13).

Annual camp at Mourne Park, 1968
L-R front row: A. Ferris, J. Kernaghan, G. Arthur, J. Gamble (Cub), A. Stevenson, M. Little, W. Porter.
2nd row: W. Kingston, T. Crawford, M. Parker, W. McConnell, N. Gray, S. Purden, I. Gamble.
3rd row: W. McAlpine CM, C. McWhirter, D. Robinson, A. Auterson, R. Little, R. Massey, C. Whiteside, T. Holmes, N. Browne, J. Gamble SM, J. Reid ACM, N. Lockington.
Back row: M. Ferris ASM, M. McWhirter, V. Wright, E. Martin, D. Gamble, J. Ferris, H. Andrews, P. Shellard, L. McCaigue, T. Auterson.

Annual camp flag break at Mourne Park, 1968

Annual camp at Mourne Park, 1968

In the canoes are Neil Lockington and Walter Porter.

Above: 1st Newry Cub Pack show off the trophies they won during the year.

Right: Parents night.

1969

The first meeting of the Group Committee in 1969 noted the death of the Rev. N. Small. The chairman referred to the work which he had done over the years for Scouting and of his interest in 1st Newry and asked the committee to stand in silence for a few moments as a sign of respect. The Venture Scout Unit held a dance in Bessbrook Town Hall which was very well supported and raised £59/10/0 (£59.50). A letter of thanks was sent to Mr Wright and his committee thanking them for their help with this event. During the year Mr Jacob Gamble, Scoutmaster, and Mr Mervyn Ferris represented 1st Newry on the Civic Week committee. A Scout convocation was held in Belfast on 29 March at which Mr and Mrs Lockington represented the Group. The Venture Scout Unit, under the tuition of Mrs Ida Norris and Dr. N. Williams, gained 13 ordinary and higher first aid certificates of the St. John Ambulance Brigade. Mr Lockington, chairman, presented Mrs Norris with a Thanks Badge on behalf of the Group in recognition of her services and for the training of the Venture Scouts in first aid. The Venture Unit also won the Roden Challenge Shield for Venture Scouts.

Members of the Newry Venture Troop pictured with the Rev. Ralph Peter's, Vicar of St. Mary's, after he had presented First Aid Certificates at the Annual Group Meeting on Thursday night 19 April 1969

Camp was once again held on the Isle of Man and a marvellous time was had by all those Scouts who took part. It was with great sadness that the Group learnt of the deaths during the year of one of our 'Old Boys' and former Scouter with the Group, Mr Sydney Sterritt, and the prominent businessman in Newry, Mr R. Haldane. Both Mr Sterritt and Mr Haldane had been involved in the Scouting Movement for many years and their service to the Movement was greatly appreciated. The quarterly account for electricity amounted to £4/3/9 (£4.18) and this was passed for payment. There was a warm welcome for Marshall McConnell and Neil Lockington both of whom took on the role of Assistant Scoutmasters. Early in the year Newry suffered a major terrorist bomb attack at the Customs Station, Dublin Road, and this had an unsettling effect on the members of the Group. The general unrest within the town was giving some cause for concern and so the leaders began taking extra precautions to ensure the safety of the Cubs and Scouts whilst attending meetings in the Scout hall.

1969 Annual camp at Quayle's Orchard, Isle of Man

1969 Cub weekend camp, Mourne Park
L-R front row: T. Pinion, M. McCaigue, W. Clarke. Back row: N. McGladdery, G. McGaffin, A. Auterson.

Cubs at Mourne Park. Note the new style uniforms.

Cubs at Mourne Park.　　　　　　　　　　Cubs' Christmas party, 22 December 1969

1970s

1st Newry Scouts Alan McGaffin (left) and Norman McNellis cooking
dinner on the open fire in Mourne Park.

1970

Unfortunately the late 1960s and early 1970s saw a great increase in terrorist activity and events, not only throughout Northern Ireland, but particularly in and around Newry, south Down and south Armagh which seriously affected the activities of the Group. These troubled times had an adverse affect on Scouting in the Newry area and particularly on 1st Newry. Many of the parents of boys in the Group belonged either to the Royal Ulster Constabulary, the RUC Reserve or the Ulster Defence Regiment. Due to the deteriorating situation and security aspects of living in or around Newry, families moved to what were considered safer areas, if anywhere in Northern Ireland could have been considered safe in those times. Parents were intimidated and forced to leave their homes, taking their families with them. Some of our most loyal and keen supporters were attacked and, in a few cases, either murdered, badly wounded or shot. The result was that the Group suffered badly over these years with reduced numbers and many activities had to be curtailed. However the Cub Pack and Scout Troop continued to function no matter what the situation and did not give in to the threat of terrorism. On many occasions the meetings were held in candlelight, torch light or with the aid of Tilley lamps and it is fair to say that no meetings were ever abandoned due to untoward events. Even during the dark days of the Ulster Workers' Council strike when the lights went out for long periods, the Cub and Scout meetings still took place. Throughout the 'Troubles', the parents of all the boys in the Group showed their faith and confidence in the leaders by continuing to allow their sons to attend the Cub and Scout meetings knowing that they were in safe hands and that all precautions were being taken to ensure their safety. The Group lost many good friends, colleagues and former members during these difficult times and will always remember them.

1970

The early months of the year were a relatively quiet time as most of the activities were held inside the hall as the leaders were concerned with the safety of our members. The 1970 annual general meeting of the Group Committee was held on 24 April in conjunction with the Cub and Scout parents night. There was a large attendance and, following the business section of the meeting, a very interesting programme given by the Cubs and Scouts entertained all present. Also in 1970 the Cubs spent quite a lot of time making recordings in the countryside in preparation for the National Recording Tape competition. Their efforts proved very successful and everyone was most delighted when they were informed that their submission had reached the finals of the National Tape competition held in London. The Venture Scout section entered a team for the Northern Ireland Venture Scout 5-a-side football competition and, after some very tough opposition, managed to achieve the runners-up position. The Cubs and Scouts together with their leaders attended Children's Day services held in Downshire Road and Sandys Street Presbyterian churches as well as the Methodist Church. The Venture Unit followed their success in the football by holding an international camp in Switzerland and Germany.

The Troop annual camp was held at our favourite camp site, Mourne Park where those in attendance had a marvellous time swimming, climbing Knockcree as well as the other many activities laid on by the leaders. Due to the ongoing situation within the area, the numbers within the Troop had reduced and this year saw one of the smallest number of Scouts attending camp for quite a few years. Later in the year the name of the Group Committee was changed to Parents Association as it was felt this would encourage more parents and friends to come along to the various meetings and give their support to the Group.

Mourne Park annual Scout camp with Scout
Billy Kingston at flag break

Parents Day at Mourne Park, 1970

Cubs at camp in Mourne Park, 23 May 1970

Scouts A. Blackadder, T. Crawford and B. Wright map reading.

L-R front row: A. Blackadder, C. Wharton,
A. Stevenson, V. Holt, J. Kernaghan.
2nd row: W. McConnell, B. Wright,
T. Crawford, W. Kingston, P. Leeson.
Back row: M. McConnell ASL,
J. Reid, ACSL, W. McAlpine CSL.

1971

During the Group's Diamond Jubilee Year an exhibition was held in the Scout hall for one week in April 1971. Notwithstanding the current unsettled conditions, the annual St George's Day service was held in Downshire Road Presbyterian Church with quite a number of our past members taking part in the parade. The guest speaker on this occasion was Mr Noel Hodgett. The Group at this time had a total of fifty nine Cubs, Scouts and Venture Scouts along with seven leaders. Plans were made to hold a special camp this year as the Group was now some 60 years old. Bob-a-job week held over the Easter week raised the sum of £147.41.

St George's Day parade. Numbered in this photograph are some of 1st Newry's Old Scouts.
1. Robert McCullough, 2. Billy Heather, 3.Sammy Crozier, 4. George McCullough, 5. William Magowan, 6. John Wylie,
7. Bill Gardner, 8. Ernest Ferris

Annual camp was held at Butcher's Coppice, Bournemouth, which is very near Brownsea Island, Poole Harbour, Dorset, where the foundations of Scouting were laid by Lord Baden-Powell at the first experimental Scout camp in 1907. Scouting has spread throughout the world, embracing every nation, colour and creed, with a total membership, in 2010, in excess of 28 million. Today there are only six countries in the world where Scouting does not exist. The Cub Sixers and Seconders held a very successful weekend Cub camp at Mourne Park. During the year Colin and Malcolm McWhirter and David Robinson gained the highest award in Venture Scouting, the Queen's Scout Badge. This year saw the departure of Mr Alex Wylie to Lisburn. Alex had been District Commissioner and Assistant Scoutleader with the Group.

1971 Annual camp at Butcher's Coppice, Bournemouth. The Falcon Patrol are ready for inspection.
L-R: Colin Whiteside (PL), Robert Ferris, Vernon Holt, Andrew Stevenson, Brian Wright.

L-R front row: D. Wilson, G. Cowan, T. Pinion, V. Holt, A. Blackadder. 2nd row: A. Stevenson, C. Watt, J. Kernaghan, B. Wright, P. Leeson, S. Purden. Back row: R. Ferris, P. Crory, W. McConnell, C. Whiteside, T. Crawford, W. Kingston.

All the section members and leaders of 1st Newry, April 1971

Cub camp at Mourne Park

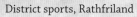

District sports, Rathfriland

Scout First Aid class

1972

The treasurer reported that the capitation fee paid this year to Headquarters amounted to £38.50. Mr J. Jones, Bessbrook, was appointed as District Commissioner in place of Jacob Gamble who was moving with his family from Newry to take up residence in Newtownards. A pleasant evening took place in the Scout hall when Mr and Mrs Gamble were entertained to supper and a presentation was made to them.

The Troop annual camp was held at Auchengillan, Scotland. During the camp, which was blessed with fine weather, the campers enjoyed the site swimming pool which although very cold was well used. Once again the Patrol system worked well, everyone being well fed and the kitchens and tents kept neat and tidy. A number of visits were made during the period to Glasgow, Loch Lomond and other places of interest.

Sixers and Seconds Cub camp at Mourne Park.
Back row L-R: Brian Cowan, Neil McIlwaine, Andrew Grills.
Front row: Alastair Holland, Michael Nixon, David McCullough, Jacob Gamble (Jnr)

Cub camp at Mourne Park,
25 June 1972

The Life and Times of 1st Newry Scout Group

On the last Saturday in August the Group had a stall selling burgers, hot dogs, tea and refreshments at the 'Black' parade . The sum of £64.83 was raised at this event. A request from Newry Olympic Hockey Club for use of the Scout hall was approved, free of charge, by the Parents Association. Due to the unsettled time with the 'Troubles' in and around the Newry area, the number of meetings of the Parents Association was curtailed and attendances at these meetings reduced in numbers.

August 'Black' Saturday with Robert McCullough (centre) selling hot dogs.

Cub Christmas party

County Flag winners at the Slieve Donard Hotel, 1972
Back row L-R: T. Pinion, A. Blackadder, G. McGaffin, G. Cunningham.
Front: J. Kernaghan, A. Auterson, R. Ferris, County Commissioner Robert Jones.

1973

At the annual general meeting of the Parents Association held in the Methodist Church Hall, it was reported that interest in Scouting among the boys and parents was going badly downwards. Unless a big effort was made by all concerned, the leaders would find it impossible to keep Scouting alive in the town. It was mainly due to the 'Troubles' in the area which was playing a major part in this downward spiral as a large number of parents had moved from Newry to safer locations in other parts of the Province. The committee hoped that the situation would improve in the future. However, despite the unrest, a successful sale of work was held on 13 April in Downshire Road Church Hall. A stall providing burgers, hot dogs and refreshments on 12 July and a cake sale in the Market had also proved most successful.

Sale of work for Group funds in Downshire Road Church Hall.
Above left: Mrs Grills, Mrs Baird, Mrs Robinson, Mrs McAlpine, Mrs White, Mrs S. McConnell (Treasurer, Group Parents Committee)

A weekend camp was held in Mourne Park for the small number of Scouts in the Troop and on this occasion they were joined by some of the older Cubs who were due to move into the Troop shortly. Unfortunately, due to the lack of numbers in the Scout section, no annual camp was held this year.

Cubs and Scouts at camp in Mourne Park. L-R: John McKee, John Knight, David McCullough,
Neil McIlwaine, Brian Cowan, Bob McCullough

However the Venture Scout Unit again visited Germany camping at Frankfurt, Mainz, Koblenz and Bonn. The Cub Pack gained top honours in county Down winning the Dora Baxter Memorial Flag in the County Competition. Also during the year Miss Joan Ferris took on the role of Assistant Cub Scout leader. During the year Mr John Henry was appointed District Commissioner in place of Mr J. Jones who had retired from the position. The Group wished John all the best in his role as D.C. This year also saw the Group obtain more spacious premises just a few yards from their existing hall. The dining hall and canteen of the Grammar School, which had been vacant for some time, was taken over by the Group and approaches were made to the Southern Education and Library Board to finalise outstanding issues on this matter.

Venture Scouts on their way to Germany, boarding the train in London, 1973

1st Newry Cubs Dora Baxter flag winners with leaders John Reid, Joan Ferris and Billy McAlpine

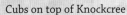

Cubs on top of Knockcree

Cub 7-a-side winners at district sports. Above left, Wilson Robinson presents the cup.

1974

New accommodation

At the beginning of the year the Group made the move, after some fifty to sixty years, to their present accommodation, adjacent to our old hall. The 'new hall' was in fact the canteen and dining hall of the now vacant Newry Grammar School, which had been amalgamated into Newry High School. When the building was taken over by the Group, the leaders and members of the Parents Association spent many hours and days dismantling all the catering equipment and gas heating system to allow it to be safely used for Scouting purposes. The facility had new toilets installed along with a complete re-vamp of the kitchen and finally painting was completed and lighting installed. This facility now caters well for all sections of the Group and allows room for most of our activities and storage space for the Group's equipment.

The minutes of the annual general meeting, held on 5 April 1974, noted that there was a large number of parents present. The Group also expressed their shock and regret at the shooting of the District Commissioner, John Henry, a Reserve Constable in the Royal Ulster Constabulary, and a suitable letter expressing the Group's best wishes for a speedy recovery was sent to John who was currently in Newry General Hospital. The finances were in the very capable hands of Mrs McConnell with the sum of £855.00 in the bank account. Mrs M. McGaffin took on the role of secretary of the Parents Association.

Once again the 'Troubles' had a detrimental affect on the Group as Job Week only managed to raise the sum of £62.05 due to the inability of the members to go around the area. A presentation of a cheque from Mr Noel Hodgett towards the purchase of equipment was greatly appreciated. The minister and committee of Sandys Street Presbyterian Church were thanked for the provision of twelve forms for use in the Scout hall. Ten photographs taken by Cub Scoutleader, William McAlpine, were accepted by the publishers of the Cub Scout Annual for inclusion in its next publication. The roof of the 'old Scout hall' was in need of repair and the Committee granted permission for repairs to be undertaken. It was felt that the Group would benefit greatly if it were possible to purchase a trailer for use in transporting gear to and from local camps. The Scoutleader and Cub Scoutleader were asked to make enquiries into obtaining one as soon as possible as prices were likely to increase over the coming years. Mr Cecil Grills, father of one of our Scouts, agreed to make a trailer for the Group with the chairman providing the wheels. Alterations to the heating system in the Scout hall were made in order to provide a warmer environment for meetings during the winter months.

Cub camp at Mourne Park, 1974

L-R: S. Wylie, R. Gray, A. Hanna, G. Jones.

L-R: M. Smyth, D. Anderson, A. Stevenson, G. Hanley, J. Gray.

Annual camp, Troon

The Troop held a most enjoyable and exciting annual camp at Fullarton Estate, Troon, in Scotland. A bequest of £25 was received from Fisher & Fisher, solicitors, from the estate of the late Mrs Thompson, Erskine Street, Newry and the chairman, Mr Lockington, expressed appreciation of this bequest. A tuck shop was opened in the Scout hall and parents agreed that this was an excellent idea. A sub committee, consisting of the chairman and Messrs Robinson, White, Parker and McGaffin, was established to take forward outstanding issues with the Southern Education and Library Board concerning the possible purchase of the building currently being used as the Scout hall. Following contact with Mr Jack Mackin, SELB, the sub committee asked Mr Hogg to carry out a valuation of the property as the youth officer with the SELB felt there was a good possibility that the Group might be able to purchase the hall. The Rev. L. McAdoo made a proposal, with Mr Handley seconding, to the Parents Association that if possible the Group should buy the hall, as this would secure premises for the future. The Cub Scoutleader, William McAlpine, received a donation of £52 for use in the Cub Pack from our great friend and supporter, Noel Hodgett, and our appreciation of his generosity was expressed by the chairman and Parents Association.

A well-attended Parents evening was held in the Scout hall when Cubs and Scouts put on a number of activities and parents also took part in a variety of events some of which raised much laughter but everyone enjoyed the evening which ended with refreshments served by the ladies of the committee. During the year Venture Scout Gary Cowan gained the Chief Scout Award. A coffee party, sale of work and funfair, held on 6 December in Sandys Street Presbyterian Church Hall, proved to be very successful with good support and the sum of £205.38 was raised. Again Sandys Street Presbyterian Church Hall was the venue for a 24-hour football marathon held by the Scout section to help raise funds for the Group. This event was extremely well supported by all the members of the Scout section with some of the older Cubs also taking part for a short period during the evening session. The marathon was a great success and enjoyed by all taking part, even though everyone had little sleep during the night. The thanks of the Group went to the many members of the Parents Association and friends who provided the meals to keep up their strength for the 24-hour period. At the end of the marathon and after scoring a total of eight hundred and sixty seven goals, everyone went home exhausted but exhilarated by the fact that they had achieved their target and also raised the sum of £245.94. The Scoutleader, Mervyn Ferris, reported that plans were progressing for annual camp in 1975 to be held in Austria and the cost would be in the region of £65.75p per member attending.

Parents night.

Cubs, June 1974

Cubs at the 24-hour football marathon where 867 goals were scored, December 1974

1975

At a Parents Association meeting on 29 January 1975, the treasurer, Mrs McConnell, reported that the Group's balance in the Group's bank account was £1045.96. Mervyn Ferris, Scoutleader, reported that he had been successful in obtaining a grant for the sum of £400 from the British Youth Council towards the cost of annual camp and he was hopeful that further grants could be available from other sources. After discussion at the Parents Association, it was agreed that the cost to each Scout attending would be £40 with any expenditure over this sum being met from Group funds. Arrangements were well in hand for this special camp which was to be held at Zellhof, situated near the beautiful city of Salzburg. It was agreed that a donation should be forwarded to Sandys Street church for the very generous use of their hall for the past two events. Jumble sales held in February and March raised the sum of £133.56. Job week this year proved to be much more successful than last year with a total of £180.20 being earned. The Cub Pack was presented with new colours by Mr and Mrs Noel Hodgett and the dedication service was held in the Methodist Church.

In May the County Down Challenge Flag Competition was held in Mourne Park. A patrol from 1st Newry Troop was entered for the competition and, after some very hard work over the weekend, gained first place. The Chief Scout, Sir William Gladstone, who was paying a visit to Scouting in the Province, came to Mourne Park on the Sunday and the patrol from 1st Newry had the honour of receiving the Challenge Flag from him.

Challenge Flag winners.
L-R: David McCullough, Paul Brown, Ivor McGaffin, Freddy White, Brian Cowan, Sir William Gladstone, Chief Scout.

Noel and Ruby Hodgett (above left) present a new Cub flag to the group

1975 Annual camp in Austria

Arrangements were made for transport to Belfast for Troop camp in Austria, from 9 July, with alternative means of travel being considered in the event of a rail strike. Parents would provide cars to Belfast and the Police Community Relations would provide a minibus for the return journey from Larne on 26 July. Amidst great anticipation and excitement, the Troop left Newry on 9 July at 5.30 a.m. for their long journey to Austria. They toured the gardens in Salzburg where scenes were shot for the film *The Sound of Music*, and paid a visit to a folk festival where the Scouts joined in the folk dancing. They travelled along the alpine roads to the Grossglockner glacier where there was plenty of snow still around in the middle of July and everyone joined in snowball fights while the sun shone brightly from a clear blue sky. Another day they travelled to see the Eisriesenwelt Ice Caves at Werfen. In later years the castle at Werfen was to feature in the film *Where Eagles Dare*. Everyone was amazed to be able to walk through some of the miles of caves running through the mountains, some of them cut through solid ice. At this camp, many friends were made with Scouts from other countries who were camping there at the same time. Friendships were developed with the staff on site which would remain for future years and a number of camps to come. This was a truly memorable camp for all who attended. Due to the troubled times it was decided that midnight hikes would be postponed until the situation improved.

Troop ready to set off for Austria, July 1975
L-R front row: G. McIlwaine, B. Cowan, R. Gray, T. Holmes, J. Kelly, I. Anderson, G. Power.
2nd row: J. McKee, D. McCullough, M. Thompson, J. McCullagh, I. Simms, G. Hanley.
3rd row: G. Hodgett, F. White, M. McCaigue, J. Knight, I. McGaffin.
Back row: R. Brown, G. McGaffin, M. McConnell ASL, R. Ferris, M. Ferris SL, R. McCullough, N. Lockington, G. Cowan, W. McAlpine CSL.

At the swimming area, Grabensee lake, Zellhof, Austria, 1975. L-R front row: B. Cowan, I. Anderson, T. Holmes. 2nd row: I. McGaffin, D. McCullough, J. McKee. Back row: G. McGaffin, F. White.

L-R: F. White, M. McCaigue, J. McCullagh, D. McCullough, T. Holmes, G. Hanley, J. McKee, M. Thompson, I. McGaffin.

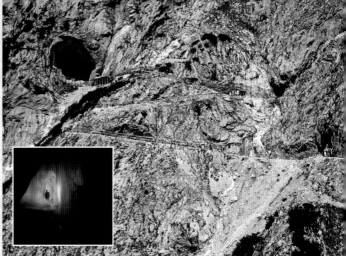

Above and left: Eisriesenwelt Ice Caves at Werfen, July 1975

1976

The year began with a donation from our very faithful friend, Noel Hodgett, who presented the Group with a cheque toward their funds. Once again the Group expressed their gratitude to Noel whose generosity toward the Group was greatly appreciated. Early on, Saturday 21 February, a party of Venture Scouts headed off into the Mourne mountains for a hike and an overnight stay at the Hares Gap. Later in the day leaders Neil Lockington, Billy McAlpine and Mervyn Ferris walked from Trassey Bridge along the Trassey track up to the Hare's Gap to visit the hikers and make sure that all was well. After chatting for a while and seeing that the group had safely arrived the leaders then returned to Newry in the early evening. Within a few hours of their return Mervyn and Billy received the very sad news that Mrs Lockington, wife of the Group's chairman Douglas Lockington, had been critically wounded when gunmen opened fire on their car while returning home from a Rugby International game in Dublin. Mrs Lockington never recovered from her injuries and sadly died later that evening in Daisy Hill Hospital. The Group received the news with great sadness and many expressions of sympathy were sent to the Lockington family.

The Scout football team won the District football tournament and were presented with the Ian McCullough Memorial shield by the District Commissioner. A presentation of Chief Scout Awards was made by one of our 'Old Boys', Mr William Magowan, to Venture Scouts Freddie White and John McKee. As this was Cub Jubilee Year, ten Cubs were invited to attend the Cub Jubilee Jamboree in Wales from 2 to 10 July. The Cub Scoutleader selected the Sixers and Seconds to attend this event. A weekend camp for the Scout section was held at one of our favourite sites, Mourne Park, where those hoping to attend annual camp received suitable training for the venture. Also during the month of June nine Cubs spent the weekend under canvas on the Three Bridges site at Mourne Park. This was a real thrill for the boys as they had never been under canvas before.

Scout football winners.
Back row L-R: Geoffrey Hodgett, James McCullagh, David Gray, Freddy White.
Front row: David McCullough, John McKee, Mervyn McCaigue.

The annual Scout camp was held at Barrwood, near Stirling, in Scotland while thirteen of the Cubs travelled to Wales as guests of the people of Cardiff for ten days. Highlights of the Cub holiday were the dinner with the Lord Mayor of Cardiff in Cardiff Castle, and visits to Barry Island, the zoo, Llandaff Cathedral and the folk museum, to name just a few places.

Cub camp to Wales, 1976
Standing, L-R: Stewart McConnell, John Lockhart, Kenny Gibson, Richard Strain, Adrian Stevenson, Neil Thompson, Ronald Boyd
Kneeling, L-R: Nicholas Gray, Rupert Pinion, Michael McParland, Roger Holland, Ivor Graham, Richard Hazley
Leaders: Billy McAlpine (CSL) and Gary Cowan (Venture Scout and helper)

1st Newry Cubs invited to tea by the Lord Mayor of Cardiff

1st Newry Cubs at Barry Island, Wales

As the Chief Commissioner for Northern Ireland, Mr David Harrison, was resigning the post which he had held for a number of years, the Group made a donation to his retirement present. Also following a request from Headquarters for a 'Good Turn' for Jubilee Year, the Group decided to send a donation of £10 towards the Save the Children Fund.

The Scout hall was now open on Sunday evenings for fourteen year olds and over following the church services, with coffee being provided by the Parents Association. A birthday party for the Cub Pack was held in October, as well as a Jubilee dinner in the Scout hall. The guest of honour at this event was the Chief Commissioner for Northern Ireland, Mr David Harrison. The Jubilee dinner proved to be a great success with the Scout hall being filled to capacity. Everyone enjoyed the entertainment and the wonderful meal provided by the Parents Association. Unfortunately the Cub Scoutleader, William McAlpine, was not able to be present on this occasion as he had been admitted urgently to hospital. However a letter, which he had written, was read out at the dinner and everyone sent their best wishes for a speedy recovery. Special badges commemorating the Queen's Silver Jubilee were purchased and given out to all members of the Group for wearing on their Scout shirts during 1977.

Cub camp, in the river at Mourne Park, 1976
Back row L-R: Kenny Cowan , Norman McNellis, Kenny Gibson. Middle row: Gareth Holt (red jumper), Ronnie Boyd, Richard Hazley. Front row: Rupert Pinion, Roger Holland, Neil Thompson.

1st Newry Cubs, 26 May 1976

Cub cup winners

1977

The Venture Scouts held a number of hikes through the Mourne Mountains and a weekend camp at Mourne Park along with the Scouts. This year Job Week proved to be another successful year with the boys earning the sum of £266.94. A presentation of a silver salver was made by Scout Martin Thompson and Cub Christopher McCullough to Mr Douglas Lockington, upon his retirement as chairman after some nineteen years of long and valued service to the Group.

The annual Scout camp was held at Ambleside in the Lake District. This was great hiking country. The work carried out by Mr Cecil Grills in constructing metal frames for the protection of the Scout hall windows, was gratefully acknowledged by the Group. A sale of work was held in Sandys Street Presbyterian Church on Friday, 21 October, with the following stalls in place; cake, pound and tombola with a silent auction also being held. The Parents Association provided refreshments. This event was well attended and the sum of £264.07 was lodged to the Group's bank account.

Billy McAlpine with Cubs Paul and Norman in Mourne Park.

1978

On Thursday, 12 January, 1978 the Group was yet again stunned by the murder of yet another of its supporters and parent of one of our ex Scouts. Cecil Grills, a very active supporter of the Group and a member of the Ulster Defence Regiment, was shot while returning home from work. Cecil died instantly from the wounds received in the shooting. The Group was deeply saddened by his death and their deepest sympathy was conveyed to his wife, Nancy, and children Michael and Anne. Members of the Parents Association and all the leaders attended the funeral service.

A coffee party and sale of work in aid of the victims of the La Mon massacre was held on 10 March in Sandys Street Church Hall. This proved to be a great success and the Group's thanks went to all those in the community who contributed in any way to this event. The death took place of Mr William Magowan, a founder member of 1st Newry Cub Pack. Venture Scout Robert Ferris, who had completed all the requirements for the Queen's Scout Award, was presented with his badge and certificate by the Northern Ireland Chief Commissioner, David Harrison. The Group's thanks were expressed to Crieve Band for their attendance at our church parades. Once again the Cubs went to Mourne Park for their weekend camp only this time they camped on the Cliff site adjacent to the old cottage belonging to Kilkeel High School.

The Scouts stayed at home for the 1978 annual camp which was held at Mourne Park, Kilkeel. Three representatives, John Kelly, John Gray and David Anderson, from 1st Newry Scout Troop, were selected from many other Scouts from county Down to take part in the World Jamboree to be held in Manitoba, Canada, in July 1979. At an event on 14 October a presentation of a Scout plaque was made by Scout David Anderson to Mrs and Mrs J. Gough, members of the Kilmorey family, in recognition of their support for Scouting in Newry District and especially for the use of camping rights at Mourne Park. A social evening for parents and friends of 1st Newry was held in the Scout hall on 20 October. This took

Cubs at camp building a shelter.
Back row: Alan Erskine, Gary Neill.
Centre: Norman McAlpine.
Front row: Stewart Stevenson, Michael McCullough.

the form of a cabaret night with entertainment provided by Mr William Cowan, Mrs Doreen Whitten and Mr John Knight, compered by Mr Noel Hodgett. The evening proved to be a great success and everyone went home well pleased with the event and looking forward to another such occasion. The Group purchased a minibus which would provide much needed transport for the Cubs and Scouts over the coming months and years. Having worked very hard over the past two years Venture Scouts, Brian Cowan and Martin Thompson, gained the Chief Scout Award following completion of all the requirements for this much-coveted award.

Cubs at Mourne Park

Robert Ferris receives his Queen's Scout Award from N.I. Chief Commissioner, David Harrison.

1979

A sale of work and coffee party was held once again in Sandys Street Church Hall on 23 February to help raise funds to send the three Scouts to the World Jamboree in Canada this summer. This event was well attended. This was followed by another social evening in the Scout hall on 23 March. The latter event was in the form of an Irish night, with supper being Irish stew. Entertainment was provided by Mr William Cowan, Mr Kenny Cowan, Mrs Violet Lowry, Mrs Doreen Whitten and Mr Derek Noble, with Mr Noel Hodgett acting as compere. Again the night proved to be a great success and enjoyed by one and all. During the annual general meeting held on 10 April 1979, the County Commissioner, Mr Jim Aicken, presented Scoutleader Mervyn Ferris with the Medal of Merit in recognition of his contribution to Scouting over the past years. At the same meeting Mr Jack White was appointed as chairman of the Group.

Buckmore Park, Kent, was the venue for the Troop annual camp. This was well attended and all present enjoyed the camp and the many and varied activities arranged. During the year some of the Venture Scouts, under the leadership of Mervyn Ferris, began the construction of three canoes for the use by the Venture Scouts and Scouts. The building of these took place in the basement of the Institute (YMCI), Hill Street and all were constructed from kit form. The Scouts and Senior Scouts continued the collection of waste paper which was then bundled up and sold to help provide additional funding for the Group. The marriage of Cub Scoutleader, William McAlpine, took place in 1979.

Cubs Roger McCullough and Gavin McCullough at Mourne Park, August 1979

Cubs at sale of work, February 1979
L-R: I. Taylor, I. McAlpine,
M. McCullough, P. McCandless,
G. Neill, M. Grills,
G. McCullough, N. McAlpine.

Annual camp at Buckmore Park, Kent, 1979
L-R front row: N. McNellis, P. Preston,
R. Pinion, A. Erskine, J. Grant,
D. Anderson, C. McCullough.
Middle row: W. McAlpine CSL, N. Baird,
K. Gibson, A. McGaffin, N. Gray,
J. Lockhart, M. Robinson, D. Mitchell.
Back row: M. Ferris SL, I. McGaffin,
D. McCullough, G. Cowan, R. McCullough.

Cub camp at Mourne Park, August 1979

1980s

1st Newry Cubs make a day trip to the Jamboree camp
at Lakeland, county Fermanagh, 1982

1980

A t the beginning of 1980 the Group held a very successful coffee party and cake sale which helped to augment Group funds to the tune of £185.57.

Job Week this year was most successful and well supported with a total of £404.81 being made due to the hard work of both Cubs and Scouts. It was noted in the minutes of the Parents Association that no beneficial progress had been made on the situation in relation to the hall and further discussions were to be considered. A patrol from the Scout section came 5th in the County Flag Competition but bettered this by taking 1st place in Newry District Flag competition. The Parents Association of the Group organised two very successful stalls selling hot dogs, burgers and minerals on 12 July, one at the Scout hall and the other was on the forecourt of Rockmount Service Station with the blessing of Mr S. Lockhart, the owner of the filling station.

This year the Troop held its annual camp at Snowball Plantation, York. The Parents Association then held a Flag Day in Newry on a very wet and cold 11 September, when a number of parents and friends turned up to support this worthwhile effort. Over the past few years the Group held a number of discos in the Scout hall. The music for these events were provided by the Blue Lamp, Police Community Relations team, and later on by supporter Roy Taylor. These discos proved to be very popular for some time with large numbers coming along on each occasion. However eventually as time went by they came to an end.

Newry Canal Festival

The Group this year took up the offer from Newry District Council and, together with members from 1st Newry Guides, entered a float in Newry Canal Festival parade. Thanks were expressed to Mr Drew Warde for providing a suitable lorry for the event and Cubs, Scouts, Venture Scouts and Guides took part in decorating the float for this special event. To the amazement of all the float took first place in the category of 'best dressed floats' and a cup was presented to the Scouts and Guides for this achievement.

1st Newry Cub Pack pictured with the District Sports Shield along with leaders Billy McAlpine (right) and Robert Ferris.

Cub Christmas party, 1980

Cub receiving the District Sports Shield.

Troop getting ready for annual camp to York, 1980

Christopher McCullough (left) and Kenny Gibson prepare lunch at York annual camp.

In the photo are M. Ferris SL, K. Gibson, A. McGaffin, N. Thompson, J. Lockhart, D. Mitchell, M. Robinson, K. Smyth, A. McTurk, W. Nummy, M. McElroy, C. McCullough, R. Ferris, J. Knight, A. Erskine, W. McAlpine CSL, D. Anderson, G. Neill, N. Gray, M. McCullough, N. Baird.

1981

70th Anniversary Dinner

The year began with a band of hard working parents and friends spending hours over a number of evenings and weeks carrying out renovations to and painting the Scout hall in preparation for the Group's 70th anniversary dinner. Finally, with all the work completed in early February, the Group held its 70th anniversary dinner in the rejuvenated Scout hall which was attended by approximately 180 former Scouts and friends of the Group. It was a most enjoyable night with many friendships being renewed. An evening of nostalgia brought a sense of all that had been accomplished over the past seventy years. During the anniversary dinner, Mrs Sadie McConnell was presented with the Chief Scout's Commendation for services rendered as treasurer to the Group for some 30 years. Mr and Mrs H. McGaffin, Mr and Mrs J. White, Mr W. Robinson and Mr R. McCullough were also presented with Thanks Badges for services rendered to the Group.

Entertainment was provided by (L-R) Lorna Hanna, Ju Gray, Bunty Kelly, Albert Jones, Maura Erskine, Marga Thompson and Billy Cowan, remembered best for rendition of the song "Old Man Rive

Former Scout Billy Smyth (centre) makes presentation of Thanks Badges to (L-R) Harry McGaffin, Margaret McGaffin, Jack White, Annie White and Robert McCullough for outstanding service to the Group.

1st NEWRY SCOUT GROUP [EARL KILMOREY'S]

70th Anniversary Dinner

SCOUT HALL · SANDYS STREET
FRIDAY · 20th FEBRUARY · 1981
At 8 p.m.   Dinner £3

A Troop weekend camp was held in Mourne Park to prepare those Scouts hoping to go to annual camp in Switzerland later in the year. All former members of the Group were invited, with many accepting, to attend the St George's Day parade and service and a very good response resulted. The Parents Association held a cake sale and a demonstration of children's clothing by Elizabeth Alexander also proved to be a great success. This year saw an increase in acts of vandalism being carried out on the Scout hall, so much so that the committee were forced to express their concerns to the local Police Inspector and, later in the year, to erect grills on the windows and doors to help secure the building. Robert Ferris who had volunteered to take on the role of Assistant Cub leader completed all the requirements to qualify for the Wood Badge.

To celebrate the 70th anniversary the Troop held their annual camp at Thun in Switzerland and visited many of the famous Swiss tourist attractions. This camp was held in a Scout chalet high on the mountainside overlooking Lake Thun.

Robert Ferris at Buckingham Palace with his Duke of Edinburgh Gold Award, December 1981

On 20 September a further act of vandalism was reported to the Group by a vigilant neighbour concerning damage caused to the 'old hall'. A youth had been seen and recognised with the result that his parents had been informed and, with police involvement, an apology and offer of repair costs was received from the family concerned.

During the month of October, car maintenance classes, under the tutelage of Mr Jack White, were held in the Scout hall each week for the benefit of the Venture Scout section. There was some bad news received from the Southern Education and Library Board indicating that the Board would be requiring possession of the Scout hall, although the Group may have the option of purchasing Windsor Bank (the preparatory school for Newry Grammar School) which was now no longer in use by the Board. In December, Assistant Cub Scoutleader Robert Ferris, who had now completed all the requirements for the Duke of Edinburgh Gold Award, took up the invitation to attend the Duke of Edinburgh award ceremony in Buckingham Palace to receive his well-earned award.

To end the year the Parents Association organised an Irish place names quiz which was given to all members for distribution to help raise funds for the Group and Mrs Nancy Grills organised a doll's name competition. These events raised the sum of £106.42.

International night with Robert Ferris (left) and
Clive Scoular, County Commissioner

International night. L-R: Karl Mulligan, Peter Whitcroft,
Denis Niblock, Richard Brown, Jeffrey McNeill

Cub camp at Mourne Park, June 1981

Robert McCullough teaches some of his
expert DIY skills to Scouts Gareth Holt
and Garry McWhirter

Cub crafts.

1982

Following correspondence from the Southern Education and Library Board informing the Group that no decision had been made by them concerning Windsor Bank, it was agreed that no further action would be taken until the Board had reached a decision and communicated again with the Group.

As 1982 was designated as the Year of the Scout, the Parents Association once again organised another dinner to celebrate this special occasion. That year was the 75th Anniversary of the formation of the Scouting Movement in the United Kingdom by Lord Baden-Powell. The Parents Association prepared a most excellent meal and again many former members and friends met to reminisce and renew old friendships. Discussions took place with a number of contractors to carry out repairs to the roof of the 'old Scout hall', especially as it was no longer watertight and subsequently temporary repairs were carried out to improve the situation. The Cubs and Scouts during Job Week raised the very useful sum of £374.60. A disco held in the Scout hall made a profit of approximately £37.00. These very popular discos continued to be provided for quite a number of years as there was very little entertainment being provided for the young people of the town. On many occasions the Scout hall was filled to capacity with some one hundred and forty to one hundred and fifty young people dancing the night away. These events were well managed with many of the parents coming along to provide security and help organise the evenings. 1982 also saw the departure from Newry of the Rev. R. Birney, our chaplain and very good friend, and the Troop marked the occasion with a small presentation to Mr Birney and wished him well in his new church in Ballymena.

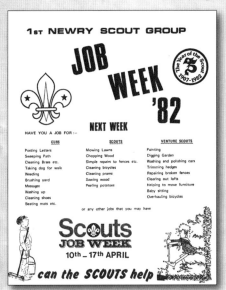

Lakeland '82

The Troop held their annual camp at 'Lakeland 82', which was a mini Jamboree held at Castle Archdale in county Fermanagh, and was enjoyed by all those attending. During the camp the Cub Scouts visited for the Saturday and all reports were good. Mervyn Ferris was responsible for the security arrangements for the Erne sub-camp, ably supported by members of the Venture Scout Unit who provided day and night security duties during the duration of the camp.

Scouts Neil Thompson and Alan McGaffin gained their Chief Scout Award with the presentation being made by the Chief Scout, Major General Michael Walsh, at an award ceremony held at Portora Royal School in Enniskillen. An excellent attendance of Cubs and Scouts together with the leaders attended the harvest service in St Patrick's Parish Church on 3 October at the invitation of the select vestry.

L-R: R. McCullough, M. McElroy, M. McCullough, W. Nummy, A. Erskine, C. McCullough, I. Taylor.

Mary Peters

County Commissioner Clive Scoular

Chief Scout Award: Neil Thompson (left) and Alan McGaffin with Mervyn Ferris (above) and County Commissioner Clive Scoular (top right).

Neil Thompson

1st NEWRY SCOUT GROUP [EARL KILMOREY'S]

YEAR OF THE SCOUT
Dinner and Entertainment

SCOUT HALL · SANDYS STREET
FRIDAY · 12th MARCH · 1982
At 8 p.m.
Dinner £3.50

The Venture Scout Unit made preparations for a sponsored car push in aid of Combat Cancer and Group funds. Then, on 1 November, all the Venture Scouts turned out and made a huge effort in pushing a car from Newry to Warrenpoint and return. In completing this wonderful achievement and showing their community spirit, they helped raise much-needed funds for a very worthwhile charity. After the event and when all the returns were collected, cheques for £150 were presented to Combat Cancer and the Group. The Cub Scout Pack was visited by the County Down International team led by Wallace Shaw and a most enjoyable night was had by all those in attendance.

L-R: Gareth Holt, Alan McGaffin, Kenny Gibson, Nicholas Gray

1983

During this year the Group saw the departure of the Assistant Cub Scoutleader, Robert Ferris, who married and moved to Banbridge where he then became a Scoutleader with one of the Banbridge Groups. The Cubs held a parents night to say cheerio to Robert and made him a small presentation for all his hard work while with the Pack. On 7 May Cubs and Scouts attended the Fun Day which was held at Saintfield. During the day all were enthralled to see one of the large Sea King helicopters give a display of rescuing an injured casualty. The Parents Association once again organised a flag day held on 12 May to help raise funds for the Group. On this occasion, however, they had competition from the Christian Brothers Past Pupils Union who had, without authorisation, held their flag day on the same date. Notwithstanding, the parents put in a marvellous effort and collected in excess of £320.00. A Scout patrol entered for the County Flag competition and due to their very hard work they managed to win the County Novice flag. The Cub football team took part in the District football competition at Warrenpoint but unfortunately did not manage to win this event although everyone enjoyed the competition.

Robert and Karen Ferris, 4 April 1983

Patrol Leader Mark McElroy receives the County Novice flag from Assistant County Commissioner (Scouts) Sinclair Trotter.

County Novice flag winners, 1983

1st Newry Cub football team at District Cub Football event in Warrenpoint, May 1983 L-R front row: Not known, C. Jones, S. Wylie. Back row: M. Smyth, Not known, J. Hamilton, A. Andrews.

The Scout annual camp was held at Bonaly Scout Camp site near Edinburgh, with 23 Scouts taking part. The site was well organised and, with many activities on hand as well as the outings planned by the leaders, everyone had a wonderful time and returned home looking forward to next year's event. One event which will be remembered by those who attended was on the occasion when the leaders decided that each patrol would have haggis for dinner. After purchasing this favoured Scottish dish the leaders got all the patrol leaders together, gave instructions on how the haggis should be cooked stating that this delicacy only required to be placed in a saucepan of water and simmered gently until cooked. The rest of the menu was then handed out and the patrol leaders left to get on with the cooking. Everything appeared to going smoothly until Venture Scout Garry McWhirter decided that he would check to see how the haggis was doing and went around the various patrols. On visiting the third patrol he discovered that the haggis was not at all well, having disintegrated into a gooey mush. When asked what had happened to cause this the patrol leader responded 'well we just took the skin off the haggis, placed it into the saucepan as you said and this is what it turned out like'. Garry then came back to the leaders and, when asked how things were progressing, stated that two patrol were having haggis with potatoes and peas while the other patrol was having haggis soup, potatoes and peas. Such are the joys of camping.

The year ended with the Cub Pack holding a well-attended Christmas party at which all the Cubs were given a small gift.

Troop at Edinburgh Castle, 1983
L-R front row: I. Craig, C. McElroy, M. Taylor, J. Lawson.
Middle row: A. Stewart, K. Gibson, A. McTurk, R. Brown, M. Annett.
Back row: C. McCullough, G. McWhirter, A. Erskine, A. McGaffin, G. Cassidy, N. Thompson ASL, M. McCullough.

From top left:
Alan Erskine's patrol.
Christopher McCullough's patrol (middle photos).

Michael McCullough and Michael Annett unpacking.

Scout weekend camp at Mourne Park

Cub camp at Mourne Park

1984

During the early months of 1984 the Venture Scouts organised a visit to the Marble Arch caves where they, together with members of Queen's University Caving club, carried out some potholing. The weather during the weekend was not at all favourable with the water flowing through the caves freezing cold. Not only was the potholing cold but the overnight accommodation left a lot to be desired. This consisted of an old ramshackle house with no windows and certainly no heating. However the Venture Scouts had enjoyed the event although returning home cold and hungry.

The Cubs and Scouts provided the entertainment for a parents night on 30 March 1984, when the Cubs performed a play while Scouts put on a display. 'Comedians' Gavin McCullough and Richard Brown provided further entertainment and, after everyone had settled down, a wonderful supper was

provided by the Parents Association. All the parents voted this a very big success. The district Cubs and Scouts visited Stormont during the year with 1st Newry being represented by Cub Scout Christopher Lyons and accompanied by Scoutleader Mervyn Ferris. During the visit they were shown around the magnificent building by the Speaker of the Assembly, Mr J. Kilfedder, and then entertained to afternoon tea.

The Troop won the County Down Novice Flag in the County Down camping competition which was held in May. The Troop held their annual camp in Mourne Park in July and had a very successful camp. They also had a most successful parents open day, even though it turned out to be rather wet. Later on in the year the Group went to visit the Craigavon Civic Centre for the visit of the Chief Scout to Northern Ireland. Also this year the Group took part in the Christmas carol service held in Rathfriland as well as putting on an abseiling display at the Newry High School open day. The Cubs and Scouts took part in the Fun Day held in Crawfordsburn and had a most enjoyable time.

L-R front row: J. Lawson, R. Armstrong. Middle row: M. Annett, D. Lawson, D. Steele, C. Lyons, J. McNeill, N. Sterritt, I. Taylor. Back row: J. Gray, R. Brown, N. Gray, N. Thompson ASL, K. Gibson, A. McGaffin, J. Lockhart, D. Mitchell, M. McCullough. G. McWhirter.

**Annual camp at Mourne Park,
July 1984**

Patrol Leaders training at Mourne Park

1985

In January, Venture Scout Neil Thompson was presented with his warrant as Assistant Scoutleader by the County Commissioner, Mr Clive Scoular, who was also guest speaker at the Parent's Association meeting. Following the business, our resident comedians Richard Brown, John Knight and Gavin McCullough entertained all present. John Knight, who was acting as Assistant Cub Scoutleader, left the Group to take up employment in South Africa and the Cubs had a farewell party to wish John all the best in his new job. In March the Parents Association organised a very successful coffee party and sale of work, which was then followed up by the Cub Pack entering a team in the District football competition and winning the event. On 28 June a 'Surprise Night Out' was organised in Kilbroney Park, Rostrevor, for members, parents and friends of the Group. The evening took the form of a treasure hunt followed by games, competitions and barbecue. This event proved most successful and was immensely enjoyed by all who attended. During this 'Surprise Night Out', Scoutleader Mervyn Ferris was indeed taken aback when the County Commissioner, Mr Clive Scoular, presented him with the Bar to the Medal of Merit. Also on the night, presentations were made to Cub Colin Jones, sportsman and footballer of the year, and to Cub Craig Peake, for his outstanding contribution during Job Week, and to Gavin McCullough and Richard Brown for entertainment during the year. The Cub Pack was visited by former Scout, Billy McConnell, an Olympic Bronze Medal winner. Billy told them all about his medal and of all the sports personalities whom he met while at the 1984 Olympic Games. The Cub Pack also started to correspond with a Cub Pack in Canada and, as a result, some Cubs continued to correspond with their pen pals in Canada.

The Scout Troop held their annual camp at Buckmore Park, in Kent, during July. The Cub Scout football team won the district football tournament and the prizes were presented by Newry Town chairman, Mr Kenny Cowan, who indeed was also a former member and leader of 1st Newry Group. The Sportsman of the Year award was awarded to Cub Scout Colin Jones. The Parents Association, aided by Venture Scouts and friends, organised and staffed two stalls selling hot dogs, burgers, minerals, crisps and tea on 'Black Saturday' which was held in Newry on the last Saturday in August. The Group's thanks go to the Henning family for providing space in the field for one of the stalls. The Cubs and Scouts continued to collect waste paper with the latest sale making a profit of £88.40. This year also saw the introduction of the new Scout badge system and all the Scouts were busily engaged in this new scheme. The Cub Scouts donated their Christmas good turn funds to Heartbeat.

County Commissioner Clive Scoular (left) presents Mervyn Ferris with the Bar to the Medal of Merit.

Former Scout, Billy McConnell, with his Olympic Bronze Medal which he won in Los Angeles, 1984. 1st Newry Cub Steven McNeill gets his hands on the medal, with Mark Smyth behind.

Above left: Cub Christmas party.
Left: Cub camp in Mourne Park.

The group at Westminster Abbey, 1985

Stuart Dillon (above left) at camp in Mourne Park and Nicholas Dulvy cooking in the hall.

Scouts at Mourne Park.

Alan McGaffin, Gavin McCullough, David Mitchell

David Steele, Richard Brown, John Lawson, Ashley Dillon

Gavin McCullough, Alan McGaffin

Neil Thompson

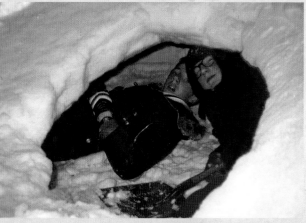

David Steele, Ashley Dillon

1986

During this 75th Anniversary year, it was good to be able to announce the formation, on 20 January, of the newest section of the Movement, Beaver Scouts, under the leadership of Jennifer Steen ably assisted by Doreen Fegan. Beaver Scouts cater for the age range 6 to 8 years and everyone wished them well and much success in the future. 1986 also marked the 70th anniversary of the formation of Cub Scouts in the United Kingdom and 1st Newry Cubs were also able to celebrate this occasion as they had been in existence from 1915 making them the oldest Cub Scout Pack in Northern Ireland.

First Beaver meeting with Leader Jenny Steen

Beaver garden barbecue

Beaver Halloween party. Leaders (above left) are
Dorrie Hamilton and Jenny Steen

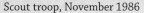

The Parents Association worked extremely hard to redecorate the Scout hall for the reunion celebration dinner which was held in the Scout hall on 14 March 1986. This was an excellent event, attended by more than 80 former members and friends of the Group. All who attended went away with many happy memories of Scouting in Newry and having met old friends and acquaintances. An exhibition was held in the Scout hall from 14 to 21 March from 7.45 each night. It was delightful to see many former members of the Group, as well as the general public, attending the exhibition. During the anniversary dinner, the McWhirter family presented the Group with new colours in memory of their late father, Frank McWhirter, who was a member of the Group for many years, Scoutleader from 1940 to 1946 and holder of many other offices within the Group. The flag was dedicated during the annual St George's Day service at Downshire Road Presbyterian Church. Job Week this year was very successful with Cubs and Scouts working very hard to raise the sum of £453.15. Beavers and Cubs took part in the District Beaver and Cub sports evening when quite a number of the boys won medals in the various events which took place. The Cub football team also won the District football tournament. The capitation fee payable to Headquarters this year amounted to £314.00 (58 Cubs and Scouts at £5 per head and 12 Beavers at £2 per head). This year the Troop held their annual camp at the Austrian Scout centre at Zellhof. A most memorable and splendid time was had by all who attended. The Venture Unit and leaders again began running discos in the Scout hall from October and these proved to be a great success.

Scout troop, November 1986   Scouts at weekend camp in Mourne Park   Cub camp, Mourne Park, 5 July 1986

1st Newry 75th anniversary celebrations. Above right (L-R): Wilson Robinson, Clifford Boyd (NI Chief Commissioner), founder member Bobby Graham, Scout Colin Jones, former Scoutmaster Sam Cassidy, Clive Scoular (County Commissioner) and Paddy Graham (District Commissioner)

The McWhirter family present a new Scout flag to the Group in memory of their late father, Frank McWhirter (former Scout Master).

District sports, 7 June 1986

Cub Christmas party

1986 Annual camp, Zellhof, Austria
Back row: Richard Brown, Richard Kellett, Garry McWhirter, David Steele, Alan Johnston, Jeffrey McNeill, Michael Annett, Neil Thompson ASL.
Front row: Ashley Dillon, John Lawson, David Lawson, Mervyn Taylor

It was John Lawson's birthday whilst at camp in Austria

Mervyn Taylor (left) and John Lawson at the Water Gardens, Salzburg

1987

The month of January saw the progression of the first two Beavers from the Beaver section into the Cub Pack. Another disco was held in the Scout hall on Saturday, 21 February, with a very large number of young people attending this event. Discussions took place with representatives of Downshire Road Presbyterian Church with a view to purchasing the 'old Scout hall' and having this in the name of 1st Newry Group. There were considerable repairs to be done to the hall and the Group felt that it would be beneficial to have the deeds held by the Group. In May the Cub Pack took part in the District football competition and although they did not manage to win the event acquitted themselves well.

The Scouts held a number of weekend camps at Mourne part as well as hiking through the Mourne mountains before heading off for a well attended annual camp which was held once again at Blackwell Court, Bromsgrove, near Birmingham. The Beaver colony held a very successful Christmas party for all the boys which was thoroughly enjoyed. The Cub Pack held their Christmas party in the hall when most of the Cubs, and indeed some of the leaders, donned fancy dress for the occasion. All sections of the Group were progressing well and membership was satisfactory.

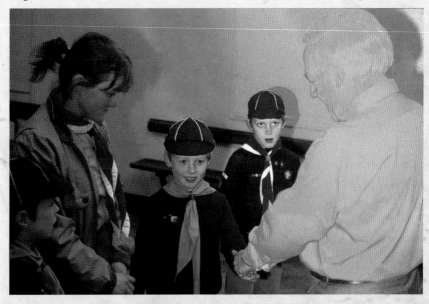

First Beaver to swim up to the Cub pack was Ray Menown, 16 January 1987

The Troop in 1987
L-R front row: R. Hamilton, I. Steen, S. Dillon, R. Baines, P. McNeill, T. Wilson, J. Lawson.
Back row: M. Smyth, D. Lawson, A. Johnston, J. McNeill, S. Smyth.

Newry Parents ladies were always on hand to help with refreshments after meetings. L-R: Florence McCullough, Annie White, Johan McAlpine, Sadie McConnell, Margaret McGaffin.

1987 Annual camp, Blackwell Court, Bromsgrove

Richard Kellett

L-R front row: P. McNeill, R. Baines, T. Wilson. Middle: S. Dillon, I. Steen, G. Kellett, R. Hamilton, S. Smyth. Back: N. Thompson ASL, J. Lawson, D. Lawson, A. Johnston, R. Kellett, J. McNeill, M. Smyth, M. Ferris SL.

Scouts at work on three bridges, Mourne Park weekend.

Scout and Cub Christmas parties.

Michael Annet (above left) and Ashley Dillon (left) getting mummified in toilet paper.

1988

The final transfer arrangements for the 'old hall' were finalised and the necessary repairs undertaken at a cost of approximately £3,500. Again these costs were fully met within the Group's own resources as no grant aid was available. The Group were extremely grateful to Downshire Road Presbyterian Church for their support throughout the years and especially for their agreement to transfer the deed for the 'old Scout hall' into the ownership of 1st Newry (Earl Kilmorey) Scout Group at a nominal figure. Gavin McCullough, who has been a member of the Group as a Cub and Scout for many years, took on the role of Assistant Cub Scoutleader. The Cub pack held their annual weekend outing to Mourne Park when all in attendance had a wonderful time. The Beaver and Cub sections had a very successful year with a wide and interesting variety of activities. The Scout Troop held annual camp at one of the Troop's most favourite camp sites, Mourne Park, and a wonderful time was had by all. A number of pioneering projects and Scouting activities were undertaken during camp. Many other activities and events were held throughout the year.

Cub camp, 25 June 1988. Above right (L-R): Philip McNeill, Keith Ferris, Nigel Henning, Roy Stevenson, Jonathan Scott

Beavers Christmas party.

Scouts practising for the County Meat Competition in the hall (above).
The competition (below) took place at Crawfordsburn, 4 June 1988.

1988 Annual camp at Mourne Park

1989

The Scouts and Venture Scouts had a very active year with activities ranging from cooking competitions, football and hockey, as well as continuing with their usual yearly programme and badge work. Work began in March on the 'old Scout hall' to replace the roof and make some other minor inside work. The Cub Pack entered two teams in the District Football competition.

Annual camp this year, which was attended by both Scouts and Venture Scouts, was held at the Welsh International Jamboree where they met Scouts from many other countries and joined in all the wonderful activities both on and off site. Members of the Cub Pack had a day out at the International Jamboree held at Gosford Park where they met many other Cubs and Scouts from different parts of the United Kingdom and other foreign countries. The Group was pleased to announce that five members of the Troop had gained their Chief Scout Award which is the highest award to be attained in the Scout section. The Venture Scouts arranged a number of discos at Newry Olympic Hockey Club with the profit helping to augment Group funds. These discos proved to be very well supported and appreciated, as there was little other activity for young people in the area. The Beaver and Cub sections had a most interesting year with many activities for the boys with numbers in both sections on the increase.

Cubs and Beavers at the International Jamboree at Gosford Park.

1989 Welsh International Jamboree

1990s

Billy McAlpine and Mervyn Ferris with their Silver Acorn Awards

1990

The year started off with the presentation of first aid certificates to a number of Scouts and Venture Scouts by Dr. McKnight. The Group thanked Dr. McKnight and Mrs Nancy Grills for their help and assistance in so ably tutoring the boys in the requirements for the public first aid certificates. This year the Group joined with the Guides and entered a float in the St Patrick's day parade in Newry and was presented with a trophy for 'Best float in parade'. Messrs. Haldane & Shields provided their support for the Group by supplying a trailer for this event. On 19 May the Beaver leaders took the Colony to Crawfordsburn Scout Activity Centre to attend the annual Beaver day out. All the Beavers and indeed their leaders had a wonderful time arriving back in Newry tired but very happy that the day had gone off so well.

The Troop annual camp was once again held in Mourne Park, Kilkeel, where the boys took part in orienteering, pioneering, swimming, hiking and many other Scouting activities. Following on from Scout camp the Venture Scout Unit for the first time held their annual outing on the Norfolk Broads where they hired a river craft for a week and navigated some of the broads. This event proved to be very successful and was enjoyed by everyone who took part. The Beaver Colony held an outing to Belfast Zoo where they all had a wonderful time seeing the many strange animals around and then finishing off their visit with ice cream and popcorn. Cubs and Scouts continued to flourish with varied and active programmes. Beaver and Cub sections held their Christmas party on 17 December with many exciting games and activities taking place as well as a surprise visit from Santa Claus. Then, for the first time, the annual district carol service was held in Sandys Street Presbyterian Church and organised by the Group. A large attendance from all Groups in the district, together with parents, friends and supporters, made this event a memorable occasion.

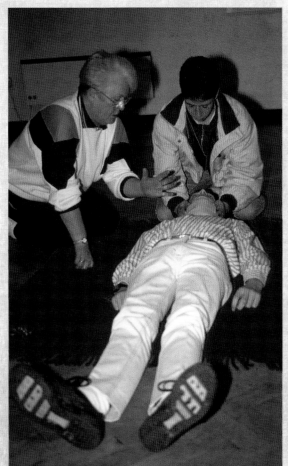

L-R front row: Dr. M. McKnight, Mrs. N. Grills, M. Ferris SL.
Middle row: John Lawson, V. Milsop, T. Wilson, E. Neill, D. Lawson.
Back row: P. McNeill, S. Finch, J. McNeill, R. Hamilton, J. Cunningham.

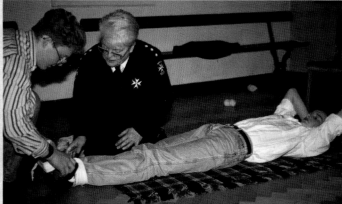

St John Ambulance First Aid course.

Presentation of first aid certificates.

Beavers at a day out to Crawfordsburn, 19 May 1990.

Beavers at a day out to Crawfordsburn, 19 May 1990.

1st Newry Beavers at a day outing to Dublin Zoo. The Beavers travelled down to Dublin by train with Beaver Leader Sandra McBlain.

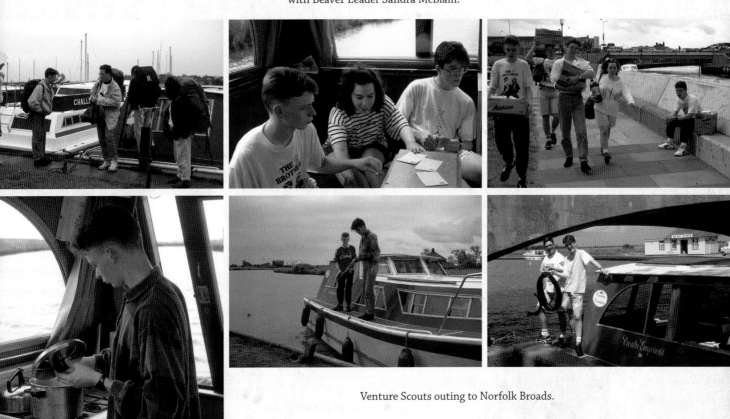

Venture Scouts outing to Norfolk Broads.

Above: 1st Newry 5-a-side hockey winners.

Left: Cub Glynn Moffett at camp lunch.

Below: Beavers and Cubs Christmas parties.

1991

All over the United Kingdom in 1991 the Cubs celebrated their 75th anniversary and Newry Cubs also took part in all the activities with enthusiasm and much enjoyment. The Group also celebrated its 80th anniversary year by holding a celebration night in the Scout hall. This event was well attended and many former members of the Group came along to celebrate this special occasion. The Beaver Colony celebrated the Silver Jubilee of the formation of Beavers in Northern Ireland in 1966 by taking part in a Northern Ireland Beaver day out to Dublin Zoo. The Cub football team won the district indoor football competition in Rathfriland while the Scout teams also won both the indoor football and hockey tournaments held in Newry High School.

The annual district St George's Day parade was held in Newry with the Service being held in Downshire Road Presbyterian Church whose support for the formation and continued existence of 1st Newry had always been greatly appreciated. The Cub Pack held its annual weekend outing to Mourne Park where once again a great time was had by all those who were present.

As part of the year's celebrations, the Troop held its annual camp at Kampeerterrein Staelduinhoeve, Gravenzande, Holland. During this camp the Scouts saw many of the wonderful places in the country, visiting The Hague and Delft by bicycle as well as many more distant places by train.

While the numbers of Beavers and Cubs continued to be satisfactory towards the end of 1991, the numbers in the Scout Troop began to decline and an effort was made to circulate the various churches about the benefits of Scouting to try to increase the membership. As was now the usual practice both Beavers and Cubs held their Christmas parties with presents being presented to each boy by Santa Claus.

Troop ready for the St George's Day parade.

Beavers ready for a day out at Crawfordsburn, May 1991.

Paul Murphy at Cub camp.

5-a-side district football, with District Commissioner David Payne and Tony Wilson.

Sadie McConnell

This year saw the tragic loss of one of the Group's longest serving members, Mrs Sadie McConnell. Sadie had been Group treasurer since 1955 and had provided sterling service, not only as treasurer, but also as a very active and enthusiastic member of the Parents Association over the many years during which she held office. Sadie was often seen serving refreshments at many of our events and was always in attendance at our numerous meetings and social occasions.

Wilson Robinson

Towards the end of 1991 another stalwart supporter of the Group, Mr Wilson Robinson, passed away. Wilson also served as district chairman and secretary for many years. He was the manager of the local Ulster Bacon factory and, as manager, often provided very valuable transport for our gear to the Troop's numerous camps at Mourne Park. It was not unknown to see our red minibus parked safely in the grounds of the factory and on many occasions Wilson persuaded some of his staff to give it a good steam hose to keep it clean and tidy.

1991 Annual camp at
Kampeerterrein Staelduinhoeve, Gravenzande, Holland

Roy Stevenson prepares for morning inspection.

David Revels (left) and Philip McNeil.

1992

In January the Chief Scout, Mr Garth Morrison, came to visit Mourne Park for the day and Newry Scouts and Cubs were there to meet and talk with him and to spend an excellent, if a somewhat very damp and cold, day out in the 'Park'. The Cub Pack celebrated winning the Northern Ireland Cub 5-a-side football competition at Omagh and later were guests of honour at a Civic Reception, hosted by Newry and Mourne District Council in the Arts Centre. The Cub Pack once again held its annual outing to Mourne Park where they made use of Kilkeel High School cottage and in what was glorious weather had a wonderful time. Owing to the declining numbers within the Scout section no annual camp was held this year but in order to make up for not holding an annual summer camp a number of weekend camps were held at Mourne Park and also quite a few hikes in the Mourne mountains. In September the District organised a Fun Day at Kilbroney Park, Rostrevor and Beavers, Cubs and Scouts from 1st Newry all attended this event and took part in the many activites which were organised during the day. Beavers and Cubs headed off on 17 October to Newcastle where they took part in a number of activities and ended the day with a campfire session organised by Gerry Watson in 1st Newcastle Scout hall. This year was not a particularly good year in the annals of the Group as it saw a decline in numbers throughout all sections of the Group although the activities and events provided continued to be of a very high standard.

Chief Scout, Garth Morrison (front row, fourth from right), with Group, District and County Scouters, January 1992

1st Newry Cubs at weekend camp at the cottage in Mourne Park. Assistant Cub leader Gavin McCullough teaches the Cubs how to pitch a hike tent.

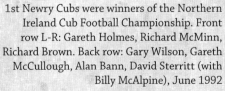

1st Newry Cubs were winners of the Northern Ireland Cub Football Championship. Front row L-R: Gareth Holmes, Richard McMinn, Richard Brown. Back row: Gary Wilson, Gareth McCullough, Alan Bann, David Sterritt (with Billy McAlpine), June 1992

Newry & Mourne District Council (NMDC) provided a civic reception in honour of the achievements of 1st Newry Cubs on winning the NI Football Cub Championship competition. Pictured here are council officials Councillors P. J. Bradley (left) and Danny Kennedy along with NMDC official Pamela Arthurs.

Cubs at camp in Mourne Park cooking and learning how to use a compass.

David Revels at a cooking competition in Warrenpoint

County Commissioner Gerry Watson at Newcastle Scout hall cub campfire, 17 October 1992.

District Fun Day at Kilbroney, Rostrevor. Cubs (L-R) David McBirney, Gareth McCullough and Alastair McAlpine are enjoying the 'snow' display kindly provided by the Fire Service, September 1992

1993

In June the Group said farewell to Assistant Scoutleader Neil Thompson who had been with the Group since 1985. The Group Committee held a family barbecue on 7 June which was very well supported and Beaver, Cub, Scout and parents games and activities were provided on the evening. During this year all of the sections took part in the Promise Appeal National Fund raising campaign and raised much needed finances for Headquarters through a wide variety of events. Cub camp was again held at Mourne Park in the cottage where activities included climbing Knockcree and swimming in the river.

The Troop held a number of weekend camps at Mourne Park and the boys were again taken by the leaders on hikes throughout the Mourne mountains. There was no annual camp this year as numbers were small and did not warrant one, however with the range of weekend activities provided the Troop did not miss out on learning new Scouting skills and having an exciting summer. Once again the committee members, together with friends and leaders, carried out minor repairs and a complete redecoration of the Scout hall. Numbers in all sections of the Group showed a small increase and leaders and committee members took a special interest in persuading young people to come along and join the Group.

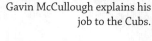
Gavin McCullough explains his job to the Cubs.

1st Newry Group at Corry Monument, 1993

1994

The year saw the Group continue with numbers being on the increase and the leaders continuing to provide an exciting and stimulating programme for all sections. The Parents Association also continued to flourish and a very successful table quiz was held in the hall on 1 February. Unfortunately our Beaver Leader, Sandra McBlain, resigned from the Group due to her home and work commitments. A Group barbecue was held at the Scout hall on 13 June. This event was well supported by parents and friends and ended with a much-appreciated slide show from Cub Scoutleader, William McAlpine. The year also saw all sections of the Group not only assisting with the district Fun Day, but also taking part in the many and varied activities held in Kilbroney Park, Rostrevor to raise funds for the replacement of the three bridges in Mourne Park. The

Cubs again held their weekend camp at Mourne Park which, as by now you will no doubt have noticed, certainly appears to be their very favourite camping ground. During the weekend they were shown how to erect a hike tent, light a fire, cook, and they also took part in the campfire. The Troop held its annual camp once again at Zellhof in Austria. The camp was well attended and those taking part enjoyed not only the hospitality of the staff at the campsite but also experienced the many and varied activities and visits arranged by the leaders.

Cub camp in Mourne Park. Above left: Alastair McAlpine, Kris Fletcher, Robert Hempkin and Gareth Warde enjoy their first night under canvass.

Mervyn Ferris is seen here investing new Scouts Mark Taylor (left) Alastair McAlpine and David McIlwrath (all holding the Scout flag). The investiture is assisted by Roy Stevenson and Garry McWhirter.

Alastair McAlpine's going up ceremony, June 1994

Scouts visit Exploris in Portaferry, July 1994. L-R: Alastair McAlpine, Roger Baines, David McIlwrath, Gareth Murphy

Annual camp at Zellhof in Austria, August 1994

Scouts at Mirabell Gardens, Salzburg where *The Sound of Music* was filmed. These are the 'Do-Re-Mi' steps.
L-R: G. McCullough ACSL, R. Stevenson, A. McAlpine, S. Revels, G. Murphy, C. Baines, R. Taylor, P. McNeill,
D. McIlwrath, G. McWhirter ASL.

Burg Hohenwerfen was the impregnable 'Schloss Adler' in *Where Eagles Dare*.

Above left: Preparing schnitzel for lunch. Tucking in (above right) are David McIlwrath (front), Colin Baines (centre) and Gareth Murphy.

217

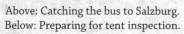

Above: Catching the bus to Salzburg.
Below: Preparing for tent inspection.

1995

On 8 February Mrs Carol McWhirter and her husband Garry, a former Venture Scout, joined the other leaders of 1st Newry and took on the roles of Beaver Scoutleader and Assistant Scoutleader respectively within the Group. Once again the Parents Association held a most successful family barbecue at the Scout hall on 26 June. Although numbers within the Troop were still very low the Troop held a very successful annual camp from 7 to 15 July at Blackwell Court, Bromsgrove, near Birmingham.

Silver Acorn for Billy McAlpine

In May 1995 Cub Scoutleader, William McAlpine, was presented with the Silver Acorn, the second highest award in Scouting, in recognition of distinguished service to Scouting. William had been a member of the Group since 1940, first as a Cub Scout and then as a Scout. In 1955 William, or Billy as he is affectonately known, took on the leadership of the Cub Pack and has continued to this day. The presentation was at Greenmount College, Antrim, where the retiring Chief Scout, Mr Garth Morrison, made the award.

Billy McAlpine (right) and his son Alastair meet up with Chief Scout Garth Morrison
after the Silver Acorn Award ceremony.

1995 Annual camp at Blackwell Court, Bromsgrove, near Birmingham

L-R: Billy McAlpine, Colin Baines, John McCague, Gareth Murphy, Mervyn Ferris, Alastair McAlpine, Garry McWhirter, Richard Strain, Stephen McAlpine, Gavin McCullough.

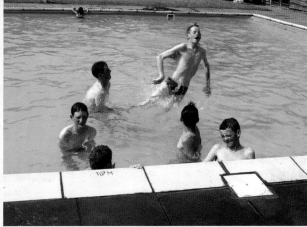

Visit to RAF Cosford.
Above: an Avro Lincoln. Right: Alastair McAlpine in an ejector seat.

Visit to Alton Towers, July 1995
Front row L-R: Gareth Murphy, Richard Strain, Alastair McAlpine.
Middle: Stephen McAlpine, John McCague, Colin Baines.
Back: Garry McWhirter ASL, Mervyn Ferris SL, William McAlpine CSL, Gavin McCullough ACSL.

Above and top: Visit to William
Shakespeare's house.
Right: Visit to Cadbury World.
Below: Billy McAlpine finds his mark.

1996

At the beginning of February all the Cubs in the Cub Pack, who had been tutored by Mrs McDonald, were able gain their First Aid certificates which were then presented on 5 February. One of the sixes from the Cub Pack took part in the Dora Baxter flag competition during a weekend in April and, although not managing to win this event, had a good time in taking part in the various activities and having new experiences.

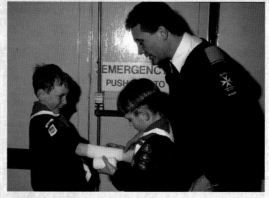

Cubs first aid training and certificate presentation.

The Newry District Fun Day which was organised in Kilbroney Park, saw all the Beavers, Cubs, and Scouts taking part in this event and having a thoroughly magnificent time. At the end of June nine Cubs, under the leadership of Billy McAlpine, held their annual weekend camp at the cottage at Mourne Park where they tried their hand at cooking on an open fire, climbed Knockcree, swam in the river and undertook many other exciting activities. All arrived home well and truly exhausted but looking forward to other such events. This year, being the 80th anniversary year of Cub Scouting, saw the Cub Scout Pack taking part in a wide range of activities with the theme being 'Around the World in Eighty Days'. One of the highlights was receiving a message of greetings from Australia sent by Mrs M. Cannon, nee Margaret McCullough. The Troop held its annual camp at Loans in Scotland. As numbers attending camp this year were small, just eight Scouts, it was decided to avail of the use of 1st Loans Scout hall instead of the usual camp under canvas.

Silver Acorn for Mervyn Ferris

In May Scoutleader, Mervyn Ferris, was honoured by the award of the Silver Acorn in recognition of distinguished service to Scouting. Mervyn had been a most active and long-serving member of the Group, first as a Scout and subsequently as a Senior Scout, Senior Scoutleader, Venture Scoutleader and Scoutleader over many years. Mervyn, currently the District Commissioner, has held this office on a number of occasions within Newry District as well as Assistant District Commissioner for Scouts and Venture Scouts and is also Warden for Mourne Park campsites, a position he has now held for thirty eight years. The presentation was made by the new Chief Scout, Mr George Purdy, the first Chief Scout to have come from Northern Ireland.

Mervyn Ferris with Chief Scout George Purdy

District Fun Day at Kilbroney, June 1996.

Cubs at the Dora Baxter competition, 20 April 1996.

80th anniversary of Cub Scouting celebrations, 'Around the World in Eighty Days'.

Cub camp at Mourne Park, June 1996.

1996 Annual camp at Loans, near Troon, Scotland

Scouts (L-R): Mark Taylor, Alastair McAlpine, Gareth Murphy, Samuel Strain, John McCague, David McIlwrath, Colin Baines.
Leaders (L-R): Gavin McCullough, Philip McNeill (Venture Scout Helper), Garry McWhirter, Mervyn Ferris, Billy McAlpine.

Scouts stayed in the Loans Scout hall instead of under canvas this year.

The troop visited the Maritime Museum in Irvine.

Above: The Troop at the Magnum Centre, Irvine.
Below: At church in Ayr.

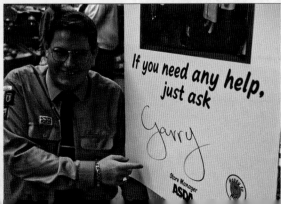

1997

The year opened with a big surprise for Cub Scoutleader, William McAlpine. Billy was indeed surprised but honoured to see his name in the New Years Honours list with the award of the MBE in recognition of services to Scouting. On Monday evening, 10 February, during Cub night, the Pack was visited by former member and long time supporter Robert McCullough who came along with a supply of timber, nails and other equipment to supervise the Cubs constructing seventeen bird boxes. All the Cubs really got involved in this activity and everyone took home a well-made box to be placed in their garden. Once again the Cub Pack entered a six for the Dora Baxter flag competition where they all had a great time but unfortunately did not manage to bring home the flag.

Former Scout Robert McCullough (left) is pictured with 1st Newry Cubs at the bird box building night. Robert helped the boys make a bird box of their own in one night and each of the Cubs is holding the finished product.

Cubs at the Dora Baxter comptition.

Then following this, on 25 April, the Group held an 80th anniversary dinner to celebrate the formation of Cub Scouts in 1916. The dinner was extremely well attended with many former members of the Group present. During the course of the dinner the Group also recognised the sterling services given by Mrs Margaret McGaffin and Mr Jack White over a long number of years by the presentation of Long Service Awards. Margaret had held the office of secretary of the Parents Association for some fifteen or sixteen years and still continued to help with the running of the Group, always taking a keen interest in all its activities. Jack White, who had held the offices of vice chairman and chairman of the Parents Association for some twenty years, continues to give his support to the Group and attends all the functions organised.

80th anniversary dinner, 25 April 1997.

At the Annual District Scout Dinner Newry's Jack White and Margaret McGaffin are presented with Long Service (15 years or more) Certificates by County Commissioner Belle Bell (left in uniform) and Hannah Webster, Newry District Commissioner.

April and May also saw the Scouts holding a number of weekend camps at Mourne Park and in the Mourne mountains in preparation for their annual camp. Flying helicopters, or rather just having a seat inside one, was the next event for the Cubs when later in the month they paid a visit to the Army barracks at Bessbrook Mill. All the Cubs were shown around the Mill with the highlight of the evening being able to clamber into a helicopter to see all the controls and be told how this huge flying machine works. Following the excitement of a few weeks earlier, the Cubs next event was their annual camp at Mourne Park where this year they were able to sleep out in one of the Scout patrol tents on a site close to the cottage.

Cub camp at Mourne Park, June 1997.
Above left: Mrs F. McCullough, Mrs M. McGaffin and Mrs J. McAlpine.

William McAlpine, MBE

On 23 July 1997 Billy McAlpine, along with his wife Johan, and son Alastair, attended Buckingham Palace where he was presented with the MBE by Her Majesty, The Queen. This was a very special occasion for all and one which will not be forgotten for a long time.

Billy with his wife and son at the Palace steps.

Billy at the Chapel of the Order of the British Empire, St Paul's Cathedral.

25 April 1997 – 1st Newry put on a special evening to mark the fact that Billy McAlpine had been awarded the MBE for services to Scouting in Newry. Here Billy and Johan McAlpine are pictured with two of the men (Robert McCullough and Noel Hodgett) who were instrumental in the background nomination work of Billy's award.

10 March 1997 – here is the whole of 1st Newry Group from the Beavers in grey tops on the front row, followed by the Cubs and then Scouts. The Leaders from the left Garry McWhirter (ASL), Tina Henry (ABSL), Mervyn Ferris (SL), Carol McWhirter (BSL), Billy McAlpine (CSL), and Gavin McCullough (ACSL).

1st Newry Cubs make a once-in-a-lifetime visit to Army base in Bessbrook Mill. The Cubs and leaders met with the 1st Battalion Welsh Guards. The Cubs were shown around the whole military base at the former Bessbrook Mill site including the helicopter pad – which, at the height of the 'Troubles', was known as the busiest heliport in Europe. Above right: Lee McWhirter fancies himself as a pilot.

From 14 to 25 August the Troop annual camp was held once again at the Hook of Holland. This was a small camp as the Scout Troop was low in numbers and only four or five members participated. Unfortunately Garry McWhirter, Assistant Scout Leader, who was to come along, had to be admitted urgently to hospital just two days before the camp and Billy McAlpine took his place at the last moment. Sadly Garry missed the camp but happily made a full recovery from his illness. Christmas time was soon upon all of the sections and once again the Beavers and Cubs held their Christmas party with Santa Claus being in attendance to give out presents.

1997 Annual camp at Hook of Holland

Above: Gareth Murphy cooks a schnitzel and the scouts visit Airborne Museum Oosterbeek

Visiting the klompenmaker, Colin Baines took the opportunity to try the clogs on for size.

Madurodam, a miniature city in Scheveningen, the Hague.

L-R: John McCague, Colin Baines, Gareth Murphy shopping for presents.

18 October 1997, Scouts Jamboree on the Air (JOTA) year. Here members of 1st Dromore CBSI invited 1st Newry Cubs down for the morning to try out the short wave band radio. CBSI Leader Paddy Trainor (wearing blue uniform) explains to the boys what it's all about. Newry Cub Gareth Young is seen here on the radio with another Scout in Europe.

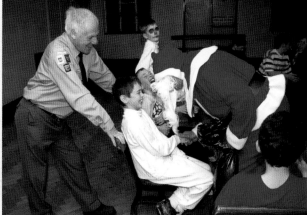

Cubs Christmas party.

Gareth Young and Chris Brown at a carol service, 21 December 1997.

1998

Saturday 25 April saw the Cub Six heading off for Crawfordsburn Scout Activity centre to take part in the Dora Baxter flag competition where the six Cubs took part in a number of marked activities and games during the day. Although everyone had a good time, the Cubs did not manage to bring home the flag. During the month of June the Cub Pack attended the County Cub Camp which was held at Mourne Park. Although the weather deteriorated during the weekend, all the Cubs enjoyed the activities and arrived home safely if rather tired and weary. Unfortunately this year, due to the shortage and unavailability of leaders, there was no Scout annual camp held but this was compensated by quite a number of weekend camps which were held in Mourne Park and hikes in the Mourne mountains.

At the beginning of August the Venture Scouts, along with leaders and other helpers, set up a number of marquees and tents to accommodate Scouts arriving from the Crawfordsburn anniversary camp. Members of the Parents Committee and others provided meals for the event whilst the leaders arranged and supervised the activities on site. On this occasion the meals were purchased from and centrally cooked at Daisy Hill hospital and brought to the site daily by Mervyn Ferris. Everyone who attended the event agreed that it was a great success.

On Monday night, 16 November, there was a great deal of noise to be heard in the Scout hall when the Cub Pack held a car rally night. The Cubs had brought their remote controlled cars along and a number of 'Grand Prix' races were held during the evening. Everyone agreed that the evening had been a marvellous success. Again in December the Beaver and Cub sections held their Christmas party and even though the years were progressing Santa Claus still managed to come along and hand out gifts for everyone.

Cubs at the Dora Baxter flag competition, Crawfordsburn.

Cubs at weekend camp, Mourne Park, June 1998

Left: Venture Scouts with leaders putting up the marquee for the Crawfordsburn anniversary camp (above), August 1998.

Cub rally night, 16 November 1998.

Cub Christmas party.
Above: Cub Robert Henry with Santa Claus

1999

The Cub Pack visited the Ardmore Police station where they were shown around the premises and the equipment used by the police for their daily duties. They were shown how fingerprints were taken and how accurate descriptions of events or people could help the police carry out their role to protect the community. The Cubs were then allowed to try out the gym equipment before finishing their visit with lemonade and crisps.

Sadly the death took place of Sam Cassidy who had been Scoutleader with the Group from 1950 until the early sixties. Sam had been instrumental in revitalising the Group in 1950 and had taken a very active role in organising and carrying out the work to construct suitable premises for the Group's meetings from the early 1950s and onwards. Also this year Mr Robert Baird, who had been a member of the Parents Association for a long time and vice president for a number of years, sadly passed away. Once again this year the Cub Pack attended the County Cub weekend camp which was held at Castlewellan Forest Park where they all had a wonderful time. Unfortunately again this year the Troop did not have an annual summer camp due to the fact that leaders were not available to take the Troop away, but the leaders did compensate by organising a number of weekend camps at Mourne Park and in the Mournes. Gavin McCullough, Assistant Cub Scoutleader, was presented with the Ten Year Certificate for service to the Group, while William McAlpine, Cub Scoutleader, was also presented with the Chief Scout's Award for 40 years' service to the Movement. The District Commissioner, Mrs Hannah Webster, made both presentations.

Cubs visit Ardmore Police Station, 1 February 1999.

Cub camp at Castlewellan, June 1999.

George Graham (left) and Ross McWhirter at camp kitchen duties.

Left, front to back: George Graham, John Taylor, Richard Taylor, Gavin McCullough. Right, front to back: Robert Henry, Paul Girvan, Billy McAlpine.

Cub camp at Castlewellan, June 1999.

Beavers' Halloween party, October 1999.

2000s

1st Newry at the Centenary Jamboree, Hylands Park, July 2007
L-R front row: B. Williamson, C. Bagnall, S. Poucher, J. Wilson, A. Hodgett,
J. Mitchell, D. Kernaghan, J. McGrath, G. Hodgett, W. Nummy.
Back row: M. Ferris SL, G. McWhirter ASL, D. Whiteside, P. Girvan,
L. McWhirter, J. Whiteside, C. Whiteside ASL, C. Baines, W. McAlpine CSL.

2000

The deaths took place of our vice president, Mrs W. Robinson, and Mrs G. Ferris and Mr David McConnell who had both been keen supporters of the Group. The Parents Association organised a flower arranging evening for all the parents and supporters. Mrs Rae Dodds, a past Cub Scoutleader in Bessbrook and District Commissioner for a time, demonstrated her flower arranging skills to those assembled and gave various hints and ideas to the parents on the best way to present flowers in their homes and churches. The evening was a wonderful success, with everyone looking forward to future events of a similar nature. A team of Cubs took part in the Dora Baxter flag competition and after completing all the requirements were delighted to have gained second place. Carol McWhirter, Beaver Scoutleader, completed the requirements for her Wood Badge training with the

Flower arranging evening.

certificate being presented on 13 April. Over the weekend 26 - 28 May the Scout Troop took part in the Millennium Celebration Camp which was held at Crawfordsburn Scout Centre with the Cub Pack coming along for a day visit on the Saturday. The Beavers, Cubs and Scouts along with their leaders took part in the St George's Day parade and service as well as attending Children's Day services in Downshire Road and Sandys Street Presbyterian churches and the Methodist Church.

This year the Troop held their annual camp, not under canvas as is the usual practice, but at Baden-Powell House in London. Garry McWhirter, Assistant Scoutleader, and Mervyn Ferris, Scoutleader, accompanied the Scouts and, whilst there, toured the sights of the city of London. All those present really enjoyed the occasion which was new to them, with some of the Scouts never having visited the capital city before. Mrs Alison Kernaghan took on the role of Assistant Beaver Scoutleader during the year. William McAlpine, Cub Scoutleader, received a Special Youth Award from the Southern Education and Library Board for his services to the youth of Newry, especially Scouting. Coming up to Christmas both the Beavers and Cubs held their annual party with Santa Claus calling in as usual to distribute the many gifts.

Dora Baxter flag competition, 1 April 2000. The cubs took second place.

L-R front row: G. Graham, I. McMillan, D. Whiteside.
Back row: W. McAlpine CSL, P. Girvan, R. Taylor, N. Irwin G. McCullough ACSL.

Millennium camp, Crawfordsburn

L-R back row: G. Hamilton, S. Lennon. Middle: R. Little, M. Kernaghan.
Front: P. Taylor, J. Kernaghan, N. Irwin, J. Lennon, B. McAlpine.

L-R: G. McWhirter ASL, J. Hanna,
J. Whiteside (hidden), L. McWhirter,
S. Henry, R. Campbell, R. Morgan,
J. McCague, G. Young.

Annual camp at Baden-Powell House, London.
Top left: Madame Tussaud's. Above left: In the changing rooms at Wembley Stadium.

Billy McAlpine cooking
sausages with cubs (L-R) David
Kernaghan, Richard Taylor,
Ross McWhirter.

1st Newry Group, 2000.

Cubs' Christmas party, 11 December 2000.

Cubs playing conkers with Gavin McCullough.

2001

The year began with Colin Whiteside, a former Cub, Scout and Venture Scout, agreeing to take on the role of Assistant Scoutleader with the Troop. The Cub Pack held a very successful first aid course run by Mrs Mary McDonald and all learnt a great deal of how to handle various situations and our thanks were expressed to Mrs McDonald for giving her time to help us in this way. In April some of the Scout Troop took part in a hike along Banns road up to Lough Shannagh where they camped overnight and then hiked out on the Sunday morning to arrive home tired and hungry and ready for a good rest.

As the Troop had been in existence for more than ninety years it was decided to celebrate this and hold annual camp abroad this year. The site chosen was one of the Troop's favourites, Zellhof Scout camp at Mattsee in Austria. There was a full attendance for this anniversary camp and everyone had a great time. Prior to a special event in November, a number of the committee and the leaders carried out renovations and redecoration to the Scout hall and the Group was particularly thankful to Mr W. V. Hogg for presenting the Group with enough carpet to lay on the floor of our hall. Thanks were also due to Sean McDonald for tiling the kitchen and helping to make it more hygienic and clean. The Group held an anniversary dinner in Sandys Street Church Hall in November to which a large number of 'Old Boys', friends and supporters came along. The evening went with a swing with everyone having a marvellous time and meeting many old friends and colleagues from 'yesteryear'. The year ended with the Beaver and Cub Christmas parties with Santa Claus paying his usual visit to a very excited audience.

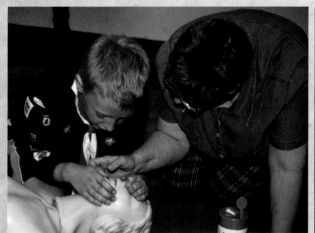 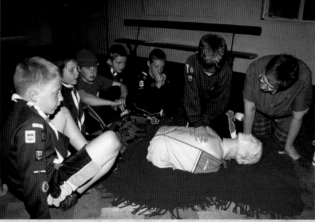

Cubs receiving first aid training from Mary McDonald.

Cubs crafts. Above right: David Whiteside.

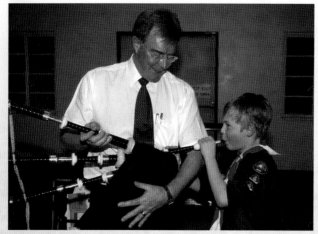

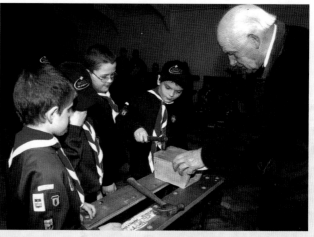

Cub David Whiteside tests his lung capacity on a set of bagpipes. Robert McCullough shows the cubs how to make a bird box.

Beaver and Cub sports, 31 May 2001
L-R back row: B. McAlpine, S. Pasparaki, G. Hodgett, S. Lennon, A. Baird, A. Hanna.
Front: N. Irwin, C. Fullerton, J. Lennon, J. Kernaghan, S. Hughes.

90th anniversary celebrations

1st Newry Group on Remembrance Sunday, 11 November 2001

Blue Peter stamps appeal

Troop ready for Austria.

Cubs' and Beavers' Christmas parties.

2002

As this was the Golden Jubilee of the Queen's accession to the throne, discussions took place as to how the Group would partake in the numerous celebrations which would be held during the year. It was agreed that the leaders would be part of the Jubilee organising committee and the Group would be responsible for undertaking some of the events. Robert McCullough once again came along to the Cub Pack and assisted the Cubs in making a number of bird boxes which they all took home to hang in their gardens. On 26 April Assistant Cub Scoutleader Gavin McCullough was married in Downshire Road Presbyterian Church. On coming out of the church both Gavin and Alison were surprised to see the Cubs and Scouts gathered there. The Scouts and their leaders took part in a number of hikes in the Mournes. Jubilee celebrations took place in Newry in June with a parade, fun fair, races and a barbecue being held in Windsor Hill school field. 1st Newry Scout Group organised and ran the fun fair, races and barbecue, as well as organising painting and poetry competitions for all schools in the Newry district.

Cubs and Scouts surprised Gavin and Alison McCullough on their wedding day, 26 April 2002.

Job Week, which was held in April, proved to be very successful. The boys and leaders also set up a display of the history of Scouting in the Scout hall. The Young Men's Christian Institute in Newry (Y.M.C.I.) presented the Group with a cheque for £500 towards the cost of running the Jubilee events and the purchase of a pool table for the use of the Group. The Group also held a sponsored balloon race by selling tickets with prizes going to the purchaser of the balloons which travelled the furthest distance. The Group organised the shooting and editing of a video of all the various Jubilee activities which had taken place during the year, and this was put on sale to the general public. The profit from this venture was distributed equally between the Northern Ireland Children's Hospice and Newry Hospice. Members of the Scout Troop and Venture Unit helped the Newry Lions Club to raise the sum of £350 from bag packing at Dunne's Stores on a number of occasions. The first bag packing proved very eventful as the weather took a turn for the worse just as the event began and, with torrential rain pouring down, the number of shoppers was drastically reduced. Then in the midst of this lighting struck and that, together with the rain, fused the electrics in Dunne's store bringing the night to an abrupt end. However the second attempt proved more successful and everyone went home well pleased with the outcome.

Although numbers in the Scout Troop remained quite low, the Troop decided to hold their annual camp at Tawd Vale near Liverpool. Eight Scouts and two leaders took part in this event under the leadership of Garry McWhirter, Assistant Scoutleader. The Cub Pack held its annual weekend outing at the Tain Centre, Omeath where all the Cubs had a wonderful time taking part in the various events as well as using the indoor swimming pool. Beaver Scoutleader Carol McWhirter organised a special Halloween party and fireworks display for the Beaver Scouts at the end of October. The Cubs also joined with the Beavers for the firework display. Scoutleader Mervyn Ferris agreed, once again, to take on the role of District Commissioner for Newry District.

Cubs and Beavers at Easter. Robert McCullough helped the Cubs build bird boxes.

2002 Annual camp at Tawd Vale, near Liverpool

Jonathan Whiteside, Gareth Young and Iain McMillan wait
their turn for the climbing wall.

Cubs and Beavers at Christmas
L-R back row: D. Williamson, S. Martin, A. Shahid, S. Hughes, A. Hodgett (on Santa's knee), H. Stinson, J. Lennon, C. Fullerton. Middle: A. Priestly, J. McKee, T. Girvan. Front: Z. Shahid, M. Davis, C. Martin, J. Kernaghan, N. McElroy.

2003

In January the Troop entered two teams in the District 5-a-side hockey competition where they managed to achieve winners and runners up medals. The previous year turned out to be the last year for Job Week as Scout Headquarters had taken the decision to cease this form of fund raising for Groups mainly due to child protections issues. Following this decision there was much discussion within the Group regarding alternative methods of funding for capitation fees and general running costs for the Group. It was decided to introduce the Gift Aid scheme which had been introduced by the government in place of the covenant scheme, and ask each family with members in the Group to pay an annual membership fee on which we could then claim Gift Aid payment from the government. The number of Scouts in the Troop had now increased to sixteen and the Scoutleaders were very pleased that things were on the 'up'. The Beaver and Cub sports were well supported by Newry Beavers and Cubs and the Beavers managed to win the cup while both Cubs and Beavers won quite a few medals in the various events. During the months of April and May the leaders again took the Scouts for a number of weekend camps and also hiked through the Mourne mountains. A very well attended parents evening was held in the garden to the rear of the Scout hall when a number of activities and games were held for both the parents and the boys.

The annual Scout camp this year was held at Fordell Firs, near Stirling, in Scotland. Eight Scouts, two Explorers and two leaders took part in this event. The Tain Centre was once again the venue in September for the Cub weekend event when ten Cubs accompanied by the leaders attended and all had a magic time. The year was brought to a close with a Cub car rally night in November and a Christmas party for the Beaver Colony and Cub Pack.

L-R: Ross McWhirter, Jonathan Whiteside, Sam Henry, Robert Henry, Iain McMillan

L-R: Lee McWhirter, John Bell, David Whiteside, Nicholas Irwin, Paul Girvan.

Beaver sports at Windsor Hill Primary School field. Above right: Zain Shahid wins the cup!

Parent's night, 27 June 2003.

Mervyn Ferris receives his District Commissioner warrant from
County Commissioner, Jack Darragh, 20 May 2003.

Scouts pony trekking at Castlewellan, May 2003. L-R: Stephen Murdock, Lee McWhirter, Sam Henry, David Whiteside.

Cubs annual outing to the Tain Centre, Omeath, 20-21 September 2003.
Above left, front row L-R: G. Hodgett, A. Patterson, P. Taylor, J. Kernaghan, C. Fullerton, J. Larkin. Back row : A. Priestley,
J. Larkin, S. Holmes, D. Henry, S. Hughes, M. Kernaghan, along with Leaders C. Baines, Alison Kernaghan, G. McCullough,
L. McWhirter and W. McAlpine.

2003 Annual camp, Fordell Firs, Stirling

L-R front row: D. Kernaghan, R. Henry, C. Fullerton, S. Murdock, J. Bell, S. Henry.
Middle: D. Whiteside, I. McMillan. Back: J. Whiteside, R. McWhirter, P. Girvan,
L. McWhirter.

Just finished caving and all found the way out:
L-R: J. Whiteside, I. McMillan, R. McWhirter, S. Henry, J. Bell.

Cubs and Beavers Halloween parties.

Pictured here along with leaders G. McCullough, L. McWhirter and W. McAlpine are Cubs J. Gray, A. Hanna, S. Pasparakis, R. Neill, S. Hughes, C. Fullerton, W. Elliott, A. Priestley, J. Larkin, A. Shahid, J. Larkin, D. Henry.

Santa Claus with David Henry.

2004

The Parents Association organised a nursery rhyme quiz to help raise funds for the Group, and the Beavers, Cub, Scouts and Explorers all sold sheets. A prize was presented to the member who sold the greatest number of sheets as well as a prize for the winner of the quiz. Mrs Joan Elliott won the quiz while Wendy O'Hagan sold the most number of quiz sheets. During the early part of the year the Scouts attended Kilkeel swimming pool where they were given tuition by Mr Newell in the handling of canoes and taught how to escape from a capsized canoe. The Beavers were very busy during the early part of the year in making Mother's Day cards as well as making gingerbread men and pancakes. Mr Jack White indicated that he wished to relinquish the post of chairman of the Parents Association so a very keen parent, Mrs Gwen Patterson, agreed to fill the vacancy. Beaver and Cub sports were held in Windsor Hill school field and both sections came away with many medals while the Cub football team won the final match to win the District cup for this event. The Scout leaders again took Scouts on a number of hikes and weekend camps in preparation for their annual camp which was to be held in England. The Beaver colony attended the Rally Day at Crawfordsburn where they all had a great time and enjoyed taking part in all the activities which were provided on site. At the end of June the Group held another successful barbecue for the parents. At the beginning of July the Group assisted the organisers of the annual golf competition, known as the Ferris Cup, held at Kilkeel

Golf Club, by obtaining sponsors for the event and in return receiving a donation from the organisers. This event proved to be very popular and the Group was handsomely rewarded with a substantial cheque from the organising committee.

Scout annual camp this year was held at Longridge Scout Water Activity Centre at Marlow in Buckinghamshire when twelve Scouts, four Explorers and four leaders took part. During camp the Scouts took part in canoeing, sailing, rowing and dragon boating as well as a number of day trips to various places of interest. Of course each patrol had to carryout their own cooking and washing up as well as maintaining their tent and kitchen area in a clean and satisfactory condition. Another of our faithful friends, Mrs McDonald, again gave her time to train the Cubs in first aid and so all managed to get their first aid badge. In October the Cub Pack held their annual outing at Shannaghmore Outdoor Pursuits centre. John McKee and Colin McElroy offered their services as Assistant Cub Scoutleaders with the Cub Pack. John was a former Cub, Scout and Venture Scout, while Colin was a former Cub and Scout with the Group. Both offers were gratefully accepted, as there was a shortage of leaders in both the Cub and Scout sections.

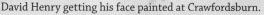

David Henry getting his face painted at Crawfordsburn.

Beaver sports, May 2004.

Cubs with the District football cup.

Scouts ready for annual camp, July 2004.
L-R front row: D. Whiteside, A. Patterson, N. Irwin, G. Hodgett. 2nd row: S. Murdock, S. Henry, J. Bell, A. Irwin, D. Kernaghan, M. Kernaghan. 3rd row: R. Fullerton, R. Henry, J. Whiteside, P. Girvan, L. McWhirter, I. McMillan, R. McWhirter. Back row: C. Baines, C. Whiteside ASL, G. McWhirter ASL, G. Irwin ASL.

2004 Annual camp, Longridge Scout Water Activity Centre, Marlow

Paul Girvan's birthday, 19 July 2004

The Troop at the Tower of London

The London Eye

Thorpe Park

Mourne hike, October 2004.
L-R: John Bell, Lee McWhirter, Jonathan Whiteside, Ross McWhirter (hidden), Paul Girvan.

2005

The Beaver Colony activities during the year included Christmas and Mothers' Day card making, pancake cooking, mobile construction, Halloween and Christmas parties and a range of craft activities, and of course a visit to see Santa when he arrived at Crawfordsburn when the Beavers had a great night playing games and learning the true meaning of Christmas. During the brighter nights some of the activities were carried out in the local park. Our Cub Pack commenced the year with 13 members on the roll. After receiving members from the Beaver section and some new recruits the Pack ended the year with a total of 18 Cubs. The Cub Pack held a number of very exciting and interesting nights in which all the Cubs took part. There was an interesting visit by the Ambulance Service and yet more pancake making. Cub football was enjoyed by all even though Newry lost to Rathfriland Cubs. A treasure hunt took place in June and Cubs came along to the Group barbecue before their summer break. October saw many of the Cubs setting off for their weekend at Shannaghmore Outdoor Education Centre where they all had a really magnificent time. They hiked up the lower slopes of Slieve Donard at night, canoed at Castlewellan and took part in climbing, a rope course, blind trails and archery. All too soon the wonderful weekend was over and all headed home again looking forward to next year's event. Cubs enjoyed a craft night in November and in December held a Christmas Party with Santa arriving to give everyone a present. At the end of the year both the Beavers and Cubs had a really good Christmas party with lots of fun and games and ending with Santa's visit.

Top: Visit from the Ambulance Service.
Above left: Cubs' pancake night. Above right: Cubs and Beavers bowling at Sheepbridge.

Cub car rally night.

Cubs prepared to get wet at Shannaghmore Outdoor Education Centre.

The announcement of the award of the Silver Wolf to former Scoutleader, Noel Hodgett, was made in January of this year. The award, which is only presented for services of the most exceptional nature to Scouting, is the highest honour bestowed upon a leader within the Scout Movement. Noel received his award from the Northern Ireland Chief Commissioner, Philip Scott, on 18 May 2005.

The Scout Troop proved to be active with a wide range of activities provided. The Scouts took part in many and varied activities both indoors and outside. Swimming at Lisburn Leisure complex, a short hike in the Mournes, ten pin bowling, archery, air rifle shooting, mini pioneering, an ice hockey visit, clay pigeon shooting and a barbecue, as well as their usual Friday night activities. Annual Camp this year was held at Crawfordsburn. Twelve Scouts and four Leaders took part and everyone had a marvellous time with many varied and exciting activities and visits having been undertaken. They went on a fishing trip off Bangor, as well as participating in artificial caving, archery, climbing,

Gavin McCullough receiving his Medal of Merit from County Commissioner Jack Darragh.

Noel Hodgett is presented with the Silver Wolf by N.I. Chief Commissioner Philip Scott, 18 May 2005

Robert McCullough receiving his Silver Acorn from N.I. Chief Commissioner Philip Scott, 18 May 2005

abseiling, swimming and hiking. Of course, as everyone knows, Scouting encourages the boys to be self sufficient and resourceful and so camp is not all fun and games as the Scouts have to do all their own cooking, washing up and keeping their kit and tents clean and tidy ready for inspection at any time. It is also an early start in the mornings with everyone having to be up by 7.30 am with breakfast cooked and all washed up for 9.00 am for inspection and ready to take part in the various activities and outings. All those taking part in the camp said that this was a good camp and everyone is now looking forward to next year's event which will be held in Austria.

All sections took part in the annual St George's Day service in Warrenpoint as well as attending Children's Day services at Downshire Road Presbyterian and Methodist churches. All our leaders and Explorer Scouts completed the first response course held in our hall during October and November and successfully gained their certificates. Again all sections attended the Remembrance Day ceremony at the Cenotaph in November. Beavers, Cubs and Scouts took part in the Christmas carol service at Clonallon Parish Church in December.

Cubs and Beavers making Christmas cards and decorations.
Above left, L-R: J. Gibson, D. Truesdale, J. Donnelly, S. Scott, C. Davis, D. J. White, J. Poucher, R. Smith.

Christmas party.   Halloween party.

2005 Annual camp, Crawfordsburn

L-R front row: A. Patterson, J. McGrath.
2nd row: D. Whiteside, J. McGuinness, S. Holmes,
D. Kernaghan.
3rd row: L. McWhirter, R. McWhirter, P. Girvan, I. McMillan.
Back row: W. McAlpine CSL, M. Ferris SL, G. McWhirter ASL.

Below: Weekend camp at Mourne Park, 2005.

Some members of the Troop and Explorers had a go at karting, 26 May 2005.

Ross McWhirter presents a cheque to the Special Care Baby Unit after getting his hair cut.

2006

As part of its community service at the end of January 2006, the Group made a presentation of a cheque to Dr Tariq to be used to help his fellow countrymen and women following the earthquake in Pakistan.

Discussions took place in respect of activities arranged to celebrate the centenary of the formation of the Scout Movement by Robert Baden-Powell. The Beaver activities during the year included Christmas and Mothers' Day card making, pancake cooking, mobile construction, Halloween and Christmas parties as well as a range of craft activities. We have also embarked upon some of the centenary activities to celebrate the 100 years of Scouting. During the brighter nights many of the activities were carried out in the local park or in the grounds of Windsor Hill primary school. Many other activities too numerous to mention were also carried out in our own hall and everyone enjoyed the excitement and fun.

During the year the Cub Pack held a number of very exciting and interesting nights in which all the Cubs took part. In June Cub football was enjoyed by all even though Newry lost to Rathfriland Cubs. Also in June the boys took part in a cycle run at Gosford Park. A treasure hunt took place in June and Cubs came along to the Group barbecue before our summer break. On 8 October many of the Cubs set off for their weekend at Shannaghmore Outdoor Education Centre where they all had a really magnificent time. They hiked up the lower slopes of Slieve Donard at night, canoed at Castlewellan, took part in climbing, a rope course, a blind trail and archery. All too soon the wonderful weekend was over and all headed home tired but very pleased that they had attended this event. Cubs enjoyed a craft night in November and in December a visit to the planetarium along with the Scouts took place. There was a Christmas Party for the Beavers and Cubs with Santa arriving to give everyone a present and this was enjoyed by all.

Following on from his Silver Wolf award in 2005, Noel Hodgett was presented with a long service award this year. Unfortunately, due to Noel's ill health, he was unable to be present at the official award presentations and so the award was made at Noel's home in Crieve Court by the County Commissioner, Mr Stephen Donaldson, accompanied by the county secretary, Mr James Dorrian.

Once again this year the Scout Troop was very active with a wide range of activities provided. We received a number of Cubs from the Pack but had a number of leavers during the year and ended the year with an overall slight reduction in numbers compared to the previous year. The Scouts took part in a wide range of activities both indoors and outdoors — swimming at Lisburn Leisure Complex, hikes in the Mourne mountains, ten pin bowling, archery, air rifle shooting, backwoods cooking, mini pioneering, clay pigeon shooting and a barbecue, as well as our usual Friday night activities.

Our various sections took part in the annual St George's Day service in Newry as well as attending Children's Day services at Downshire Road Presbyterian and the Methodist churches. Beavers, Cubs, Scouts and Venture Scouts along with the leaders attended the Remembrance Day ceremony at the Cenotaph in November. As part of its community service some of our older Scouts helped with the Remembrance evening in Bessbrook Town Hall in November, where they sold programmes and directed people to their seats.

Top and above left: Cubs on a cycle run in Gosford Park. Above right: Pancake night.

2006 Annual camp, Zellhof

Of course the highlight of any Scouting year is annual camp which this year was international. On 27 June 2006 we jetted off to Zellhof in Austria where we camped for the next eight days until our return flight home on 6 July. During our stay everyone had a great time and enjoyed the hospitality and kindness of our brother and sister Scouts at the wonderful setting beside the lake near the lovely village of Mattsee. While at camp all took part in a number of visits to see the wonderful sights in Austria. Just across the border into Germany, we visited some of the locations where *The Sound of Music* was filmed, went to see the salt mines and also the Eagle's Nest, where Hitler stayed during the 2nd World War. The scenery from this vantage point was

breathtaking and all enjoyed the day out. We also toured the lovely city of Salzburg and paid a visit to the wonderful Water Gardens just outside the city. Everyone was taken by surprise with the ingenuity of the water displays and almost everyone got wet and cooled down during their visit. The Scouts also took part in a number of very interesting and thrilling activities during their stay. These included partaking in the high rope course, very high indeed, and canyoning in the very deep gorges of the Salzach River in its very cold water. On another day the Scouts went abseiling and rafting on the Salzach River. While the junior Scouts were rafting the Explorers took part in hydrospeed, again on the cold and fast flowing Salzach River. While in camp we met other Scouts from different countries and many new friendships were formed. This is truly the spirit of Scouting. Only too briefly the camp soon came to an end and all paid our thanks to the staff at Zellhof and made our way to Salzburg Airport and our homeward journey. Everyone enjoyed this international experience immensely and will no doubt remember it for many years to come.

L-R front row: Geoffrey Hodgett, Andrew Patterson. Middle row: Josh McGuinness, David Whiteside, Samuel Holmes, David Kernaghan. Back row: Lee McWhirter, Iain McMillan, Paul Girvan, Jonathan Whiteside.

Preparing for a canyoning expedition.

Sam Holmes and Andrew Patterson get wet at the
Water Gardens, Salzburg, Austria 2006.

Venture Scouts Ross McWhirter, Iain McMillan, Lee McWhirter and Paul Girvan try their hand at hydrospeed on the cold waters of the Salzach river.

Front Row: Geoffrey Hodgett, Ali Kronberger, Andrew Patterson, Monica Kronberger, Sam Holmes
Second Row: David Whiteside, Josh McGuinness, David Kernaghan
Third Row: Mervyn Ferris SL, Ross McWhirter, Paul Girvan, Iain McMillan, Jonathan Whiteside
Fourth Row: Colin Baines, Lee McWhirter, Garry McWhirter ASL, Colin Whiteside ASL

Andrew Patterson (left) and David Whiteside make friends with two Danish Scouts.

Cubs at Shannaghmore, October 2006

Scouts took part in the British Amateur Shooting and Conservation Association event, October 2006.

Cubs at the Armagh Planetarium, December 2006.

Above and above left: Beavers and Cubs Christmas parties.

2007

On 5 January the Troop was privileged to have four of our Scouts attend the presentation of Chief Scout Gold Awards in Belfast City Hall. This was a wonderful occasion and a fitting tribute for the hard work which David, Andrew, David and Geoffrey had put into gaining this very coveted Scout award. The event was attended by the boys' parents and family as well as their leaders. Afterwards everyone was entertained to a wonderful buffet.

L-R: David Whiteside, Geoffrey Hodgett, David Kernaghan and Andrew Patterson with their Chief Scout Gold Award certificates along with N. I. Chief Commissioner Dr. Wilfred Mulryne, OBE.

During the year the Beaver Colony took part in the joint Beaver/Cub sports event as well as attending the Beaver Rally Day at Crawfordsburn where a great day was had by all. A good attendance of Beavers took part in the special St George's Day parade and service in Bangor this year to celebrate the Scout Movement's centenary year. A campfire was held to finish off our session in June before taking a well earned holiday. Activities during the year included pancake cooking, craft work, fancy dress Halloween party and Christmas party as well as going to visit Santa, Mrs Claus and their many elves at Crawfordsburn. The Beavers got really involved in many of the centenary activities to celebrate the 100 years of Scouting as well as working on the various Beaver badges. All enjoyed working on the badges and were thrilled when these were presented to them. As in past years when the brighter nights came some of the activities were carried out in the local park or in the back garden. The Beavers also attended the Children's Day services and went to the Cenotaph for Remembrance Sunday in November. There were many activities which took place both inside our own hall and outside and everyone enjoyed the excitement and fun.

At the beginning of Scouting's Centenary Year the Cub Pack set a target to gain 100 proficiency badges. April saw the Pack continuing to gain these badges and then the Pack took part in the St George's Day parade in Bangor. During the month of May the Cubs visited the centenary exhibition in Bagenal's Castle and held the Grand Howl in the banqueting hall much to the delight of the curator. The Cubs took part in the district sports, winning 11 medals and then it was off to the centenary camp

Cubs displaying their proficiency badges, April 2007.
L-R front row: M. McDonald, Not known, J. Lawrence, S. McCammon, M. Kernaghan, Not known, A. Graham, J. Donnelly.
2nd row: C. Davis, G. Bingham, G. Dunne, J. Whiteside, N. McElroy, J. McKee, R. Milne, Z. Shahid, D. White, D. Quigley, J. Fearon
Back row: J. McKee ACSL, W. McAlpine CSL, L. McWhirter ACSL, C. McElroy ACSL.

Cubs visiting the local fire station, May 2007.
L-R Front row: J. Donnelly, D. J. White, C. Davis, G. Bingham, G. Dunne, M. Kernaghan, S. Scott.
2nd row: R. Milne, N. McElroy, Z. Shahid, J. McKee, S. McCammon, J. Whiteside, D. Quigley, A. Graham.
Back row: C. McElroy ACSL, G. McCullough ACSL, L. McWhirter ACSL, J. McKee ACSL, W. McAlpine CSL.

at Crawfordsburn for the Cub Fun Day. 1st Newry hung their banner on the totem pole and joined the Scouts for lunch as well as taking part in lots of activities. Cubs spoke with Scouts in Scotland as part of the Communicator Badge. During May the Pack also visited the local fire station where they enjoyed a talk given by the Chief Fire Officer and tried to hold the high pressure fire hoses. June saw the Pack attending Children's Day services at Downshire Road and Sandys Street churches as well as taking part in the Group end of term barbecue. There was great excitement when the Pack assisted in letting off more than 700 balloons later in the evening. In July some of the Pack took part in the photo call of the floral display at the Dublin Road and then later met some of the Swedish Scout Jamboree contingent. Stuart Scott and Toby Girvan chatted with the Swedish Cub Leaders and asked about Scouting in Sweden.

After the summer break the Cub Pack then went on an activity weekend in September to Shannaghmore Outdoor Education Centre where they all had a really magnificent time. Everyone went canoeing at Castlewellan, took part in climbing, a rope course, a blind trail, orienteering and archery. Some of the Cubs even managed to rescue two people who got lost in the maze and escorted them out to safety. All too soon the wonderful weekend was over and all headed home again looking forward to next year's event. Cubs enjoyed a visit to the police station in October and were allowed to see the working of the station along with the police cars and Land Rovers. At the end of the month there was a Halloween party which was enjoyed by all. In November the Pack held an indoor golf tournament and then took part in the Remembrance Sunday parade to the Cenotaph. During December there was a quiz about the centenary exhibition in the Scout hall, a first aid night, craft nights and of course a Christmas Party with Santa arriving to give everyone a present which was enjoyed by all.

Shannaghmore Outdoor Education Centre, September 2007

1st Newry Group at St George's Day, 22 April 2007

Centenary camp at Crawfordsburn, 26 May 2007

During the year the Scouts again took part in a range of activities in the hall and outside. During the months of April through to June, our usual Friday night activities included backwoods cooking, pioneering, compass and mapping, orienteering and a number of outings. Our first major event was the county St George's Day Centenary parade held in Bangor on 22 April. The Troop had a good turn out at this event and all the members were surprised to see so many Scouts on parade. May saw the attendance at the County Down Centenary Camp at Crawfordsburn where all who camped had a wonderful time with lots of activities and splendid weather. At this camp the Scouts were accompanied on the Saturday by the Cub Pack which attended the Cub Open Day. Following on from this the Troop attended Children's Day service at Downshire Road and Sandys Street churches. On 14 June some of our older members attended the Veterans Day celebrations in Poyntzpass where they helped to distribute leaflets and manned a photographic display showing Scouting over the years in Newry District. The end of June saw the Troop taking part in the Group's annual barbecue and treasure hunt. At this event all the members of the Group released more than 700 balloons which Beavers, Cubs and Scouts had sold during the year to raise funds for the two main charities supported by County Down Scouting for the centenary year. Later in the year cheques were presented to Help the Aged and the Children's Hospice.

Beaver pancake day, 19 February 2007
L-R back row: M. Kinnin, E. Quigley, J. Poucher, J. Fearon, D. Truesdale, D. Bingham, R. Smith, I. Hamilton. Front: M. McElroy, T. McCammon, J. Magowan, M. O'Brien, R. Murphy, L. Wilson, H. Gamble, C. Quinn. Flipping pancake: D. Corkey.

Beaver and Cub sports, 21 May 2007

July saw the Troop attending a number of very special events especially organised for Scouting's centenary year. These included a photo call with local councillors at the floral display which was planted by Newry and Mourne Council to commemorate our centenary. Later in the month the District hosted the Swedish Jamboree contingent to Newry when again the Council came up trumps by providing a meal and a visit to Bagenal's Castle for our Scouting friends.

Meeting Swedish Scouts, 26 July 2007.

Cubs performed the Grand Howl in
Bagenal's Castle Museum.

Beaver and Cub Halloween parties

At the end of July the Troop held annual camp at Phasels Wood in Essex where they took part in a large number of exciting activities such as caving, climbing, a cresta run, abseiling, canoeing, shooting, archery, climbing an artificial ice wall and of course a visit to the Centenary Jamboree at Hylands Park. No doubt the visit to the Jamboree was the highlight of the camp as our Scouts were amazed to see and meet some of the 40,000 plus Scouts from around the world who were encamped for around ten days. Scouts from nearly 200 countries took part and our Scouts were privileged to be able to attend this great event on the open day. Now as we are all aware, the purpose of annual camp is not just to have a holiday but it is to put into practice the various skills which Scouts have been shown over the years and to fend for themselves. The two patrols were required to prepare and cook their own meals as well as wash up and tidy up after each meal. In the mornings all had to get up very early to prepare for daily prayers, flag break and inspection before taking part in the planned programme. As well as visiting the Jamboree the Troop visited Thorpe Park for a wonderful day of fun and excitement on the many breathtaking rides. Another day took us on a visit to the RAF Museum at Duxford where the members saw lots of famous aircraft from former years as well as some of the most up to date planes currently in service with the RAF, and were then treated to a fly past by one of the few remaining Spitfires. On the day before leaving camp a visit to the nearby town of St Albans was a must to buy some presents to take home to Mum and Dad. Everyone returned home having had a wonderful camp with a full and active range of activities as well as 'wall to wall' sunshine for the whole camp. William Nummy, our transport officer, accompanied us to this camp and was at our beck and call during the whole event.

It was quickly round to September again when the Troop restarted after the short break and was soon involved in the programme of activities to take us up to Christmas. As the dark nights were upon us most of our programme was indoors and included indoor cooking, mini pioneering, knotting, first aid, origami and mapping and compass work. Our indoor programmes were supplemented with visits to the swimming pool at Lisburn, ten pin bowling and a visit to Fun World at the King's Hall. The Troop also took part with Beavers and Cubs in the parade and service to the Cenotaph in Newry on Remembrance Sunday.

In November the Troop was honoured when David Whiteside was selected to take part in LIVE07, the Scout Movement's Centenary celebration show, at The O2 in London. This was the largest show ever staged by Scouting and involved a cast of many thousand Scouts. David had a wonderful experience and enjoyed every minute of taking part in this historic event. At the end of the year the Group was in a very healthy state now with some sixty four members and a good band of supporters.

David Whiteside with the LIVE07 flag

2007 Annual camp at Phasels Wood (Essex) and World Jamboree (Hylands)

L-R front row: J. Mitchell, A. Hodgett, C. Bagnall, S. Poucher, B. Williamson, J. Wilson, J. McGrath.
Back row: W. McAlpine CSL, L. McWhirter ACSL, W. Nummy, G. McWhirter ASL, G. Hodgett, C. Baines, D. Kernaghan,
M. Ferris SL, P. Girvan, D. Whiteside, C. Whiteside ASL, Jonathan Whiteside ASL.

David Whiteside taking part in the human version of foosball.

Andrew Hodgett (left) and Ben Williamson become gladiators.

8am, 1 August 2007. This was part of the the world wide renewal of the Scout Promise. It was led by the
Chief Scout, Peter Duncan, from Brownsea Island, the site of the first experimental camp for Scouts in 1907.

Above and left, L-R: C. Baines, W. McAlpine, W. Nummy, G. McWhirter.

David Kernaghan brings the shark home.

Garry McWhirter shows off his cooking skills.

Mervyn Ferris and Billy McAlpine with two of the camp staff.

Former Scouts Stanley Ferris and Robert McCullough along with N.I. Chief Commissioner Dr. Wilfred Mulyrne, OBE cut the Scouting centenary cake.

Centenary dinner, 30 November 2007.

Christmas party and Cubs show off the new Scouting Centenary scarves, 11 December 2007.

2008

The year commenced with the announcement of the award of the Silver Wolf to Scoutleader and District Commissioner, Mervyn Ferris. This is the highest honour given to leaders within the Scout Movement and is only presented for services of the most exceptional nature to Scouting.

Above: Meryn Ferris receiving his Silver Wolf from Northern Ireland Chief Commissioner Dr. Wilfred Mulryne, OBE.

Right: The Troop celebrated Mervyn's award with a *This is Your Life* event, 20 June 2008.

Below: Ben Williamson and Matthew McElroy also celebrated birthdays at Mervyn's event.

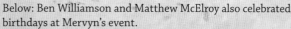

From the beginning of January the Scouts held a number of evenings spent outside at the field where activities included air rifle shooting, a barbecue, outdoor games and bivouacking. Then in early February a team of Scouts took part in the County Down Scout quiz at Inch Scout hall where they acquitted themselves quite well although did not manage to win any awards. The Troop was also represented at the County Down Founder's Day Service at Down Cathedral on Sunday, 24 February, where the guest of honour was Lord Baden-Powell, grandson of our founder, BP.

Every year, the Beavers take part in a varied programme. Before the summer

Lord Baden-Powell (centre) with Troop representatives at the County Down Founder's Day
service at Down Cathedral, 24 February 2008.

break, the Colony visited the annual Northern Ireland Beaver Rally Day at Crawfordsburn, where a day of numerous activities took place. An emphasis this year was placed on badge work throughout the year and the good attendances at the St George's Day parade and service, the Cenotaph on Remembrance Sunday and local Children's Day services helped contribute to the boys' Faith Badge. Badges were also completed in Creativity, Hobbies, Healthy Eating, Animal Friends, Exploration, Imagination and Safety. Unfortunately the visit to Northern Ireland Beaver Zoo Day had to be cancelled but, rather than miss out, the leaders Carol and Alison took the boys during the Halloween school break to Belfast Zoo for the day. Beavers always enjoy a party and there was no shortage of fun with the Fancy Dress night at Halloween and Santa Claus' visit to Newry Scout hall during the Christmas party. Indoor and outdoor games, crafts, baking, art and discussion are some of the activities used when Beavers remember St Patrick's Day, Mothers' Day, Easter, Fathers Day and the other important dates throughout the year.

Later in the year, on St George's Day in April, Mervyn was invited to attend the annual St George's Day service at St George's Chapel, Windsor Castle, and to be present at the parade of Queen's Scouts in the quadrangle of the castle. Mervyn was greatly thrilled by the award and with his visit to Windsor, which he will recall for many years to come. Mervyn is only the second leader in 1st Newry and first leader holding a Newry District appointment to receive this high honour, following the same award being presented to Noel Hodgett in 2006.

St George's Day, 24 April 2008.

From January to March the Cub Pack had a film show, went ten pin bowling and tried their hand at pancake making. April saw the Cub Pack gaining activity badges and then joining with the Beavers and Scouts in the District St George's Day parade and service hosted by 1st Poyntzpass. In May the Cubs took the train from Newry to the County Fun Day at the Ulster Folk Park, Cultra. Cubs saw the Transport Museum and the Titanic exhibition. Everyone enjoyed the novelty of going by train to this event and all had a great day out. In June, as the District Cub Sports Day was not held this year, the Cubs held their own Pack sports night and many of the Cubs gained their Athlete's Badge. They also held a treasure hunt around the local area, and

Cubs ten pin bowling, March 2008.

this was enjoyed by all. The Pack also took part in the District Cub football tournament and won the District Cup. Also in June the Pack attended Children's Day services at Downshire Road and Sandys Street churches as well as taking part in the Group end of term barbecue.

After the summer break the Cub Pack got up and running with a new system of correct uniform, attendance and behaviour at the meetings with marks being allocated and a pennant being presented by Lee for the best Six. Once again the Cub Pack went on an activity weekend in September to Shannaghmore Outdoor Education Centre where we all had a really magnificent time. Everyone went canoeing at Castlewellan, took part in climbing, a rope course, a blind trail through the trees, orienteering around the lake and archery. On the Saturday evening after the activities everyone gathered around the campfire for a sing-a-long with musical accompaniment by Billy on the mouth organ. Then it was off to bed where all fell quickly to sleep. All too soon the wonderful weekend was over and all headed home again in Mr Nummy's bus and looking forward to next year's event. Also in September more Beavers were transferred into the Cub Pack. At the end of October we held a Halloween party, dunking for apples and a rummage in the 'gunge', which was enjoyed by all. November saw the Pack take part with the Beavers and Scouts in the Remembrance Sunday parade to the Cenotaph. This turned out to be a very wet event but we all managed to cope well. During December the Cubs had a race evening with radio controlled cars when all proved to be budding Jenson Buttons, at least indoors. This was followed by a craft night and later on attendance at the District carol service at Drumgooland, where we had a good turn out. One of the lessons was read by Cub Matthew McElroy. Soon it was around to the Christmas Party where there was fun and games as well as a visit from Santa Claus who presented gifts to all the Cubs. During the year the Pack gained a total of 86 proficiency/activity badges.

The Scouts took part in many and varied activities both indoors and outside. The Scout Troop started the year with healthy numbers and during January to March much of the programme was of necessity held indoors. Once the weather had improved the Troop was able to get out and about and take part in many of the Scouting activities which Scouts really enjoy, which included backwoods cooking, pioneering, compass and mapping, orienteering and outings. Our first major event was the District St George's Day parade and service at Poyntzpass where we had quite a good turn out. During May and June we had a number of evenings in the field at Mervyn's house where we bivouacked overnight, did some backwoods cooking, participated in air rifle shooting and enjoyed some outdoor games. Following on from this the Troop attended Children's' Day service at Downshire Road and Sandys Street churches. The end of June saw the Troop taking part in the Group's annual barbecue and fun evening at which quite a number of parents came along for the fun and excitement.

During the year the Troop received a number of Cubs from the Pack and ended with 20 Scouts and 4 Explorers.

Cubs Fun Day at Cultra, 24 May 2008.

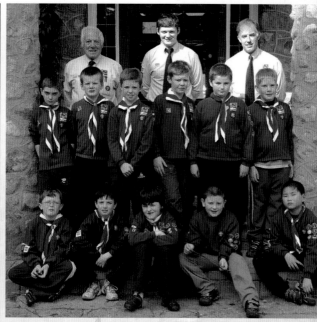

Cubs at Shannaghmore Outdoor Education Centre.

Christmas and Halloween parties.

2008 Annual camp, Linnet Clough, Stockport

On Wednesday, 30 July at 6.30 a.m., members of 1st Newry (Earl Kilmorey) Scout Troop and their leaders met at the Scout hall in Sandys Street to begin their annual camp. This was to be held at Linnet Clough Scout Activity Centre near Stockport and last for eight days with many activities and visits planned. The Troop travelled from Newry to Dublin where they took the ferry from there to Holyhead in Wales. From Holyhead the minibus then travelled through Wales into England and on to the site, arriving some 3 hours later around 3.30 p.m. Immediately each Patrol began setting up camp, pitching tents, setting up dining shelters and generally preparing for their eight day camp. At the end of a very tiresome and exhausting day everyone retired to bed and had a good night's rest. The following day saw each patrol putting the final touches to their tents and kitchen areas and organising cooking and washing schedules. In the afternoon the Scouts had a break when they headed off for a canoeing session on the nearby lake. This was thoroughly enjoyed by all. After this energetic activity each patrol came back to the campsite where dinner was prepared and quickly eaten. Later on in the evening the Group enjoyed a spell on the site's marvellous climbing wall with some members excelling by reaching the top of the wall. Some of the younger members took the opportunity to try this activity for the first time. The evening continued with some football and other games before each patrol prepared supper and retired to bed ready for the following day's activities.

Another day dawned and all were up early for inspection before heading off for some adventure to the Blue John Caves near Castleton. Here the party descended into the world famous Blue John cavern where the mineral known as Blue John is still mined to this day. Stalactites and stalagmites were seen in abundance along with seams of the famous Blue John stone. After descending more than 300 feet underground and having reached the Grand Crystallised cavern with its multi-coloured dome, it was time to ascend the many steps to the entrance. The trip was a great educational experience for young and old alike. It was then time for a snack and so a visit to the nearby town of Castleton was in order. Here the Scouts had something to eat and did some window-shopping before heading back to their campsite for dinner. Dinner however was to be something special in that the Troop was invited by the captain of Mellor and Townscliffe Golf

L-R front row: J. Wilson, B. Williamson, J. McKee, S. Poucher, T. Girvan, G. Bingham, J. McGrath, W. Nummy. Back row: G. McWhirter ASL, A. Patterson, D. Kernaghan, L. McWhirter ACSL, M. Ferris SL, C. Whiteside ASL, J. Whiteside ASL, D. Whiteside, W. McAlpine CSL.

Club Captain Victor Wright presents Scoutleader
Mervyn Ferris with souvenir score card.

Club to the clubhouse for the evening meal. The captain was none other than one of our former members, Victor Wright, who had gone to live and work in England many years ago. The meal was thoroughly enjoyed by all and following this Victor presented the Troop with a souvenir score card from the golf club. Our thanks go to Victor for all his help and the wonderful meal at the golf club. The evening finished off with games and various activities and then supper before retiring to bed.

The next morning and part of the afternoon were spent orienteering and taking part in the low ropes course as well as preparing lunch. In the afternoon the Troop visited the swimming pool at the nearby town of Stockport where all enjoyed the various slides. A walk around the town allowed the Scouts to do some shopping and then it was back to camp for the evening meal. On the following morning, everyone was up early preparing breakfast, washing and getting ready for the morning inspection. After breakfast and morning prayers there followed inspection with each patrol being marked on cleanliness of cooking equipment and other utensils and how tidy they had left their kitchen area. Then it was time to go into Mellor for the morning church service. After church it was time for lunch which was then followed by rafting and other activities during the afternoon. After dinner everyone took part in the wall traverse, which was indoors, and which gave some cover from the rather wet conditions outside.

Next day we were all up early for inspection before heading off for some fun at Alton Towers. This park was a short drive from the campsite and soon the Scouts were enjoying the many rides and activities which were available at this wonderful theme park. The older Scouts enjoyed the roller coasters, water flumes and the more adventurous rides while the younger Scouts tried the calmer rides and sideshows. Again, after a wonderful and exciting day out, all returned tired but exhilarated by the activities. After an evening meal the Scouts then took part in the on site activities. After a shower to get rid of the dirt and grime, each patrol then had supper and retired to bed for a well earned rest. There followed another early start to the day, in preparation for a visit to Waterworld at Chester. Here the members saw a wide and wonderful variety of fish and other amphibious creatures from various parts of the world. This was a wonderful experience and everyone saw some of the fish and sharks being fed by the staff. It was then time for lunch in the nearby city of Chester and then shopping for presents to take home to Mum, Dad, brothers and sisters. On arrival back at the campsite, dinner was prepared and after cleaning up all took part in air rifle shooting. Then it was time for supper and bed but not before some tents were dismantled to get ready for the journey home the next day. It was then time to leave the site for the journey home, the Scouts travelled across England into Wales, thence to Dublin where they were then transported home again to Newry where the Scouts were met by parents and friends. We would especially thank William Nummy, our transport officer, who accompanied us to this camp and was at our beck and call throughout our stay.

Troop attended a Sunday Children's Day service in the local Methodist Church.

L-R : Ben, Jake, Toby, Johnny, George and Sheehan enjoy their lunch of chicken, peas, potatoes and gravy with a sweet of fruit salad and fresh cream to follow.

Noel Hodgett

On Tuesday 18 March the Group was greatly saddened by the news of the death of one of its former members and great supporter, Noel Hodgett.

Noel had been a member of the Group, first as a Scout and later as Assistant Scoutmaster, Scoutmaster and Group Scoutleader as well as taking on the role of District Commissioner for Newry District. Noel was always at our beck and call as well as being a very generous benefactor to the Group. Following the funeral service in Newry Methodist Church members of 1st Newry Scout Group and Newry District Scout Council provided a guard of honour as the cortege left the grounds of the church.

Noel is sadly missed for his good humoured banter and craic, especially around the now famous campfires at Mourne Park.

2009

At the beginning of the year the Cub Pack had 14 Cubs on the roll. April saw the Pack gaining activity badges and then joining with the Beavers and Scouts in the District St George's Day service held in Warrenpoint. In May the Cubs began practising for the District Cub football tournament and, as the saying goes, 'practice makes perfect' as we went on to win the Wilson Robinson Cup in June. Following this the Pack went off to Crawfordsburn to the Cub Fun Day with the theme of the Wild West. All those attending thought it was great with the one exception of line dancing which did not go down so well. In June the Pack gained 10 sports medals in the District Cub Sports but this year did not win the Cup which was won by 1st Drumgooland Pack. All attended Children's Day services at Downshire Road and Sandys Street churches as well as taking part in the Group end of term barbecue.

Beavers, Cubs and leaders enjoying pancake night.
Above left, L-R back row: B. Moffett, J. Jennings, J. Wilson. Middle: E. Quigley, M. McDonald, R. Clements, T. Dodds, J. Ferris.
Front: C. Moffett, H. Bingham.

The Cub football team.

After the summer the Cub Pack, once again went on an activity weekend in September to Shannaghmore Outdoor Education Centre where all had a really magnificent time. The Cubs went canoeing at Castlewellan, took part in climbing, a rope course, a blind trail through the trees, orienteering around the lake and archery. On the Saturday evening after the activities everyone gathered around the campfire for a sing a long with musical accompaniment by Billy on the mouth organ. Then it was off to bed where all fell quickly to sleep. All too soon the wonderful weekend

Cubs day out at Crawfordsburn, May 2009.

was over and all headed home again in Mr Nummy's bus looking forward to next year's event. At the end of October the Cub Halloween Party was held which was enjoyed by all. In November the Pack took part with the Beavers and Scouts in the Remembrance Sunday parade to the Cenotaph. During December the Cubs had a craft night which was closely followed by the Cub Christmas party where there was fun and games as well as a visit from Santa Claus who presented gifts to all Cubs. Unfortunately our usual Santa was not available due to illness but an excellent replacement, in the form of our esteemed Treasurer, was found to continue the Christmas tradition for the Cubs.

Plans were made by the Executive Committee for a range of events to take place over the following year to celebrate the Group's centenary. Applications forms were completed in August and forwarded to the National Lottery Awards for All office seeking funding to cover some of the costs for our planned celebrations. Later in the year the Group received a positive response from Awards for All and so plans were firmed up and finalised for our 'big year'. The Executive Committee members have been in discussion with the Southern Education and Library Board on the matter of repairs to the building currently being used as the Scout hall. Following much discussion and conversations with the SELB, progress, although rather slow, was at last being made and it was hoped that repairs would be effected to the hall in the very near future.

Scout annual camp this year was held at Auchengillan Scout Centre, Scotland, when thirteen Scouts, four Explorers and five leaders took part. The weather was very poor with incessant rain every day. Eventually the ground became so waterlogged that the campers were forced to move to indoor accommodation on site. Morale picked up and everyone began to enjoy the camp much more. It was quickly round once again to September when the Troop restarted after the short break and into our programme of activities to take us up to Christmas. As the dark nights were upon us most of our programme was indoors and included indoor cooking, mini pioneering, knotting, first aid and mapping and compass work. Our indoor programmes were supplemented with visits to the swimming pool at Lisburn. October saw the commencement of our Centenary Year and the Scouts were asked to bring forward some ideas as to how the Group would celebrate their centenary. The Troop took part in the British Legion parade along with Beavers and Cubs to the Cenotaph in Newry on Remembrance Sunday.

Towards the end of 2009, work commenced to refurbish the 'old Scout hall' to bring it into use for our centenary anniversary celebrations during 2010 and the following years. A group of dedicated volunteers and leaders worked hard for many weeks to carry out necessary renovations and rewiring required to allow the building to be used safely again.

Beaver and Cub sports day, 8 June 2009.

Jonathan Whiteside (left) and Toby Girvan hiking in the Mournes, June 2009.

Shannaghmore Outdoor Education Centre, September 2009.

2009 Annual camp, Aughengillan

En route to Auchengillan. L-R front row: M. Kernaghan, S. Poucher, A. Graham, D. Quigley, G. Bingham, T. Girvan, A. Hodgett. Middle row: S. Scott, N. McElroy, H. Stinson, J. Wilson, J. Kernaghan, C. Bagnall, G. Hodgett, D. Kernaghan. Back row: M. Ferris SL, L. McWhirter ACSL, D. Whiteside, W. Nummy, C. Whiteside ASL, G. McWhirter ASL.

George Bingham tries his hand at circus skills.

Jack McGrath and Colin Whiteside washing up after dinner.

Ashley Graham's birthday   Jake Wilson

Toby Girvan (left) and Stuart Scott   Chris Bagnall's patrol inspection

Chris Bagnall takes the lead during a karting race at Loudon Castle.

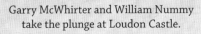

Garry McWhirter and William Nummy
take the plunge at Loudon Castle.

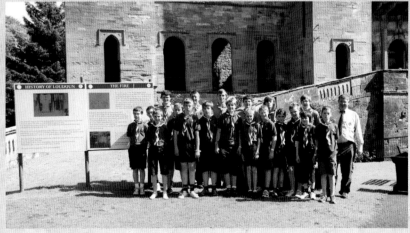

The Troop at Loudon Castle.

Beaver and Cub Halloween and Christmas parties 2009.

2010

Work commenced again following the Christmas break to finalise the renovations to the 'old Scout hall'. Further meetings and follow up discussions were held with members of the Southern Education and Library Board with regard to arranging a licence for the use of the Scout hall and to take forward the much needed repairs, especially to the existing asbestos roof which is now leaking badly. It was hoped that work would commence as soon as the licence had been finalised and signed and that repairs be completed before our St George's Day service and parade in Newry on 18 April. The Executive committee met early in the year to put the final touches for the number of events which were planned to take place throughout our centenary year 2010, as well as information regarding progress on the commemoration window for Downshire Road church. The events planned were a Fun Day, fly the logo, 100 good turns, scarf up 100, centenary badge design and a centenary concert to end the year.

January

In early January two teams of Scouts from the Group took part in the district Scout quiz held at Drumgooland where one of the teams claimed the runners-up prize out of eight teams from the district. The other team managed a very worthy fourth place in this event. The runners-up went on to take part in the county quiz finals held in Inch Scout hall at the end of February where they performed exceptionally well in gaining third place. This county event was a closely fought battle with 1st Newry's team only being one point behind the top two teams who tied for first place. Following this event the team members were presented with a gift from the Group for their very worthy performance. In February and March the Scout Troop entered a number of teams in the district 5-a-side hockey and football tournaments and acquitted themselves well at both events.

February

The Group was extremely upset when, on Monday 23 February, a bomb explosion took place next to the Court House in the town causing severe damage to Downshire Road Presbyterian church which is close by. Unfortunately this meant that design work could not be go forward on our centenary window which it was hoped would be dedicated at the St George's Day service on 18 April. February and March saw Cub Scout David Bingham taking part in the N.I. Scout Council's Big Communications project. This project entailed David giving a presentation, lasting no longer than three minutes, to a panel of three judges at the District, County and Northern Ireland heats. Not only was David successful in the District and County heats but he also went on to win the Northern Ireland final stage and win the coveted award of being the best Cub in Northern Ireland. David was rewarded with a gift from 1st Newry in appreciation of his success and in representing the Group so well.

Beavers flipping pancakes.

Jim Baines, Group Treasurer, received his Long Service award from Mervyn Ferris, District Commissioner 27 February 2010.

David Bingham, best Cub in Northern Ireland 2010.

March

At the beginning of March the Group learned that Scouting HQ in London was showing their support to Newry Scouts by sending the UK Chief Commissioner, Wayne Bulpitt, to join them at their special centenary St George's Day parade. 1st Newry Scout Leader and District Commissioner Mervyn Ferris commented, 'Wayne Bulpitt leads a very busy Scouting schedule and we are absolutely thrilled and delighted to have him with us on the Sunday for our parade. Wayne will be joined at a special salute base in the centre of the city, by the Northern Ireland Chief Commissioner, Dr. T. W. Mulryne OBE, County Commissioner, Stephen Donaldson, and Executive Commissioner, Ken Gillespie.'

April

On Saturday, 17 April, the Group held a wonderful Fun Day in Mervyn Ferris's field on the Cloghanramer Road where they put on a magnificent variety of entertainment for all the members, parents, friends and the general public. The day's activities included archery, climbing/abseiling wall, bouncy castle, slides, laser clay pigeon shooting, bungee run, police information display unit and barbecue as well as a dog training demonstration. Car parking to accommodate this had to be provided at the nearby Mourne Country Hotel with a shuttle bus service to and from the site. The event, which required many weeks of planning and organisation, was attended by more than five hundred people. During the event the Explorer Scouts provided assistance with the running of the various activities as well as taking part with the other Scouts, Cubs and Beavers from the Group. As the Group had previously received permission from Newry District Scout Council to hold the annual

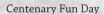

Centenary Fun Day

Mayor Feehan finds his target.

St George's Day parade and service in Newry to coincide with our other celebrations, this took place on the following Sunday, 18 April.

It had been anticipated that for the first time in Scouting history in Newry a high ranking Scouting official from London HQ, Wayne Bulpitt, would visit the city and 1st Newry had hoped to make the day memorable both for him and the Scouts in attendance. However no one could have predicted the volcanic ash cloud which so suddenly covered the British Isles at the time when their esteemed visitor was due too arrive. Unfortunately this unforeseen event caused the cancellation of all flights thus preventing Mr Bulpitt from coming to Newry's centenary celebrations. 1st Newry Cub Scout Leader Billy McAlpine MBE commented, 'We were disappointed that Wayne was unable to join us – it's hard to believe volcanic ash caused such travel chaos - let's hope it will be another 100 years before the next ash cloud'.

However despite the bomb attack on the Court House a few months earlier, the resultant damage to Downshire Road church and the disappointment due to the Icelandic volcanic ash cloud, the

St George's Day and Centenary parade.
Above left: Members of the McConnell family present new colours to the Group.

Group's centenary parade and service took place to Sandys Street Presbyterian church. The parade was well attended by current members of 1st Newry Group, by Newry Scout district and by more than 50 'Old Boys' who had all been former members or connected with 1st Newry Group. The Northern Ireland Chief Commissioner, Dr. T. W. Mulryne OBE, and County Commissioner, Stephen Donaldson, both joined in the parade and service. Newry and Mourne District Council was represented by Mayor John Feehan and Council Clerk and Chief Executive, Thomas McCall. Mayor Feehan personally welcomed members of 1st Newry Scouts at the church and extended the Council's best wishes to the Group on their 100th Anniversary year. The service was conducted and lead by Rev. Brian Colvin and Rev. Dr. Michael Barry. The organist for this special event was none other than Rowland Anketell, a former 1st Newry Scout. During this service, members of the McConnell family presented new colours to the Group, which were dedicated by the Rev. Colvin. Marshall McConnell handed over a newly inscribed Union flag in memory of his mother, Sadie McConnell, who had been Group Treasurer during the period 1955 – 1991. After the parade, members and friends met in the church hall for refreshments.

Following the two very successful events earlier in April, the Group was delighted to be informed on 20 April that their application to Awards for All, Young Roots, had been approved and their centenary project could go ahead. This project included the publication of a book on the history of 1st Newry since its inception, the development of a Group website, the creation of an exhibition centre and display as well as training for the members of the project team and Explorer Scouts. This project would take some years to complete, as much in depth research required to be completed and interviews with former members undertaken.

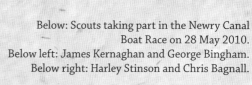

Above and left: Cubs and Beavers taking part in sports day on 9 May 2010.

Below: Scouts taking part in the Newry Canal Boat Race on 28 May 2010.
Below left: James Kernaghan and George Bingham.
Below right: Harley Stinson and Chris Bagnall.

May

On 5 May the Beavers, accompanied by their leaders, attended the Northern Ireland Beaver Rally Day where all the Beavers had a wonderful time in fine weather. This event was closely followed on 9 May when all the Beavers and Cubs took part in a wonderful sporting day out and everyone arrived home tired but well pleased with their efforts. Later in May the Scouts took part in a weekend hike and camp in the Mourne mountains and, on 28 May, some of the older Scouts constructed a raft and took part in the Newry Canal boat race. Once again the Beavers were busy when they went on a day visit to Delamont Country Park and then took the ferry across Strangford Lough to the aquarium at Portaferry. The Beavers were thrilled to view the amazingly and diverse marine life that exists around the sea in this part of Northern Ireland. A week later those busy little Beavers were out and about again when they visited a local dog kennel run by Mr William Berry. Here they were shown how the dogs were kept and Mr Berry then showed them how he trained some of his own award winning black Labradors.

June

June saw all the members of the Group taking part in the evening Children's Day services in Downshire Road and Sandys Street Presbyterian churches. The Group has been attending these services now

Cub football.

Presentation to David Bingham, 25 June 2010.

Below: Cubs visit Ulster Museum, Belfast, 26 June 2010

Cubs enjoying Botanic Gardens, 26 June 2010.

Cubs displaying the design of the new 1st Newry centenary badge.

Sir Alex Ferguson and Ryan Giggs with the 1st Newry centenary scarf.

Wallace (where's Gromit?) wearing the 1st Newry centenary scarf and holding the badge.

for more than fifty years. For our centenary badge design, the Beavers, Cubs, Scouts and Explorers were asked to draw up designs for our badge which would then be worn on our new scarves in future years. Many wonderful and unusual designs were received and it was finally agreed to settle on one which depicted Newry City Hall and the date of our original formation. New centenary scarves were purchased and our new badge sewn on to each and then it was time to make the various presentations. The scarf up event required each member to nominate a number of citizens throughout the United Kingdom whom they thought were well deserving to receive and be presented with our new centenary scarf and badge. There was a great response for grannies, uncles, teachers, brothers, sisters, footballers and comedians to this, with many and varied names being provided. Throughout the year presentations were made to local dignitaries as well as to popular sports, radio and TV personalities, footballers, a football manager and former Olympians. The highlight for many of the members was when photos were received from Ryan Giggs, Alex Ferguson and Wallace (of Wallace & Gromit fame) as well as photos taken with Rose Neill, Mary Peters, Frank Mitchell, Seamus Heaney and Paul Clark.

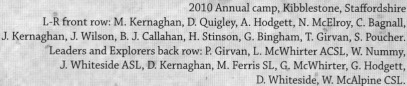

2010 Annual camp, Kibblestone, Staffordshire
L-R front row: M. Kernaghan, D. Quigley, A. Hodgett, N. McElroy, C. Bagnall, J. Kernaghan, J. Wilson, B. J. Callahan, H. Stinson, G. Bingham, T. Girvan, S. Poucher.
Leaders and Explorers back row: P. Girvan, L. McWhirter ACSL, W. Nummy, J. Whiteside ASL, D. Kernaghan, M. Ferris SL, G. McWhirter, G. Hodgett, D. Whiteside, W. McAlpine CSL.

L-R: Matthew Kernaghan, Andrew Hodgett and Harley Stinson stock up on some sweets before returning to camp.

July

On 28 July twenty two members of the Troop attended annual camp at Kibblestone Scout Activity Centre, Staffordshire, from 28 July to 3 August. Everyone present enjoyed the on site activities such as canoeing, climbing, abseiling, orienteering, as well as a number of visits to places of interest. During their visit to one of the Stoke potteries, the Scouts actually took part in creating some pottery to their own design which they were then able to bring home to Mum and Dad.

The centenary 100 good turns project involved each member of the Group carrying out a number of good turns throughout the year, such as helping other people, assisting the elderly with messages, visiting and other similar tasks. Also for this event Scouts and Explorer Scouts assisted with and raised funds for a sponsored walk on 9 October from Newry to Portadown in aid of the Pakistan Flood Disaster Appeal as well as visiting a home for the elderly around Christmas time. During the visit to the elderly the Scouts and Explorers spoke with all the residents and then had a short sing along before presenting the home with some gifts for the elderly.

Gold Chief Scout Award hike in the Mournes, August 2010
L-R: James Kernaghan, George Bingham, Andrew Hodgett, Harley Stinson.

Cubs at Shannaghmore, 2 October 2010.

Cubs and Beavers at Halloween.

Pakistan flood relief appeal, 9 October 2010.
Scouts, front row L-R: Sheehan Poucher, George Bingham, Toby Girvan, Jordan Whiteside.

August

During the month of August eight Scouts took once again to the Mourne mountains to complete their Chief Scout Gold Award hike which brought them just one step nearer to gaining the highest award available to members of the Scout Troop. At the beginning of October, members of the Cub Pack took part in their now almost ritual weekend residential experience at Shannaghmore Outdoor Pursuits Centre near Newcastle. All the Cubs had a wonderful time and everyone arrived home safely, tired but happy.

From 3 August, for one week, as part of the centenary celebrations, an exhibition was held in Newry Museum. The staff at Bagenal's Castle, together with a number of our own boys, assisted in the organisation of the exhibition which was a great success with many members of the public visiting and enjoying the various excellent displays.

October

The Beavers and Cubs held their annual Halloween party when all the members were encouraged to attend the meeting in fancy dress. Many memorable and indeed scary creations were on view that Monday evening.

November

On Friday 26 November, to finalise their centenary celebrations, 1st Newry (Earl Kilmorey) Scout Group held a fund raising celebratory concert in Newry High School at 7.30pm. The evening's

Scouts ready for the fund raising concert at Newry High School, 26 November 2010. L-R: George Bingham, Harley Stinson, Chris Bagnall, Johnny McKee, Sheehan Poucher, Sam McCammon, Steven McCammon, James Kernaghan.

Scouts visiting a home for the elderly, 5 December 2010.

entertainment consisted of a medley of music and songs to suit all tastes, including performances from the Commons Silver Band, soloist Judith McCabe, the Hunter Moore Memorial Flute Band and percussionist Natalie Chambers. The evening's events were compered by well known local artiste, Charlie Smyth, who had everyone in tears during his time on the stage. The concert proved to be a great success with more than two hundred people enjoying the various performances and everyone went home well pleased.

December

In the weeks coming up to Christmas the Beavers and Cubs once again had their Christmas parties and they all got very excited when Santa Claus appeared through the door to distribute a variety of presents to all of them. At the end of the evening the Beavers and Cubs returned home, even more eager for Christmas to arrive.

2010 concluded with all eight of the Scouts who had completed the requirements for the Chief Scout's Award being informed that the presentation would take place in January at the City Hall, Belfast.

L-R: Jake Wilson, Harley Stinson, George Bingham.

Scouts hiking in the Mournes, 5 December 2010.

Centenary Celebrations

On Friday 29 October, the Group held a magnificent centenary celebration dinner at Newry High School in the company of some one hundred and eighty Scouts, leaders, former Scouts and friends of 1st Newry (Earl Kilmorey) Scout Group. Several guests travelled in from Great Britain and from the southernmost point of Ireland. 84 year old former Scout, Leslie Truesdale, together with his wife made the trip all the way from Australia just to be present at this special event. Leslie met up with his former Scouting pals Stanley Ferris, John Bradfield, George McCullough, Leslie Dalzell and Robert Hutchinson at the dinner.

The room was very tastefully decorated with Scouting memorabilia and photographs from the past 100 years. Included in the display was the old 1st Rover Crew bass drum which had last been used in the 1st Newry Scout bugle band more than 65 years ago. The drum was recently refurbished and its former player, Robert Hutchinson, was also in attendance. Northern Ireland Chief Commissioner, Wilfred Mulryne OBE, County Commissioner, Stephen Donaldson, Cllr. Andy Moffett, representing Newry and Mourne District Council, and Terry Duffy of 1st Dromore Newry Scouts, representing Scouting Ireland, were all present. The evening was suitably compered by former Scout and Group treasurer, Jim Baines. 1st Newry Group chairman, Alan McGaffin, welcomed all in attendance and especially those who had travelled a distance. Chief Commissioner Mulryne then presented the Newry Scouts and leaders with a new red, yellow and blue bordered scarf which will now replace the traditional red and white bordered scarf which had been associated with 1st Newry for nearly half a century. Dr Mulryne wished Newry every success with their Scouting for the next 100 years and paid tribute to their dedicated team of leaders over the years and especially for their commitment and dedication throughout the troubles in Northern Ireland. Stephen Donaldson, County Commissioner, also spoke briefly and then awarded Mervyn Ferris with his 50 year service certificate. He then presented the following lay people with Scout Thanks badges and certificates for services to 1st Newry Scout Group – Linda Bingham, Alan McGaffin, Jim Baines, Joe Berry, David Campbell, William Nummy and Bill Rees. Group Scoutleader Mervyn Ferris complimented them by saying that 'The Group was indebted to them for their dedication and practical help to the Group over the past number of years. It is without doubt that 1st Newry could not have survived the last 100 years had it not been for generations of faithful servants such as themselves – and to each and every one we extend our thanks'.

Cllr. Andy Moffett spoke on behalf of Newry and Mourne District Council and sent good wishes from the Council. He then presented Mervyn Ferris, on behalf of the Group, with a specially engraved cut glass bowl as a memento of their centenary year. Former 1st Newry Scout Bill Pollock proposed the toast to 1st Newry and Colin Whiteside proposed the toast to HM the Queen. The centenary cake was cut by five of the oldest former 1st Newry Scouts in attendance - Stanley Ferris, Leslie Truesdale, George McCullough, Leslie Dalzell and Harry McGaffin.

Entertainment on the evening was provided by the Hunter Moore Memorial Flute Band ensemble; a monologue was recited by Joe Berry; a comical 'Letter from a Scout Camp' was read by Scout George Bingham; Billy McAlpine provided some memorable photographs on the big screen and John Bradfield played his accordion to accompany a number of old camp fire songs to end a very successful and extremely enjoyable evening.

Former members cutting the centenary cake.
L-R: Harry McGaffin, Leslie Truesdale, Stanley Ferris, Leslie Dalzell, George McCullough

An interview with former Scout and Scoutmaster Robert McCullough

by Gavin J. McCullough
18 May 2010

Robert Savage McCullough was born on 24 December 1925 and was the son of the late Robert and Hilda McCullough (the local midwife) of 'Trebor', Armagh Road, Newry.

What follows now is Robert's own story and words, which were recorded on 18 May 2010, of some of his life time experiences with the Scouts in 1st Newry whenever he knew there was to be a centenary book.

Robert explained that he started with 1st Newry (Earl Kilmorey) Scout Troop in the early 1930s in the Bulldog Six of the Wolf Cubs. The Cub Scoutmaster at that time was Jimmy Cowan, who was the bookkeeper in Sandys Mill in Newry at the time.

The weekly meetings took place upstairs in the old stone building (known now as the old Scout hall) in Sandys Street, Newry which, at that time, had wooden steps. Robert recalled other Cubs from that era - Leslie Truesdale, a lad called Thompson, Jim Mitchell and the McClean brothers from Canal Street. Games that they played in those days were blindfold boxing, hardy cross (which was an adventurous leap frog type game) and paper chase trails out on the Belfast Road in Newry. Football matches were played by all sections in the Grammar School field (now Windsor Hill Primary School).

Robert went on to the Scouts and the leaders were Norman McMinn (who wore glasses) and Jack Smith (who had a sister called Jean who was a singer in England at the time). Other leaders around that time were Albert and Jimmy Mateer from the Armagh Road. Robert's main friends in the Scouts were Kenny McClean, Sammy Jones, George 'Ginger' McCullough, Billy Smith, Leslie Truesdale, Walter Meek and Jim Mitchell (from the Dublin Road area and whose father was a policeman at the time). Robert recalled as a young Scout seeing Albert going to work at night to the printers at around 11pm. 'Albert was on a bicycle going down Canal Street but he had no lights on his bike; but he stuck to the Scout motto of Being Prepared, by holding his lit cigarette at his back and the glow of the cigarette end acted as his back red light', Robert laughed.

Another well-known and respected Scoutmaster in those days was Frankie McWhirter. Robert recalled that when he was doing his Scout Cooking badge, he and other Scouts were taken to Frankie McWhirter's sister's house on the Armagh Road to an area known as 'The Rocks' which was to the rear of her house. Here the Scouts had to set up a fire. They were only allowed one or two matches and then had to cook a meal. Frankie's sister did the cooking inspection and decided on who had passed the badge.

In Frankie McWhirter's era there were up to 75 boys in the Troop throughout all the sections. While in the Scouts Robert recalled doing quite a lot of tracking type activities such as paper and chalk arrow trails. He remembered one trail taking the Scouts through a yard known locally then as 'Kelly the Knackers' yard which this was out on the Belfast Road near to what is now Henning's Steel yard.

The Scouts camped a lot in Mourne Park, Kilkeel, in those days, which was during the Second World War. During one weekend camp 3 or 4 Scouts including Robert, were walking on the main road into Kilkeel on a Sunday morning en-route to church. To their surprise the then Earl of Kilmorey (who resided at Mourne Park House) pulled up in his big car and offered the boys a lift into Kilkeel which was considered to have been a great honour in those days. When the Scouts were camping at the Park they got their milk from a farmhouse on the main Newry to Kilkeel Road.

Robert remembered that when camping down at Mourne Park one summer they decided to stay a few extra days and two boys were dispatched back up to Newry to collect food at the homes of the boys who were camping. The food was brought back down to Kilkeel.

During the Second World War the American army was camped and stationed within the Mourne Park grounds. The military had permanent guard posts at the gates into the Park. Robert recalled the Scouts often chatted to the American soldiers and on one occasion the soldiers were playing a game of cards and gave the Scouts their rifles for a short while to 'do guard' while they finished off their card game. The army also had large canvas water tanks to store water and these were kept adjacent to the Whitewater river.

After Scout age Robert then progressed into the Rover Crew. One of the leaders was 'Frosty' Lawson from Dundalk. Lawson cycled from Dundalk to Newry for the weekly meeting. Robert explained why 'Frosty' got his nickname. When the Scouts were camping in early spring it would have been very cold in the mornings. But regardless of the weather conditions outside Lawson instructed the boys to tie up the brailing sides of the tents and this is how he got the name 'Frosty'. The Rover Scout Crew assisted a lot with the war effort at the time to help with the fund raising.

Robert explained that Doctor Williams's trailer was borrowed and the Scouts went around Newry doing door-to-door collections of old newspapers. The papers were brought back to the Scout hall for packaging and would then be collected on a regular basis by a 20ft lorry (which coincidentally was driven by ex-Scout Freddy Jess). Robert told the story about Freddy Jess whenever he was Scoutmaster and at camp in Mourne Park. There was torrential rain one weekend and Jess told the boys to get out quickly and tighten up the guy ropes. The lads apparently tried to tell him that this wasn't a good idea but he wouldn't listen and of course the inevitable happened – the poles ripped through the canvas.

The copper bugle used by Robert McCullough in the Rover Crew band.

The Rover Crew also formed a bugle band. A man called Pat Campbell from Sinclair Street (who used to be involved with St Joseph's band in Newry) was the conductor. The Rover Crew band played in many concerts and events in the Newry Town Hall. The second hand bass drum was acquired from a local band and it was played by Robert Hutchinson. Earlier in 2010 Robert, despite illness, ensured that the drum was refurbished (by his drum maker friend, David Alexander from Markethill), and restored to its original condition. It now sits proudly in the Scout museum for all to see. Robert retained his original copper bugle with green tassels which he diligently cleaned and polished to perfection. It is thought that this may well be the only instrument left from the Rover Crew band and is still with the McCullough family. Robert also spoke about the talent of Billy Kernaghan from Sandys Street. 'Billy could play any instrument – no problem'.

Robert went on to explain that during the war each church in Newry took its turn to supply tea and sandwiches to the troops stationed on the Newry streets. This entertaining took place in Newry Institute building on Hill Street (above what in more recent years was known as the Ambassador Restaurant). 1st Newry Scout Troop supplied two Scouts each night in the capacity as waiter staff. The Scouts also volunteered as medical casualties for the ARP and Rescue Service. Robert told the funny story that during one of these so called 'exercises' with the local Air Raid Precautions (ARP) personnel, the Scouts were placed in a makeshift ambulance. The ambulance went up Sandys Street and Windsor Hill en-route to Rathfriland Road hospital but Robert nearly needed real

hospitalisation after he fell out of the back doors of the ARP ambulance at Windsor Hill corner. It turned into a real life 'Carry On' hospital, Robert laughed.

Robert of course went on to be Scoutmaster of the Troop taking over from Frankie McWhirter. He was helped then by Harry Crawford (who was from the Hilltown area and worked in Fosters in Newry) and Norman McMinn. He recalled one camp at Silver Strand in county Wicklow and the Scouts all went by bus. Robert took an Austin 12 car (registration EZ 463) which had been kindly loaned to him for the weekend by his uncle, Joe McCullough. This car in later years was given to Robert and, after extensive restoration some 15 years ago, remains in the McCullough family to this very day.

The Scouts also camped at Ballyedmond Castle, Killowen, Rostrevor and in those days they used bell tents which were a natural colour. Robert explained that when you camped you signed your name on the inside tent panels to prove what camp you had attended.

1st Newry Troop remained strong throughout the war years until Tommy Caldwell and Jimmy O'Neill started 2nd Newry Scout Troop. Whilst initially a number of the Scouts from 1st Newry went to 2nd Newry, they soon returned and the breakaway Troop didn't last.

Robert told another story which happened during his time as Scoutmaster. He was taking a group of boys to camp at Ballyedmond. One of these Scouts was Robin Patterson from the Armagh Road. His father came to say that Robin was a very fussy eater at home and he and his wife were concerned that this might be a problem at camp. But after a few days out in the open air Robin Patterson soon changed his eating habits and by the end of the camp he would have eaten anything going. A few days after the camp had ended, Robin's father came to see Robert, declaring 'You made a great job of our Robin – he would eat anything now'. Robert chuckled at the thought of this.

He told another story about a Scout called Bertie Smith from the Patrick Street area. Bertie was at the Scouts in the upstairs hall when a few of the others decided it would be a bit of a laugh to remove the wooden steps from the doorway. Of course Bertie stepped out expecting to put his foot on the wooden stairs which had been removed as a prank. Smith fell to the ground. Thankfully he was uninjured and lived to tell the tale himself.

Robert undertook the role of Scoutmaster for a number of years and he thought that Noel Hodgett took over from him, for he remembered giving Noel his Scout trousers.

Robert McCullough continued his lifetime association with 1st Newry Scout Troop. His own family of three boys, Bob, David and Gavin, joined the Troop and he became involved in the Parents Committee (along with his wife Florence) and regularly helped out at fundraising events. One of Billy McAlpine's famous pictures of Robert sees him sitting on a chair selling hotdogs in Sandys Street. He was well known for his excellent DIY skills and would be called upon to tackle repairs at the hall over the years. For many years he also officiated on the Newry District Scout Council and held the office of Chairman and latterly President. He received many Long Service Awards over the years as well as the much coveted Silver Acorn.

Just a few days before my father's passing he told me, 'You know, I really loved the Boy Scouts – they were great fun'. This statement truly summed up Robert's commitment to 1st Newry and the passion he had for the Group for so many years.

Nothing would have pleased my father more than to know that his story was to be given pride of place in the history of the Group - marking their 100 years of Scouting in Newry.

Sadly Gone Home **O** 18 June 2010

Robert McCullough

On 18 June 2010 the Group lost one of its former members and loyal supporters when Robert McCullough passed away after a relatively short illness. Robert had been a member of the Group in years past as a Cub, a Scout, Rover Scout and Scoutmaster as well as in later years taking on an active role as a lay member. He was also and active member of the District Scout Council taking on the roles of Chairman and President. For his services to Scouting Robert was presented with the Silver Acorn which is awarded for especially distinguished service to Scouting. The Group was represented at the funeral service by members of the Scouts and leaders in full uniform.

Jack White

On Wednesday, 4 August 2010, 1st Newry Scout Group was saddened by the death of one of its lay members, Jack White. Jack first became connected with the Group when his son 'Freddie' joined the Group as a Cub Scout many years past. Jack took a great interest in the activities of the Group and was always willing to help in whatever way possible. He took on the role of Vice Chairman from 1976 to 1979 when he than was appointed Chairman. Jack continued as a very active Chairman until 2005 when at his request he relinquished the post and took on the lesser role of Vice Chairman until his retirement in 2009. The Group was well represented at the funeral service with leaders appearing in full uniform.

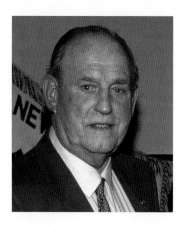

2011

The eight Scouts who had achieved the Chief Scout's Gold Award attended the presentation of these and other awards at Belfast City Hall. The presentations were made by the outgoing Chief Commissioner, Dr Wilfred Mulryne OBE, and the newly appointed Chief Commissioner, Colin Lammey. The Scouts, who were accompanied by the their parents and Scoutleaders, were entertained to a buffet before the event. The boys and their parents were very impressed with the manner in which the event had been organised and the ceremonial aspects of the evening.

Chief Scout's Gold Award presentation on 7 January 2011.
Front L-R: George Bingham, Sheehan Poucher, Toby Girvan, Andrew Hodgett.
Middle: Christopher Bagnall, James Kernaghan, Jake Wilson, Harley Stinson. Also present were: Stephen Donaldson County Commissioner, Mervyn Ferris District Commissioner, Garry McWhirter ASL, Billy McAlpine CSL, Lee McWhirter ACSL.

The district Scout quiz took place on 21 January when 1st Newry entered two teams for this event. After some fairly tough rounds of questions by the quizmaster, Jim Baines, one of our teams managed to achieve second place while the other came in a respectable third. The Scout 5-a-side district hockey tournament took place on 25 February when a number of teams from the Group took part and managed to achieve runners up position against some very tough opposition from Drumgooland. This event was soon followed up on 24 March when the district 5-a-side football tournament took place at Newry High School and, despite the Troop having a number of teams entered, they did not manage to gain any medals. However everyone thoroughly enjoyed the event.

On 17 April, once again thanks to the Newry District Scout Council, the annual St George's Day parade and service took place in Newry. The Squirrels, Beavers, Cubs, Scouts and Explorer Scouts, together with members of the Guide Association, paraded through the city to Downshire Road Presbyterian Church. At the church they were welcomed by the minister, the Rev. Brian Colvin, who officiated at the service and carried out the dedication of the newly installed Scout window. Again the Group was honoured to have a large number of former members among its ranks and present during the dedication service.

Beetle drive winners Mrs C. Holmes, Mrs T. Holmes, along with Scout Toby Girvan and Garry McWhirter, ASL, 3 February 2011

Throughout the months of April and May, the Scouts and Explorers took part in a number of weekend hikes and camps in the Mournes and made preparations for their annual camp which was to be held In Switzerland. On 9 May the District Cub football tournament took place in Drumgooland with Cubs from all the district taking part. Unfortunately the Newry Cubs did not manage, on this occasion, to win the competition but all had a good time and enjoyed meeting the other Cubs. Following on from this event 1st Newry Beavers and Cubs again headed off to Drumgooland to take part in the District Beaver and Cub sports day. Both Newry Beavers and Cubs proved to be more successful this time and managed to bring home a variety of medals and the cup. Again the members of the Group accompanied by their leaders attended Children's Day services to Downshire Road and Sandys Street Presbyterian churches.

As has been the practice now for some years a Group barbecue was held on Friday, 24 June, to bring our seasonal activities to an end for a few months. The event was well attended and the parents and friends took part in a number of games and activities during the evening. On 26 June the Group leadership team was increased with the addition of Robert Henry as Assistant Cub Scoutleader.

On 24 September the Explorer Scouts turned out in aid of the Overseas Plastic Surgery Appeal when they took part in the sponsored walk and also raised funds for this very worthy cause. During the

Martin Lynch

Dame Mary Peters

Frank Mitchell

Paul Clark

Rose Neill

month of October and, as part of the requirement of the Young Roots grant, media training sessions were held for the Explorer Scouts. This was to enable all the Explorers to enhance their interview techniques and then put these newly acquired skills to use when carrying out future interviews of some of our former members. At the end of October, the Cub Scouts once again headed off on their annual pilgrimage to Shannaghmore Outdoor Pursuits Centre where they had a wonderful time in the foothills of the Mournes. All took part in canoeing, archery, blind trail and many other exciting activities over the weekend. The extensive work on the development of a website for the Group and exhibition centre, as well as ongoing and time consuming research for the publication of our book on the history of 1st Newry, continued unabated. Garry McWhirter, Assistant Scoutleader, Colin McElroy and Lee McWhirter, both Assistant Cub Scoutleaders, gained their Wood Badge training certificates on 6 December after completing the necessary training. Beaver and Cub Christmas parties were welcomed by all and especially the visit from Santa Claus with his usual Christmas gifts for everyone. The Beaver leaders took all the Beavers to the magnificent Christmas festival at Crawfordsburn Scout Activity centre where the Beavers were again thrilled to meet Santa in his grotto and receive a small present. Finally the year came to a close with all members taking part in the Christmas carol service organised by 1st Drumgooland Scout Group in Drumgooland Parish church after which everyone was treated to refreshments before heading off home.

Centenary Scarf Up presentations, 21 February 2011
Above: Beavers with Chief Inspector Michael Kirby
L-R back row: J. Boyd, J. Nummy, J. Sterritt, J. Porter, B. White, C. McCullough, M. Sutton, J. Murphy.
Front: K. Dodds, R. Moran, D. Wilson, J. McCullough, C. McElroy, H. Murdoch, H. McCartney, S. Dunn, M. Mulligan, S. Suresh.

Below: Beavers and Cubs with Stanley Bond and John Dalzell.

Mervyn Ferris (left) presents UK Chief Commissioner, Wayne Bulpitt with the Group's Centenary Scarf, February 2011.

Cubs dressing up during a visit to the museum at Bagenal's Castle.

Cubs and Beavers sports day, 19 May 2011

The Group barbecue was held indoors due to the wet summer weather!

The Beavers on a trip to Gosford Park, June 2011.
Above left, L-R back row: J. Porter, M. Sutton, J. Sterritt, H. Murdoch, B. White. Middle: K. Dodds, R. Moffett, J. Nummy, L. Chapman, J. Boyd, S. Dunn, S. Suresh. Front: R. Moran, M. Mulligan, C. McCullough, J. McCullough, H. McCartney, D. Wilson.

Scout weekend camp, Crawfordsburn, 3 -5 June 2011. Above L-R: Toby Girvan, David Bingham, Jordan Poucher.

Scouts carrying out research of war memorials in St Mary's and St Patrick's churches for the Centenary exhibition.

2011 Annual camp, Switzerland

The Troop annual camp this year was held at Kandersteg International Scout Centre, Switzerland, from 28 June to 6 July when twenty three Scouts, Explorers and leaders took part. In the early hours of the morning, 4.00 a.m., the party was transported to Dublin where they took a flight to Geneva and hence by train and bus, arriving at the site at 3.00 p.m. The Troop was then allocated a site and camping gear by the very helpful staff at Kandersteg. Soon the tents and dining shelters were erected and everyone settled in for their first night away from home. During the following eight days the Scouts got to meet a great number of other Scouts from various different countries and quickly became friends. Hikes were undertaken into the beautiful Swiss Alps around Kandersteg and to the lovely lake Oeschinensee, about 1600 metres above sea level, where the boys were amazed by the surrounding scenery. On the way down all the Scouts, and indeed some of the leaders, paid a visit to the Rodelbahn, an extremely long luge, which snaked down the hillside. The Scouts and leaders descended on the sledges which quickly sped downwards along the straights and around the various bends before coming to an end many hundred of metres lower down the hillside. All enjoyed the thrill and it was difficult to tear everyone away and move down into the village. On another occasion the Scouts hiked along the trail to Blausee where everyone saw the lovely lake formed after the glaciers had retreated and left a wonderful blue lake which is now filled with many hundreds of rainbow trout. Lying in the bottom of what is a fairly shallow lake, are many fallen trees which are preserved by the cold waters.

Early one morning the Group took the trail from the site to take part in a high ropes course which was located a short distance away and on top of a high ridge above the valley floor. This was indeed the highest one which the boys had ever seen and took them very high into the tree canopy and, with some amazing rope climbs, ended with a zip wire down to the ground again. Of course a visit to Switzerland would not have been complete without going to see a local Swiss folk evening which was held in the nearby village of Kandersteg. This was enjoyed by all but on the walk home the heavens opened and the subsequent torrential downpour soaked everyone before they arrived back at the

campsite. On a glorious warm and sunny day a trip was undertaken to visit the Schilthorn mountain, which is around 2970 metres high, and the famous Piz Gloria restaurant. This place was where one of the James Bond films, *On Her Majesty's Secret Service*, was filmed. To get there everyone had to take the cable car from Stechelberg way down in the valley below to Gimmelwald and Murren and then again up to the Piz Gloria. There were amazing sights from this high vantage point and all were able to look across the valley to the Eiger, Monch and Jungfrau mountains. Of course everyone had to visit what is claimed to be the world's first revolving restaurant and watch the mountains pass slowly by as the restaurant rotated. The afternoon was then spent in Interlaken where the Scouts did some shopping for presents to take home to Mum, Dad and little brothers and sisters. This break gave the leaders the opportunity to relax for a while until it was time again to head home to Kandersteg. On another day the Group visited the city of Berne and had the opportunity to see the magnificent town clock as well as the famous 'Barengraben' – the bear pit. Nowadays the bears roam in a special area alongside the river and are able to roam around rather than being in captivity in the cages and pits. During the stay at Kandersteg, the Scouts made many friends with Scouts from a number of different countries and joined in the evening on site activities such as camp fires, an international night, eco trails, a bat watch, pioneering and many other new and exciting activities. Sadly the camp very soon came to an end but all those who had taken part had had a thoroughly marvellous time, making many friends with whom they are still in touch.

Right: Having a rest at Oeschinensee at around 1600m after a long climb.

Visiting the Piz Gloria where this is a rotating restuarant and where the James Bond film *On Her Majesty's Secret Service* was filmed. There is a spectacular view from this high vantage point.

International scouting in action — 1st Newry Scouts meet up with other Scouts from Europe and USA.

Below: Outside Kandersteg International Scout Chalet
L-R front row: G. Bingham, M. Kernaghan, I. Hamilton, J. Mulligan, D. Quigley, J. Poucher, D. Bingham, B. J. Callahan.
Back row: G. McWhirter ASL, J. Wilson, R. Henry ACSL, J. Kernaghan, L. McWhirter ACSL, T. Girvan, C. Bagnall, W. Nummy,
H. Stinson, A. Hodgett, C. Baines, S. Poucher, Z. Shahid, M. Ferris SL, W. McAlpine CSL.

Cubs at Shannaghmore, September 2011.

Christmas and Halloween parties.

1st Newry (Earl Kilmorey) Scout Group 2011

Appendices

Awards

King's Scout Award
D. O. Mahood

Queen's Scout Awards
Jim Dalzell
Marshall McConnell
John McWhirter
Tom Weir
Ronald Baird
Jim Ferris
Malcolm McWhirter
Colin McWhirter
David Robinson
Robert Ferris

Duke Of Edinburgh Gold Award
Robert Ferris — 1981

Chief Scout's Awards
Gary Cowan — 1975
Freddie White — 1976
John McKee — 1976
David McCullough — 1977
Martin Thompson — 1978
Brian Cowan — 1978
John Lockhart — 1980
Nicholas Gray — 1980
John Kelly — 1980
Kenny Gibson — 1981
Michael Robinson — 1981
Alan McGaffin — 1982
Neil Thompson — 1982

Chief Scout's Gold Awards
David Whiteside — 2007
David Kernaghan — 2007
Geoffrey Hodgett — 2007
Andrew Patterson — 2007
Christopher Bagnall — 2010
George Bingham — 2010
Toby Girvan — 2010
Andrew Hodgett — 2010
James Kernaghan — 2010
Sheehan Poucher — 2010
Harley Stinson — 2010
Jake Wilson — 2010

Medal of Merit
Noel Hodgett — 1961
W. John Wylie — 1965
W. John Wylie (Senior) — 1965
William McAlpine — 1972
Mervyn Ferris — 1978
Wilson Robinson — 1980
Gavin McCullough — 2005

Bar to the Medal of Merit
W. John Wylie — 1980
William McAlpine — 1980
Mervyn Ferris — 1985

Silver Acorn
William McAlpine — 1995
Mervyn Ferris — 1996
Noel Hodgett — 1997
Robert McCullough —2005

Silver Wolf
Noel Hodgett — 2005
Mervyn Ferris — 2008

MBE
William McAlpine — 1997

Former Scouts who have taken on leadership in Groups around the Province and beyond:

Judge William Johnson — 78th Belfast, Northern Ireland Chief Commissioner

Billy Pollock — County Commissioner, ACC (PR), Antrim

Edwin Mitchell — District Commissioner, Antrim

Alex Wylie — Lisburn District

Billy Smith — Greenisland

Leslie Truesdale — Tandragee and Australia

John Wylie — 4th Bangor

John McWhirter — Malvern, England

Godfrey Ferris — District Commissioner, Lisburn and the Wirral, England

John Reid — Markethill

Robert Ferris — Banbridge

Kenny Gibson — Yorkshire

These are the names of just a few of whom we know.

349

Office Bearers

Chairmen/Chairwomen
S. Sterritt	1950 - 1953
Mrs C. McAlpine	1954 - 1955
E. Whitehead	1955 - 1956
Mrs C. McAlpine	1956 - 1957
S. Cassidy	1957 - 1958
D. Lockington	1958 - 1977
M. Baird	1977 - 1979
J. White	1979 - 2005
Mrs G. Patterson	2005 - 2009
A. McGaffin	2009 - Date

Vice Chairmen/Chairwomen
Mrs C. McAlpine	1955 - 1956
S. Sterritt	1956 - 1957
D. Pollock	1957 - 1958
R. Baird	1958 - 1976
J. White	1976 - 1979
S. McCullough	1979 - 1986
B. McNeill	1986 - 1994
H. McAlpine	1994 - 1997
N. Thompson	1997 - 2000
Mrs J. McMillan	2000 - 2001
Mrs H. Young	2001 - 2003
G. Irwin	2003 - 2004
J. Gibson	2004 - 2005
J. White	2005 - 2009

Secretaries
Miss O. Manderson	1950 - 1951
Mrs C. McAlpine	1951 - 1954
Mrs W. Wylie	1954 - 1964
Mrs G. Ferris	1964 - 1965
H. Parker	1965 - 1973
Mrs M. McGaffin	1974 - 1976
Mrs J. Anderson	1976 - 1977
Mrs D. Baird	1977 - 1979
Mrs M. Erskine	1979 - 1981
Mrs M. McGaffin	1981 - 1992
C. Whiteside	1992 - 2001
Mrs J. McMillan	2001 - 2008
Mrs E. Whiteside	2008 - 2009
Mrs L. Bingham	2009 - Date

Treasurers
Mrs S. Sterritt	1950 - 1951
Mrs Wilson	1951 - 1952
Mrs S. Sterritt	1952 - 1955
Mrs S. McConnell	1955 - 1991
Mrs M. Baines	1991 - 2005
J. Baines	2005 - Date

Scouters / Leaders 1910 - 2011

W. H. Scott	1910 - 1913
R. Scott	1913 - 1916
W. J. Wylie	1919 - 1921
J. Lambe	1919 - 1921
W. J. Sterritt	1919 - 1927
D. Graham	1921 - 1923
G. Agnew	1926 - 1929
J. Cowan	1928 - 1940
S. Sterritt	1928 - 1932
S. Graham	1928 - 1932
S. Crozier	1928 - 1935
G. Clarke	1930 - 1933
Miss L. Lockhart	1930 - 1931
Miss S. McClelland	1930 - 1931
Miss S. A. Lockhart	1930 - 1933
Miss M. Lockhart	1931 - 1933
J. Smith	1933 - 1939
J. Mateer	1935 - 1937
A. Mateer	1936 - 1937
G. Kennedy	1936 - 1940
G. Clarke	1938 - 1939
D. McConnell	1938 - 1940
T. McWhirter	1938 - 1940
Miss M. Mateer	1939 - 1940
A. E. Truesdale	1939 - 1940
A. R. Hunter	1939 - 1940
B. Baird	1939 - 1940
F. McWhirter	1939 - 1946
F. Jess	1941 - 1946
B. Blair	1941 - 1947
N. McMinn	1941 - 1947
W. Hammond	1945 - 1946
J. Lawson	1945 - 1947
L. Truesdale	1945 - 1948
R. McCullough	1947 - 1949
G. McCullough	1947 - 1949
H. Crawford	1947 - 1949
B. Smith	1947 - 1950
H. McKnight	1948 - 1950
Miss T. Hamilton	1949 - 1950
Miss McKee	1949 - 1950
A. Storey	1949 - 1950
W. Bryson	1949 - 1950
Miss D. Manderson	1950 - 1952
Miss M. Hewitson	1950 - 1952
Miss A. Mitchell	1950 - 1952
J. Dalzell	1950 - 1952
S. Cassidy	1950 - 1964
J. Wylie	1950 - 1964
K. Cowan	1951 - 1953
Miss M. Porter	1953 - 1959
Miss M. Dalzell	1953 - 1954
Mrs Dover	1953 - 1954
T. McCullough	1953 - 1957
T. N. Hodgett	1953 - 1963

W. McAlpine	1955 - Date		Mrs D. Fegan	1986 - 1990
G. Ferris	1954 - 1958		Mrs D. Hamilton	1986 - 1987
H. Crawford	1956 - 1959		Miss D. Brown	1986 - 1990
Miss E. Wylie	1957 - 1963		G. McCullough	1987 - Date
Miss A. Porter	1957 - 1964		Mrs S. McBlain	1990 - 1994
M. Ferris	1958 - Date		Mrs C. McWhirter	1995 - Date
J. Gamble	1964 - 1972		G. McWhirter	1995 - Date
S. Lockhart	1965 - 1967		Mrs T. Henry	1996 - 1999
J. Reid	1967 - 1974		Mrs A. Kernaghan	2000 - Date
Miss J. Ferris	1973 - 1975		C. Whiteside	2000 - Date
M. McConnell	1969 - 1978		J. McKee	2005 - 2008
N. Lockington	1969 - 1976		C. McElroy	2005 - Date
R. Ferris	1978 - 1983		L. McWhirter	2006 - Date
N. Thompson	1985 - 1993		J. Whiteside	2007 - 2009
Mrs J. Steen	1986 - 1989		R. Henry	2011 - Date

Annual Camps

1911 — Portrush, county Antrim

1912 — Dhu Varren, Portrush, county Antrim

1913 — Bushmills, county Antrim

1914 — Sandhills, Portrush, county Antrim

1915–21 — Due to war only short camps held at Mourne Park

1922 — Mourne Park, Kilkeel, county Down

1923 — Mourne Park, Kilkeel, county Down

1924 — Cranfield, Kilkeel, county Down

1925 — Cranfield, Kilkeel, county Down

1926 — Not known, Scotland

1927 — Girvan, Ayrshire, Scotland

1928 — Cranfield, Kilkeel, county Down

1929 — Jamboree, Birkenhead, England

1930 — Cranfield, Kilkeel, county Down

1931 — Bray, county Wicklow

1932 — Newton Abbott, Devon, England

1933 — Aberystwyth, Wales

1934 — Vrom Farm, Colwyn Bay, Wales

1935 — Dane's Dyke, Bridlington, England

1936 — Hengwm Farm, Aberystwyth, Wales

1937 — Training camps at Mourne Park

1938 — Dane's Dyke, Bridlington, England

1939 — Not known

1940 — No annual camp due to war situation

1941 — Mourne Park, Kilkeel, county Down

1942 — Ballyedmond, Rostrevor, county Down

1943 — Dundalk, county Louth

1944 — Mourne Park, Kilkeel, county Down

1945 — Mourne Park, Kilkeel, county Down

1946 — Mourne Park, Kilkeel, county Down

1947 — Annesley Estate, Castlewellan and Mourne Park, Kilkeel

1948 — Silver Strand, county Wicklow

1949 — Not known

1950 — Ashgrove, Newry, county Down

1951 — Mourne Park, Kilkeel, county Down

1952 — Quayle's Orchard, Ballasalla, Isle Of Man

1953 — Newcastle, county Down

1954 — Tawd Vale, Liverpool, England

1955 — Powerscourt, Enniskerry, county Wicklow
1956 — Colwyn Bay, Wales
1957 — Jubilee Jamboree, Coventry, England
1958 — Tollymore Park, Newcastle, county Down
1959 — Ballasalla, Isle of Man
1960 — Powerscourt, Enniskerry, county Wicklow. Senior Scouts car tour of west of Ireland.
1961 — Noirmont Farm, St Brelade, Jersey
1962 — Mourne Park, Kilkeel, county Down
1963 — Wiltz, Luxembourg
1964 — Ely Lodge, Enniskillen, county Fermanagh
1965 — Mourne Park, Kilkeel, county Down
1966 — Lord Meath's Estate, Bray, county Wicklow. Senior Scouts to Germany.
1967 — Fullarton Estate, Troon, Scotland
1968 — Mourne Park, Kilkeel, county Down
1969 — Union Mills, Isle of Man
1970 — Mourne Park, Kilkeel, county Down. Venture Scout Unit, Germany.
1971 — Butcher's Coppice, Bournemouth, England
1972 — Auchengillan, Glasgow, Scotland
1973 — Venture Scout Unit, Germany
1974 — Fullarton Estate, Troon, Scotland
1975 — Zellhof, Mattsee, Austria
1976 — Barrwood, Stirling, Scotland. Cubs, Diamond Jubilee, Wales.
1977 — Ambleside, Lake District, England
1978 — Mourne Park, Kilkeel, county Down
1979 — Buckmore Park, Kent, England
1980 — Snowball Plantation, York, England
1981 — Wendelsee, Thun, Switzerland
1982 — Lakeland Jamboree, Castle Archdale, county Fermanagh
1983 — Bonaly, Edinburgh, Scotland
1984 — Mourne Park, Kilkeel, county Down
1985 — Buckmore Park, Kent, England
1986 — Zellhof, Mattsee, Austria
1987 — Blackwell Court, Bromsgrove, England
1988 — Mourne Park, Kilkeel, county Down
1989 — Welsh International Jamboree, Wales
1990 — Mourne Park, Kilkeel, county Down. Venture Scout Unit, Norfolk Broads, England.
1991 — Hook of Holland, Holland
1992 — Training camps at Mourne Park
1993 — Training camps at Mourne Park
1994 — Zellhof, Mattsee, Austria
1995 — Blackwell Court, Bromsgrove, England
1996 — Loans, Ayr, Scotland
1997 — Hook of Holland, Holland
1998 — Training camps at Mourne Park
1999 — Training camps at Mourne Park
2000 — Baden Powell House, London, England
2001 — Zellhof, Mattsee, Austria
2002 — Tawdvale, Liverpool, England
2003 — Fordell Firs, Stirling, Scotland
2004 — Longridge, Buckingham, England
2005 — Crawfordsburn, Helen's Bay, county Down
2006 — Zellhof, Mattsee, Austria
2007 — Phasel's Wood, Essex, England
2008 — Linnet Clough, Stockport, England
2009 — Auchengillan, Glasgow, Scotland
2010 — Kibblestone, Oulton, Staffordshire
2011 — Kandersteg International Scout Centre, Switzerland